To my wife, Faith, and my daughter, Vicky.

Chapter 14

Deemed Asset Sales under IRC Sections 338(h)(10) or 338(g)   237

PREFACE

I wrote this book as an accounting desk reference for investment banking, credit, and equity analysts, and I also recommend it for investment banking track upper-level undergraduates and graduate students who have already mastered the basics of financial accounting. Financial accountants may find it useful as another perspective on some of the less frequently encountered areas of financial reporting and transaction analysis.

This is not, by any means, another financial accounting textbook. Instead, I intend it as a sort of spotlight illuminating what I have found in my investment banking experience to be the "black holes" of accounting. These are the areas that, for one reason or another, junior analysts (or junior accountants) view as great voids or accounting mysteries. In reality, this book is merely the collected answers to the questions that analysts (associates, vice presidents, managing directors, and clients) asked me during the time I spent giving accounting advice on Wall Street.

This text is distinguished from other texts in four respects. The first is its focus. My experience with analysts, either investment banking, equity, or credit, is that they generally understand the basic elements of financial accounting but not some of the finer points. For the most part, I skip the basics (although there are some points I feel the need to review) and focus narrowly, providing answers to the questions analysts repeatedly ask. These answers range from providing the next level of understanding needed for applying a seemingly simple topic, to carving out the essential portions of meatier topics like deferred income taxes.

Second, the book takes an investment banking perspective. Most accounting texts are written either for the staff accountants inside the company or junior auditors that do not encounter many of these topics. Those texts take a reporting perspective on how to present information to outsiders in compliance with Generally Accepted Accounting Principles. At the other end of the spectrum are financial statement analysis texts, written for analysts, but often lacking enough of the accounting details to allow an analyst to understand how to properly model the information.

The third is the integration of financial modeling. Most, if not all, analysts use spreadsheet models for forecasting and analysis and ultimately need to incorporate these accounting treatments in their models. Where appropriate, the text suggests proven approaches to modeling the topics. Supporting this, simplified accounting entries are included as part of the explanation and examples.

Finally, the treatment of items for enterprise valuation and business combination (purchase accounting) transactions is discussed. This includes the potential effect on forward earnings per share and alternate ways of considering items when valuing a firm.

Introduction

CONVENTIONS

Accountants, like other professions, develop spelling conventions differing from traditional usage. Many of these, such as omitting hyphens after non, as in non-cash, or combinations, such as carryforwards, are now generally the commonly accepted and preferred spellings. In some rare instances, however, it appears that the language is still evolving to accept the jargon of the profession, and the accounting and common usages are not yet the same. In those cases, where a conflict exists between spellings found in authoritative accounting literature or regulations and traditional language references, I have opted to use spelling forms found in the accounting literature.

 ## ICONS

Anyone following business events in the recent past must recognize that the accounting landscape is undergoing almost tumultuous change. Without elaborating my view that these issues should have been resolved decades ago, or offering my opinion as to why they are still evolving, suffice it to say that what follows in this work represents current requirements, but some of this will not endure. Specific items having changes pending are explained from the perspective of both the current and proposed rules. In many instances these issues only exist as proposals or as uncodified decisions of the Financial Accounting Standards Board (FASB) that are subject to further change before being implemented into Generally Accepted Accounting Principles (GAAP). I have highlighted these types of issues with an "icon" as a reminder for you to "watch for changes" if that topic is material to your analyses.

LIST OF ABBREVIATIONS

ABO	Accumulated benefit obligation
ADSP	Aggregate deemed sale price
AGUB	Adjusted grossed-up basis
APB	Accounting Principles Board Opinion
APBO	Accumulated postretirement benefit obligation
ARB	Accounting Research Bulletin
cr.	Credit
dr.	Debit
EBIT	Earnings before interest and taxes
EBITDA	Earnings before interest, taxes, depreciation, and amortization
EBO	Expected benefit obligation
EBT	Earnings before taxes
EPBO	Expected postretirement benefit obligation
EPS	Earnings per share
ERISA	Employee Retirement Income Security Act of 1974 (as amended)
FAS	Financial Accounting Standard
FASB	Financial Accounting Standards Board
FIN	FASB Interpretation
GAAP	Generally accepted accounting principles
IAS	International Accounting Standards
IASB	International Accounting Standards Board
IFRS	International Financial Reporting Standards
IRC	Internal Revenue Code
IRS	Internal Revenue Service
MACRS	Modified accelerated cost recovery system
NOL	Net operating loss
NOLs	Net operating losses
P&L	Profit and loss
PBGC	Pension Benefit Guarantee Corporation

PBO	Projected benefit obligation
PIK	Payment-in-kind
PV	Present value
SAB	Staff Accounting Bulletin
SEC	Securities and Exchange Commission
VBO	Vested benefit obligation

CHAPTER 1

Equity Method of Consolidation

INTRODUCTION

When dealing with firms that account for investments using the equity method of accounting, analysts often find the reality of applying the equity method to be more complex than the simple one-line consolidation they had envisioned. Beyond that initial hurdle lies the complexity of accurately projecting the effect of equity method investments on the firm's earnings-per-share and cash flow.

To work through some of the more common areas of uncertainty, I begin with a basic introduction of the equity method, recognition of affiliate income, and the receipt of dividends. The next level involves considering the tax implications of the equity method; a common trap is ignoring the taxes because equity earnings and the associated taxes are noncash when, in actuality, they are only noncash *for now* and impact future cash flows. Following are two more subtle and less well-understood topics: equity method goodwill and intercompany transactions. Finally, we examine the analysis of cash flows from equity method investments and how all of the aspects of the equity method of accounting for investments are properly modeled together in a projection/valuation framework.

DESCRIPTION OF THE EQUITY METHOD

The equity method of accounting for investments describes how corporations and other entities account for the investments they make in other firms. It is the appropriate accounting method for them to use when the investments that they make are large enough to exert significant influence yet too small to require full consolidation accounting. The equity method is generally used for investments of greater than 20-percent ownership (delineating where significant influence is assumed

1

to exist) and less than 50-percent ownership (delineating where consolidation is required). These are nominal measures and, as we see later in this chapter, it is possible for investors to structure aspects of their ownership to extend the range over which they may use the equity method. Figure 1-1 illustrates the accounting relationship between an investor and its investee that it consolidates using the equity method.

Accounting Standards

Accounting Principles Board Opinion No. 18, The Equity Method of Accounting for Investments in Common Stock (APB 18), summarizes the process of accounting for an investment using the equity method as[1]:

- An investor initially records an investment in the stock of an investee at cost, and adjusts the carrying amount of the investment to recognize the investor's share of the earnings or losses of the investee after the date of acquisition.
- The amount of the adjustment is included in the determination of net income by the investor, and such amount reflects adjustments similar to those made in preparing consolidated statements, including adjustments to eliminate intercompany gains and losses, and to amortize, if appropriate, any difference between investor cost and underlying equity in net assets of the investee at the date of investment.
- The investment of an investor is also adjusted to reflect the investor's share of changes in the investee's capital.
- Dividends received from an investee reduce the carrying amount of the investment.
- A series of operating losses of an investee or other factors might indicate that a decrease in value of the investment has occurred that is other than

FIGURE 1·1

Accounting for Investments by Using the Equity Method

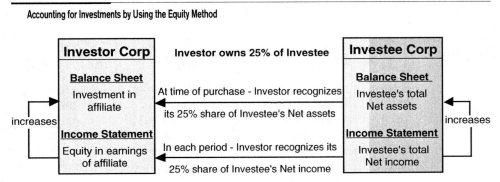

temporary and that should be recognized even though the decrease in value is in excess of what would otherwise be recognized by application of the equity method.

Accounting Under the Equity Method— Fundamental Approach

The fundamental approach for accounting for investments under the equity method is referred to as a one-line consolidation. Using the one-line consolidation approach, the investor presents her portion of the investee's net income as a single line on the income statement and the inferred value of the investment in the investee (historical cost plus the accumulated share of earnings) as a single line on the balance sheet. So, for the simplest of investments, the investor represents the impacts of the entire investment with one line on the income statement and one line on the balance sheet.

Less commonly, when the investee presents either discontinued operations, extraordinary gains and losses, or the effects of changes in accounting principle on its income statement separately after net income, the investor reports them the same way.

EXAMPLE **1-1.** Accounting for the Investor's Portion of Investee's Net Income

Assume that on 31-Dec-20X0 Investor paid 1200 for 25 percent of the common stock of Investee. Investor recognizes the investment on its 31-Dec-20X0 balance sheet in the account titled *Investment in affiliates* as 1200. (Any income tax effects are initially ignored for this discussion.)

Investee's net income for the period ending 31-Dec-20X1 is 400. Investor recognizes $25\% \times 400 = 100$ in its income statement in the account titled *Equity in earnings of affiliates*. The balance sheet account increases by the amount from the Equity in earnings of affiliates income statement account making the 31-Dec-20X1 balance 1300.

dr:	Investment in affiliates	100.0	
	cr: Equity in earnings of affiliates		100.0
memo:	To record 25% share in Investee earnings (400.0 × 25%)		

Income Statement	31-Dec-20X1
Equity in earnings of affiliates (400.0 × 25%)	100.0

Balance Sheet	31-Dec-20X1
Investment in affiliates—beginning balance	1,200.0
+ Equity in earnings of affiliates (from income statement)	100.0
Investment in affiliates—ending balance	1,300.0

EXAMPLE **1-2.** Accounting for Investor's Portion of Investee's Extraordinary Items

Assume the same fact pattern as above except that Investee also reports an extraordinary gain of 200. Investor recognizes $25\% \times 400 = 100$ in its income statement as equity in earnings of affiliates (same treatment as above) and also recognizes $25\% \times 200 = 50$ as equity in extraordinary gain of affiliates. If Investee has reported any items for discontinued operations or effects of changes in accounting principle, they would be presented similarly on Investor's income statement.

dr:	Investment in affiliates		100.0	
	cr:	Equity in earnings of affiliates		100.0
memo:	To record 25% share in Investee earnings (400.0 × 25%)			
dr:	Investment in affiliates		50.0	
	cr:	Equity in extraordinary gain of affiliates		50.0
memo:	To record 25% share in Investee extraordinary gain (200.0 × 25%)			

Income Statement	31-Dec-20X1
Equity in earnings of affiliates (400.0 × 25%)	100.0
Equity in extraordinary gain of affiliates (200.0 × 25%)	50.0

Balance Sheet	31-Dec-20X1
Investment in affiliates—beginning balance	1,200.0
+ Equity in earnings of affiliates (from income statement)	100.0
+ Equity in extraordinary gain of affiliates (from income statement)	50.0
Investment in affiliates—ending balance	1,350.0

If Investee pays a common dividend, Investor reduces its investment account by the amount of the dividend received. Note that receipt of the dividend is not recognized as income in Investor's income statement and is actually a capital transaction affecting only the balance sheet accounts (because we are ignoring, for the moment, any income tax effect). Investor treats the dividend distribution as a capital transaction because the dividend is merely a cash distribution of income that Investor has previously recorded as equity in earnings of affiliates.

EXAMPLE 1-3. Accounting for Investor's Receipt of Dividends from Investee

Assume the same fact pattern as in Example 1-2 above, except that on 31-Dec-20X1 Investee pays a total dividend of 80 to all holders of common stock. The first two entries are the same as in the previous example:

dr:	Investment in affiliates		100.0	
	cr:	Equity in earnings of affiliates		100.0
memo:	To record 25% share in Investee earnings (400.0 × 25%)			
dr:	Investment in affiliates		50.0	
	cr:	Equity in extraordinary gain of affiliates		50.0
memo:	To record 25% share in Investee extraordinary gain (200.0 × 25%)			

The new entry accounts for the cash received as a cash dividend from Investee that reduces the amount carried in Investor's Investment in affiliates account.

dr:	Cash (25% × 80.0)		20.0	
	cr:	Investment in affiliates		20.0
memo:	To record receipt of 25% of Investee's dividends (80.0 × 25%)			

Income Statement	31-Dec-20X1
Equity in earnings of affiliates (400.0 × 25%)	100.0
Equity in extraordinary gain of affiliates (200.0 × 25%)	50.0

Balance Sheet	31-Dec-20X1
Investment in affiliates—beginning balance	1,200.0
- Dividends received	(20.0)
+ Equity in earnings of affiliates (from income statement)	100.0
+ Equity in extraordinary gain of affiliates (from income statement)	50.0
Investment in affiliates—ending balance	1,330.0

TAX CONSIDERATIONS WHEN USING THE EQUITY METHOD

When assessing the tax effects of equity investments, our first reaction is to sometimes think that the Investee has already paid income taxes on its earnings and that, because of that, there should be no additional tax impact to Investor. While it is true that Investee pays income taxes on its earnings, under U.S. tax law, any gain that Investor realizes on its investment is generally subjected to a second level of taxation, i.e., double taxation; those tax effects must be reflected in Investor's accounting. The general tax effects of an equity method investment include the:

- Recognition of book taxes in each period to reflect the accrued tax burden associated with the equity in earnings of the affiliates
- Realization of a cash tax burden in periods when dividends of cash or property are actually received

WATCH THIS ISSUE

Under recently enacted changes to the tax code, dividends paid from earnings to individual taxpayers that have been taxed once at the corporate level are distributed at preferential tax rates. Because equity method investments dividends are paid to entities and not natural persons (people), the dividends are still subject to double taxation at the corporate level. Because tax laws designed to stimulate the economy can frequently be enacted, modified, or repealed, it is generally a good idea to review current taxation of dividends when analyzing companies having equity method investments. Whenever Congress enacts changes to the taxation of dividends paid to corporate shareholders, the effects of those changes can easily be incorporated into projection/valuation models by simply adjusting the tax rate used to calculate the deferred taxes for equity method investments.

Book Tax Considerations

The tax burden or benefit associated with a firm's financial reporting, or *book* earnings, is often referred to as its *book taxes*. Similarly, the taxes actually paid (or sometimes received as refunds) by a firm are referred to as *cash taxes*. Because the goals and objectives of financial reporting and income tax reporting are different, book taxes and cash taxes are never the same. The matching principle of financial accounting requires that the income tax burden on the investment's earnings be recognized, for book purposes, in the same period as those earnings. Federal income tax reporting, on the other hand, is not interested in when the earnings actually occurred but rather when the cash from those earnings passes to Investor. This creates a disconnect between the book taxes that Investor recognizes and the cash taxes that Investor pays.

Accounting for the accrued tax burden of an equity method investment becomes a matter of calculating the book taxes on the equity in earnings of affiliates. This appears relatively straightforward but requires Investor to estimate the appropriate tax rate based on how the investment is expected to be recovered. Investments under the equity method are recovered in one of four ways, by:

1. Receiving a stream of cash dividends
2. Realizing a gain on the sale of the investment
3. A combination of dividends and gain on sale, or
4. The less common case, never directly recovering the investment in cash

The tax rate for the first case, receiving a stream of dividends, can be as low as 8 percent due to the dividends received deduction. Corporate investors may usually exclude 80 percent of the dividends received from their equity investments from taxable income. The remaining 20 percent of the dividends are taxed at the corporate tax rate (which we will estimate as being 40 percent for our discussion, which approximates the combined effects of state and federal taxes). (20% × 40%) = 8%.)

In the second case, realizing the entire gain from the sale of the investment, the gain is taxed at the corporate capital gain rate, which is currently the same as the corporate tax rate for ordinary income. As before, using our estimate, gains from the sale of the investment would be taxed at 40 percent.

More practically, the investment would be recovered using the third approach, partially through receipt of dividends, with the remainder being realized as a gain on the sale of the investment. Investor determines the amount of the investment he expects to recover from each method, dividends or gain on sale, and apportions the amounts to calculate an effective blended tax rate between 8 percent and 40 percent.

Finally, there are instances where strategic investments, usually those involving true joint ventures (where control of the joint venture is truly shared and no single party has control), are accounted for using the equity method. These investments may never be directly recovered because all profits may be reinvested, and the strategic nature of the investment would bar Investor from ever selling. Recovery of the investment would occur indirectly, often in the form of reduced costs of goods sold. In these situations, the appropriate tax rate to use for the equity method investment may actually be zero. An example of such an investment might be a brewer's investment in a joint venture of a beer can manufacturer. The beer can manufacturer uses all of the capital that it generates to maintain and expand production so it never has or intends to pay a dividend. The brewer needs a secure source of beer cans at predictable prices, so its strategy precludes it from ever selling or disposing of its investment in the beer can manufacturer. To account for its investment in the beer can manufacturer, the brewer would use the equity method and calculate the deferred tax items associated with the equity method investment using a zero-percent expected future tax rate.

When accounting for the income tax effects of equity investments, recognizing amounts of equity in earnings (loss) of affiliates requires that Investor recognize income taxes for book purposes before they are actually paid in cash. Because in most cases, the taxes will eventually be paid in cash (either when the earnings are paid to Investor in cash or when Investor sells its investment for cash), the difference between book taxes and cash taxes is only temporary. This type of temporary difference, taxes recognized for book purposes before they are for federal tax purposes, gives rise to a deferred tax liability equal to the amount of the expected future tax burden (income taxes that Investor expects to pay in the future). In future periods when either the cash dividends are actually received or the investment eventually sold, Investor reverses the recorded deferred tax liability to offset the cash taxes actually being paid.

EXAMPLE 1-4. Investor's Treatment of the Tax Effects of Income from Equity Method Investments

Assume that on 31-Dec-20X0 Investor paid 1200 for 25 percent of the common stock of Investee. Investor recognizes the investment on its 31-Dec-20X0 balance sheet as an investment in affiliates of 1200. Also at that date, the tax basis of the investment is equal to the cost basis of 1200.

Investor holds the investment unchanged and Investee's net income for the period ending 31-Dec-20X1 is 400. Investor recognizes (25% × 400) = 100 in its income statement as equity in earnings of affiliates. Investor also increases the balance sheet account, Investment in affiliates, by the same amount recognized as equity in earnings of affiliates (100) making the 31-Dec-20X1 balance (1200 + 100) = 1300.

For federal income tax purposes, the 100 of income recognized by Investor in tax year 20X1 is attributed to appreciation of the equity asset, which is not taxable until Investor eventually recovers it by either receiving cash dividends or gain on sale. For book accounting purposes, Investor recognizes a deferred income tax expense for the income received in 20X1. However, the actual cash tax expense is not realized until the period in the future when the cash is received. To account for this temporary difference, a deferred tax liability is funded as a noncash expense in the current period.

dr:	Income tax expense (book taxes)	8.0	
	cr: Deferred tax liability		8.0
memo:	To record taxes on Investee earnings (400.0 × 25% = 100.0 × 8% = 8.0)		

8% is used because only 20% of the dividends are taxable at a 40% rate. (20% × 40%) = 8%.

Cash Tax Considerations

Because Investor intends to realize its investment by receiving a stream of dividends, no cash effect occurs until cash dividends are actually received in the future. At that point, Investor pays income taxes on the cash taxes received in each future period, and the deferred tax liability on Investor's balance sheet reverses by an amount equal to the cash taxes as they are paid.

EXAMPLE 1-5. Investor's Treatment of the Tax Effects of Dividends Received

Assume that on 31-Dec-20X2 Investee declares and pays a cash dividend of 80 to all holders of common equity. Remember that the dividends are generally a distribution of earnings from prior periods, i.e., the dividends that Investee pays in 20X1 may have been earned in 20X0. Those earnings, and their associated income tax expense, have already been accounted for on Investor's income statement in the prior periods. Because of this, when Investor receives its portion $(80 \times 25\%) = 20$ of dividends from Investee, it is not recognized in Investor's income statement, but only as an adjustment to the Investment in affiliates balance sheet account. The tax effect of receiving the dividend is payment of cash taxes on 20 percent of the dividends received (because under U.S. tax law, 80 percent of the dividends received are excluded) and reversing the associated portion of the deferred tax liability. Investor pays cash taxes on 20 percent of the 20 received $(20 \times 20\%) = 4$ at a tax rate of 40% $(4 \times 40\%) = 1.6$.

dr:	Deferred tax liability	1.6
	cr: Cash	1.6
memo:	To record taxes on dividends received $(20 \times 20\% \times 40\% = 1.6)$	

ACCOUNTING UNDER THE EQUITY METHOD— EXCESS OF COST OVER EQUITY PURCHASED

Another aspect of the equity method that is often overlooked or underexplained is the allocation of any excess cost of the equity investment to the underlying accounts and to goodwill. The basic approach is the same as that used under purchase accounting. The purchase price (amount of the investment) is allocated to the assets and liabilities of Investee according to their fair market value at the time of purchase, and the remainder is allocated to goodwill. Because these allocations appear in only Investor's working papers and not in the financial statements, they are sometimes referred to as "phantom write-ups" or "phantom goodwill."

This allocation only occurs in Investor's working papers for purposes of determining the correct amount of additional depreciation and amortization to use when adjusting the Investment in affiliates account. Investor's balance sheet reflects the investment in Investee at cost, and no goodwill is recorded on the balance sheet for the purchase. Where the effect of the allocations is primarily felt is in the recognition of Investor's proportionate share of Investee's earnings, which is reduced in each period to reflect the additional depreciation and amortization.

Many find this approach far from intuitive, so let me begin by framing the problem that this approach is intended to resolve. Recall that the *fair market value* purchase price paid is initially recorded in the Investment in affiliates account and is increased (or decreased) in each subsequent period by the proportionate share of Investee's earnings. Investee's earnings result, in part, from reducing its revenues by the expense associated with depreciation and amortization of the *historic book values* of the assets employed to generate those revenues. This produces a disconnect between the amounts recognized in Investor's and Investee's books because the depreciation based on historic book values is not the same as the actual depreciation based on the fair market value at the time of purchase. If the lower depreciation based on Investee's historic book values is not adjusted for by Investor when recognizing the equity in earnings of affiliates, Investor ends up overstating earnings, assets, and owner's equity. The next example illustrates more clearly how this occurs.

EXAMPLE 1-6. Overstatement of Investor's Financials Resulting from Failure to Properly Allocate the Equity Purchase Price

Assume that Investee is a very simple company employing a single asset to generate revenues and, other than the depreciation of that asset, incurs no other expenses. Investor purchases 20 percent of Investee for 1200 at the end of year 20X0 when the asset has a book value of 3000 and a remaining useful life of three years. Investee realizes revenues of 2000 in each of the subsequent three years. To simplify further, Investor holds a single asset, its investment in Investee, and generates no other revenues. As we see in Figure 1-2, Investee completely consumes its only asset and fully depreciates it by the end of 20X3.

At the end of 20X0, Investee has a single asset with a fair market value of 6000 and a recorded book value of 3000. In each subsequent period, Investee's revenues directly increase its cash account because the reduction to earnings is caused by depreciation, a noncash expense. Consequently, at the end of the three projected years, the asset is entirely consumed and Investee has accumulated cash of 6000.

FIGURE 1-2

Investee's Actual and Projected Financial Statements for Years 20X0 Through 20X3

Investee's Financial Statements				
Income Statement	**20X0**	**20X1**	**20X2**	**20X3**
Revenues		2,000.0	2,000.0	2,000.0
Less: depreciation		1,000.0	1,000.0	1,000.0
Net income		1,000.0	1,000.0	1,000.0
Balance Sheet				
Cash	-	2,000.0	4,000.0	6,000.0
Asset	3,000.0	2,000.0	1,000.0	-
Owner's equity	3,000.0	4,000.0	5,000.0	6,000.0

Investor records its initial investment and the periodic results in the financial statements presented in Figure 1-3. Investor recognizes 20 percent of Investee's net income or (20% × 1000) = 200 in each of the three projected periods, as equity in earnings of affiliates. The initial investment of 1200 is increased by that amount in each period so that at the end of year 20X3, the Investment in affiliates account has increased to (1200 + 200 + 200 +200) = 1800. Similarly, Investor's Owner's equity account has also increased by 200 each year to 1800. In reality, Investor paid 1200 for 20 percent of an asset initially worth 6000 and ended up with 20 percent of 6000 in cash and an asset worth 0, a total value of 1200 (6000 × 20% = 1200 + 0) = 1200. Because Investor neglected to properly allocate the purchase price, an investment worth 1200 ends up significantly overstated on the balance sheet valued at 1800.

To avoid this overstatement, Investor allocates the excess of the purchase price over the book value received up to the fair value of the assets purchased. In this case, Investor paid 1200 for 20 percent of Investee, having assets with a book value of (3000 × 20%) = 600. This left the difference (1200 – 600) = 600 to be allocated to the asset up to its fair value (6000 × 20%) = 1200. In this case, the full 600 of excess payment is allocable to the asset (600 + 600 = 1200). Investor records an allocation write-up equal to the full 600 with nothing allocated to goodwill. Notice in Figure 1-4 that, because the asset has a three-year remaining life, Investor adjusts the reported equity in earnings of affiliates to reflect the additional deprecation. Investor then reports the adjusted equity in earnings of affiliates on its income statement.

In the previous examples, the effect of goodwill is ignored. Beginning with the implementation of *FAS-142, Goodwill and Other Intangible Assets,* goodwill is no longer amortized, and instead is tested periodically for impairment and written down if necessary. Absent impairments in future periods, any goodwill existing as a result of an investment under the equity method would not affect any of Investor's accounts.

ACCOUNTING UNDER THE EQUITY METHOD– INTERCOMPANY TRANSACTIONS

A second potential source of overstating Investor's Net income, Investment in affiliates and Owner's equity accounts commonly comes from transactions where Investor regularly purchases goods from the Investee and subsequently resells them. This is

FIGURE 1·3

Investor's Actual and Projected Financial Statements for Years 20X0 through 20X3, Overstated Before Adjusting for the Purchase Price Allocation

Investor's Financial Statements - overstated				
Income Statement	**20X0**	**20X1**	**20X2**	**20X3**
Equity in earnings of affiliates		200.0	200.0	200.0
Net income		200.0	200.0	200.0
Balance Sheet				
Cash	-	-	-	-
Investment in affiliates	1,200.0	1,400.0	1,600.0	1,800.0
Owner's equity	1,200.0	1,400.0	1,600.0	1,800.0

FIGURE 1·4

Investor's Actual and Projected Financial Statements for Years 20X0 through 20X3, Correctly Stated After Adjusting for the Purchase Price Allocation

Investor's Working Papers

Income Statement	20X0	20X1	20X2	20X3
Unrecorded depreciation		200.0	200.0	200.0
20% x (6,000 - 3,000) / 3				
Reported earnings of affiliates		200.0	200.0	200.0
Less: unrecorded depreciation		200.0	200.0	200.0
Adjusted equity in earnings of affiliates		-	-	-

Investor's Financial Statements - correctly stated

Income Statement	20X0	20X1	20X2	20X3
Equity in earnings of affiliates		-	-	-
Net income		-	-	-
Balance Sheet				
Cash	-	-	-	-
Investment in affiliate	1,200.0	1,200.0	1,200.0	1,200.0
Owner's equity	1,200.0	1,200.0	1,200.0	1,200.0

usually the case with strategic investments, such as our earlier example of the brewer having an equity investment in a beer can manufacturer. These are often referred to as "upstream sales" because they are from the Investee up to the Investor (subsidiary to parent). The potential source of overstatement is the amount of the profit on Investee's sales that still remains, unrealized, in Investor's inventory at year-end.

EXAMPLE **1-7. Overstatement of Investor's Financials Resulting from Unrealized Upstream Profits**

Consider simply structured Investor having assets of 100 in cash and 100 as a 25-percent investment in Investee, capitalized with owner's equity of 200. During 20X1, Investor purchases 100 of merchandise from Investee, who has a net after-tax margin of 24 percent, resulting in net income of 24. Investor has no other source of income in 20X1 other than its proportionate share of Investee's earnings, $(24 \times 25\%) = 6$, and at year-end, all of the merchandise purchased from Investee remains in Investor's inventory. Investor pays taxes at a 33-1/3 percent rate and applies this rate to equity in earnings of affiliates. In Figure 1-5, the Overstated Financial Statements illustrate how the 6 of Investee's profit remaining in Investor's inventory causes overstatement of Investor's Net income, Investment in affiliates, and Owner's equity accounts. The overstatement is apparent because Investor really has done nothing more during the year than to buy some inventory, and consequently, Owner's equity should not have changed.

To eliminate the effect of the unrealized intercompany profits, Investor's Inventory account is reduced by the amount of the unrealized profits, and both the Equity in earnings

FIGURE 1·5

Investor's Overstated and Adjusted Financial Statements for 20X0 and 20X1

Overstated Financial Statements		
Income Statement	**20X0**	**20X1**
Deferred tax expense		(2.0)
Equity in earnings of affiliates	-	6.0
Net income	-	4.0
Balance Sheet		
Cash	100.0	-
Inventory	-	100.0
Deferred tax asset	-	-
Investment in affiliates	100.0	106.0
Deferred tax liability	-	2.0
Owner's equity	200.0	204.0

Adjusted Financial Statements		
Income Statement	**20X0**	**20X1**
Deferred tax expense		(2.0)
Equity in earnings of affiliates	-	2.0
Net income	-	-
Balance Sheet		
Cash	100.0	-
Inventory	-	94.0
Deferred tax asset	-	2.0
Investment in affiliates	100.0	106.0
Deferred tax liability	-	2.0
Owner's equity	200.0	200.0

of affiliates and Deferred tax asset accounts are debited. In our example, the adjusting entry is:

dr:	Equity in earnings of affiliates	4.0	
dr:	Deferred tax asset	2.0	
	cr: Inventory		6.0
memo:	To adjust for unrealized profits in inventory of 6.0 by recognizing a deferred tax asset $(6.0 \times 33\ 1/3\%) = 2.0$ and increasing Equity in earnings of affiliates by the amount of after-tax profits $(6.0 - 2.0) = 4.0$		

Completing the example, assume that in 20X2 Investor sells the entire inventory at the original cost of 100, resulting in earnings before taxes of $(100 - 94) = 6$. At a tax rate of 33-1/3 percent, Investor has book income tax expense of $(6 \times 33\ 1/3\%) = 2$ and cash taxes of 0 because the proceeds of the inventory sale were equal to their cost. Investor recognizes Net income of 4 for the period.

GUIDANCE FOR APPLYING THE EQUITY METHOD

Accounting Principles Board Opinion No. 18, The Equity Method of Accounting for Investments in Common Stock (APB 18) provides guidance for accounting for investments under the equity method. These guidelines are designed to be presumptive, but the standards also provide for exceptions where those presumptions may be overcome.

General Application Guidelines

- Investors should account for investments in corporate joint ventures by the equity method in consolidated financial statements.[2]

■ The equity method should also be followed by an investor whose investment in voting stock gives it the ability to exercise significant influence over operating and financial policies of an investee, even though the investor holds 50 percent or less of the voting stock.[3]

■ Ability to exercise significant influence may be indicated in several ways.[4]
  1. Representation on the board of directors
  2. Participation in policy-making processes
  3. Material intercompany transactions
  4. Interchange of managerial personnel
  5. Technological dependency

■ The ability to exercise influence is not always clear, but an investment (direct or indirect) of 20 percent or more of the voting stock of an investee should lead to a presumption that in the absence of evidence to the contrary an investor has the ability to exercise significant influence over an investee.[5]

Table 1-1 summarizes the U.S. and international requirements for using the equity method of consolidation. Both U.S and International accounting standards require using the equity method when the parent (investor) exhibits significant influence over the investee. Both standards presume that significant influence exists for investments of greater than 20 percent of the voting control and both standards also allow that presumption to be overcome by evidence to the contrary.

Exceptions for Investments of Greater Than 20 Percent

Situations may exist when an investor owns more than 20 percent of an investee's voting stock but cannot, in fact, exercise significant influence. FASB guidance for these situations is found in *FASB Interpretation No. 35 (FIN 35), Criteria for Applying the Equity Method of Accounting for Investments in Common Stock.*

■ The presumption that the investor has the ability to exercise significant influence over the investee's operating and financial policies stands until overcome by predominant evidence to the contrary.[6]

■ Examples of indications that an investor may be unable to exercise significant influence over the operating and financial policies of an investee include:
  1. Opposition of the investee, such as litigation, challenging the investor's ability to exercise significant influence.
  2. Investor and investee sign an agreement under which the investor surrenders significant rights as a shareholder. (This is also construed to include some stand-still agreements.[7])
  3. Majority ownership of the investee is concentrated among a small group of shareholders who operate the investee without regard to the views of the investor.

T A B L E 1 · 1

Significant Influence and the Equity Method Under U.S. GAAP and IAS

SEC Regulation S-X	U.S. GAAP	IAS
Current Accounting and Disclosure Issues June 30, 2000 An investment must be accounted for using the equity method if the investor has significant influence over the investee's operating and financial policies. Significant influence is presumed to exist where the investor owns 20-50% of the investee's voting stock.	**APB18 §17** The Board concludes that the equity method of accounting for an investment in common stock should also be followed by an investor whose investment in voting stock gives it the ability to exercise significant influence over operating and financial policies of an investee even though the investor holds 50 % or less of the voting stock. ...the Board concludes that an investment (direct or indirect) of 20% or more of the voting stock of an investee should lead to a presumption that in the absence of evidence to the contrary an investor has the ability to exercise significant influence over an investee.	**IAS 28.4** If an investor holds, directly or indirectly through subsidiaries, 20% or more of the voting stock of the investee, it is presumed that the investor does have significant influence, unless it can be clearly demonstrated that this is not the case. Conversely, if the investor holds, directly or indirectly through subsidiaries, less than 20% of the voting power of the investee, it is presumed that the investor does not have significant influence, unless such influence can be clearly demonstrated.
Current Accounting and Disclosure Issues June 30, 2000 ...In addition to factors identified by FIN 35, the staff considers the nature, form and significance to the investee of all of the investor's financial and operating interest in the investee, the protective and participating rights of the investor and other investors, and whether the investor's participation in the board is disproportionate to its common stock voting interest.	**APB18 §17** ...Ability to exercise that influence may be indicated in several ways, such as representation on the board of directors, participation in the policy-making processes, material intercompany transactions, interchange or managerial personnel, or technological dependency.	**IAS 28.5** The existence of significant influence by an investor is usually evidenced in one or more of the following ways: (a) representation on the board of directors or equivalent governing body of the investee; (b) participation in the policy-making processes; (c) material transactions between the investor and the investee; (d) interchange of managerial personnel; or (e) provision of essential technical information.
Current Accounting and Disclosure Issues June 30, 2000 ...In some circumstances, that presumption is overcome by predominant evidence to the contrary. FASB Interpretation No. 35 sets forth indicators, which are not all-inclusive, that an investor may be unable to exercise significant influence. Disclosure must be made if the registrant accounts for an investment differently than would be presumed for the voting interest held.	**FIN35 §3** Evidence that an investor owning 20 percent or more of the voting stock may be unable to exercise significant influence over the investee's operating and financial policies requires an evaluation of all the facts and circumstances relating to the investment. The presumption that the investor has the ability to exercise significant influence over the investee's operating and financial policies stands until overcome by predominant evidence to the contrary.	

4. The investor needs or wants more financial information to apply the equity method than is available to the investee's other shareholders, tries to obtain that information, and fails.
5. Investor tries and fails to obtain representation on the investee's board of directors.

Exceptions for Investments of Greater Than 50 Percent

Investments of greater than 50-percent ownership in subsidiaries are normally consolidated with the parent's financial statements. The underlying presumption for consolidation is the ability of the investor to control, usually through a majority ownership of the voting stock, the subsidiary's assets. Under certain circumstances, the ownership of a majority *economic* interest may not result in operational control of the subsidiary. This can occur when the investor separates the economic and operational ownership by contract or agreement, allowing another party to have operational control. This means that an investor with a *nearly* 100-percent ownership of a firm could, under the right operating agreement, account for the investment under the equity method. Regulatory agencies look for the operator to have some financial interest in the subsidiary. If the investor were to retain a full 100-percent interest and grant operational control to a third party, it begins to appear more like the third party is a hired manager rather than an independent operator. Other situations may preclude consolidation, such as planned temporary control, operation of law, or bankruptcy.

Table 1-2 summarizes the accounting definition of control, the conditions defining it, and the exceptions to the general rules under U.S. GAAP and International Accounting Standards (IAS). Both U.S. and international authorities recognize that there are cases when majority-owned subsidiaries should not be consolidated in the parent company financial statements because the parent has a majority economic interest but is not actually in control of the financial and operating decisions of the subsidiary. In these situations, the parent company must decide the correct method of reporting the investment in the subsidiary, whether the cost or the equity method. In most cases, the parent, although not in control of the subsidiary, has significant influence through board representation to warrant using the equity method of consolidation.

Exceptions for Investments of Less Than 20 Percent

Other situations may exist where an investor holds less than 20 percent of a company but is still able to exercise significant influence. *FIN 35* does not provide point-by-point examples of when significant influence exists at a level of voting stock ownership less than 20 percent.

Instead the Board expresses the position that the interpretation, *FIN 35*, states that the presumptions in paragraph 17 of *Opinion 18 (APB 18)* can be overcome. That statement plus the examples in *Opinion 18 (APB 18)* of ways an investor

TABLE 1·2

Accounting definition of control under U.S. GAAP and IAS

SEC Regulation S-X	U.S. GAAP	IAS
17 CFR 210.1-02.(g) *Control.* The term *control*... means the possession, direct or indirect, of the power to direct or cause the direction of the management and policies of a person, whether through the ownership of voting shares, by contract, or otherwise.		**IAS 27.6** <u>Control</u> (for the purposes of this Standard) is the power to govern the financial and operating policies of an enterprise so as to obtain benefits from its activities.
17 CFR 210.3A-02.(a) *Majority ownership:* Generally, registrants shall consolidate entities that are majority owned and shall not consolidate entities that are not majority owned. The determination of *majority ownership* requires a careful analysis of the facts and circumstances of a particular relationship among entities. In rare situations, consolidation of a majority owned subsidiary may not result in a fair presentation, because the registrant, in substance, does not have a controlling financial interest (for example, when the subsidiary is in legal reorganization or in bankruptcy, or when control is likely to be temporary). In other situations, consolidation of an entity, notwithstanding the lack of technical majority ownership, is necessary to present fairly the financial position and results of operations of the registrant, because of the existence of a parent-subsidiary relationship by means other than record ownership of voting stock.	**FAS94 §13.** The usual condition for a controlling financial interest is ownership of a majority voting interest, and, therefore, as a general rule ownership by one company of over fifty percent of the outstanding voting shares of another company is a condition pointing toward consolidation. However, there are exceptions to this general rule. A majority-owned subsidiary shall not be consolidated if control does not rest with the majority owner (as, for instance, if the subsidiary is in legal reorganization or in bankruptcy...) **APB18 §3c** ...The usual condition for control is ownership of a majority (over 50%) of the outstanding voting stock. The power to control may also exist with a lesser percentage of ownership, for example, by contract, lease agreement with other stockholders...	**IAS 27.12** ...Control is presumed to exist when the parent owns, directly or indirectly through subsidiaries, more than one-half of the voting power of an enterprise unless, in exceptional circumstances, it can be clearly demonstrated that such ownership does not constitute control. Control also exists even when the parent owns one-half or less of the voting power of an enterprise when there is: (a) power over more than one-half of the voting rights by virtue of an agreement with other investors. (b) power to govern the financial and operating policies of the enterprise under a statute or an agreement. (c) power to appoint or remove the majority of the members of the board of directors or equivalent governing body; or (d) power to cast the majority of votes at meetings of the board of directors or equivalent governing body.
17 CFR 210.3A-02.(d) *Foreign subsidiaries:* Due consideration shall be given to the propriety of consolidating with domestic corporations, foreign subsidiaries which are operated under political, economic or currency restrictions.	**FAS94 §13.** (...or operates under foreign exchange restrictions, controls, or other governmentally imposed uncertainties so severe that they cast significant doubt on the parent's ability to control the subsidiary).	**IAS 27.13** A subsidiary should be excluded from consolidation when: (a) control is intended to be temporary...; or (b) it operates under severe long-term restrictions which significantly impair its ability to transfer funds to the parent.

might indicate an ability to exercise significant influence provide adequate guidance on accounting for investments of less than 20 percent.[8]

SEC STAFF VIEWS CONCERNING THE EQUITY METHOD

The SEC tends to favor the use of the equity method over the cost method. Investments under the cost method are marked-to-market, if a market exists; otherwise they are carried at historic cost. The equity method offers superior disclosure as to the proportionate amounts of earnings and classification for those earnings arising from the investee's extraordinary items, discontinued operations, or changes in accounting principle. When evaluating whether the equity method is the most appropriate means for accounting for an investment, the SEC staff looks at the following factors together with those prescribed in *FIN 35*.

- Nature and significance of the investor's investments in the investee
- Investee's capitalization structure
- Voting, veto, and other protective and participation rights held by the investor
- Participation on the investee's board regardless of whether the right to participate is granted by contractual or other means
- Whether the investor's board participation is disproportionate to the voting interest held[9]

The SEC has, after investigation, required an investor holding 19 percent of the voting common stock to account for the investment under the equity method because the investor was entitled to select more than 20 percent of the seats on the board of directors.[10] A similar outcome may occur if the investor provides substantial amounts of investee's capitalization through investments in its preferred equity or debt securities.

WHEN TO USE THE EQUITY METHOD—SUMMARY

The 20-percent "test" for reporting under the equity method is intended as guidance and not as a bright line determinant. The proper starting point is an examination of all of the facts and circumstances to determine if an investor is able to exercise significant influence over the investee. If examination of the facts is consistent with the 20-percent presumption, then the question is settled. If, however, the facts conflict with the presumption, then they must further be assessed to determine if they are sufficient to overcome the presumption.[11]

Regulatory Perspectives

In the views of both the FASB and the SEC, it is no single criterion but rather the totality of the facts and circumstances that determines the appropriate method for accounting for investments. The underlying precept is that in cases where the investors are able, through their influence, to take "a degree of responsibility for the return on their investment," then the equity method is most appropriate.

Controlling Versus Economic Interests

It is important to remember when structuring or analyzing investments under the equity method that the investor's controlling interest and the economic interest do not have to remain coupled. In the extreme it might be possible to account for a 20-percent investment under the equity method where the investor, due to the structure of the operating agreement, benefits from *nearly* 100 percent of the economic return of the investee. Realistically, the SEC is reluctant to recognize a controlling interest in an enterprise when that interest does not have some nominal economic interest at risk. That interest may, however, be greatly disproportionate to the controlling interest, as long as the associated economic interest is at least 1 to 3 percent. It is possible to have an investor that holds a 20 percent controlling interest and a much larger, i.e., 90-percent economic interest.

ACCOUNTING FOR CASH FLOWS FROM EQUITY METHOD INVESTMENTS

In each period, Investor recognizes its proportionate share of Investee's net income as equity in earnings of affiliates. This share of Investee's earnings is an estimate of how much the economic value of the investment might have appreciated or depreciated in that period. When analyzing cash flows, an obviously important aspect of the equity in earnings of affiliates recognized by Investor is that it is merely an estimate of cash flows that may occur in the future and does not represent a cash event in the present period.

In the discussion of book tax considerations, we described four schemes that Investor could employ to recover its investment made and accounted for under the equity method. One of these, the purely strategic investment, does not produce directly measurable cash in-flows. Instead, cash in-flows generally occur as reductions in the transfer prices of vertically integrated entities, which then ultimately increase Investor's net income. This effectively increases the cash flows from operations but not as an individual, identified cash in-flow. The other methods of realizing a benefit from or recovering an investment under the equity method is to either receive a stream of cash dividends, receive cash when the investment is sold, or a combination of the two, usually selling the investment after receiving dividends for a period of years.

Analyzing cash flows related to equity method investments requires the proper classification and recognition of five different items:

- The amount of Investee's net income included in Investor's net income as equity in earnings of affiliates as noncash income or loss
- The noncash deferred tax expense related to the equity in earnings of affiliates
- Cash dividends distributed from an equity method investment to Investor

- The cash tax effect of receiving cash dividends from Investee
- Cash proceeds from a sale of the equity method investment less tax on any gain

The cash flow effects of an equity method investment can be determined from the following additions and subtractions to Investor's net income:

- − Equity in earnings of affiliates
- + Deferred tax expense related to the equity in earnings of affiliates
- + Cash dividends received from Investee
- − Cash taxes attributable to the dividends received
- + Proceeds from the sale of the investment
- − Cash taxes on the gain from sale of the investment

Classification of Cash Flow Items

If an amount for equity in earnings of affiliates is included as a component of net income, then that amount is subtracted when calculating cash flows from operations because it is a noncash item. Under U.S. GAAP, *FAS-95, Statement of Cash Flows*, dividends received from equity method investments are presented as cash flows from operating activities[12] whereas proceeds from the sale of an equity method investment are classified as cash flows from investing activities.[13] Similarly, for credit analysis, cash dividends received are included as a component of funds from operations or core earnings, whereas proceeds from a sale are usually included in noncore earnings or cash available for debt service.

MODELING THE EQUITY METHOD OF ACCOUNTING IN PROJECTION MODELS

It is not uncommon to see projections where both the Equity in earnings of affiliates account on the income statement and the Investment in affiliates account on the balance sheet are projected forward "flat," meaning at the same value as the last reported results. This approach, which sometimes is an estimate based on imperfect information, may not be the best possible estimate. The errors introduced in Investor's financial statements, misstatement of earnings, long-term assets, and owner's equity are typically small and arguably conservative but in some cases avoidable.

Elements Needed to Model an Equity Investment

To accurately model an investment in an affiliate under the equity method, an analyst needs to know or estimate the elements discussed above, the:

- Investor's proportionate share of Investee's earnings
- Appropriate tax rate
- Dividends paid by Investee

This information covers a broad spectrum from poorly disclosed investments in private companies to fully disclosed investments in publicly traded or registered corporations. Although the quality and quantity of data vary from case-to-case, in each situation it is the analyst that ultimately derives or estimates any missing pieces based, in part, on available historic information and on professional judgment and experience.

Dynamically Modeling the Elements of the Equity Investment Accounts

When adding the items necessary to model an equity method investment, the starting point is adding a noncurrent asset account to the balance sheet titled as Investment in affiliates. Depending on the number of equity method investments being modeled, the information that is known and the level of detail you desire, this can be a single account representing all of the equity method investments in the aggregate, or you could actually present a separate account for each investment. A corresponding item, Equity in earnings of affiliates, is added to the income statement below after-tax earnings. The two accounts are linked so that the balance of the Investment in affiliates account is equal to the previous period balance plus the current period's Equity in earnings of affiliates.

EXAMPLE 1-8. Modeling an Equity Method Investment

Assume that Investor acquires a 25-percent interest in Investee on December 31, 20X0. Investee currently pays dividends and Investor estimates that, because of the dividends received deduction, the appropriate tax rate for the equity in earnings of affiliates is 8 percent. Investor's proportionate share of Investee's net income is projected to be 100, 110 and 120 in 20X1-20X3 respectively. The first step, or the basic account linkage, for modeling this investment using the equity method is shown in Figure 1-6.

The basic account linkage captures the major share of the impact of an equity method investment on the earnings, asset, and capital accounts. Because taxes on the equity in earnings of affiliates are not taken into consideration, Investor's earnings are still slightly overstated but, for an investee that did not pay dividends, stopping here may provide an adequate estimate. A further refinement, displayed in Figure 1-7, is the proper accounting for the deferred tax expense arising from the equity investment. The associated tax effects are calculated by multiplying the equity in earnings of affiliates by the appropriate tax rate.

In the case of equity method investments paying dividends, Figure 1-8 illustrates the changes needed to reflect the return of investment as a reduction to the Investment in affiliates account and to account for the cash taxes being paid. This results in the calculation of a cash tax expense that is treated as the reversal of deferred tax liabilities that were recognized in prior periods. Investor received its proportionate share of the cash dividends paid by Investee equaling 20 in each of the three projected periods. As expected, the dividends are subject to the dividend received deduction, making the actual cash tax rate on the dividends 8 percent.

FIGURE 1·6

Investor's Actual and Projected Financial Statements for Years 20X0 Through 20X3, Modeling the Basic Equity Method Investment

Investor's Financial Statements - Basic equity method accounting

Income Statement	20X0	20X1	20X2	20X3
Gross profit	900.0	1,000.0	1,200.0	1,400.0
Tax rate on earnings	40.0%	40.0%	40.0%	40.0%
Less: Taxes @ 40%	360.0	400.0	480.0	560.0
After-tax earnings	540.0	600.0	720.0	840.0
Equity in earnings of affiliate	-	100.0	110.0	121.0
year-over-year growth percent			10.0%	10.0%
Net income	540.0	700.0	830.0	961.0

Balance Sheet - Assets				
Cash	540.0	1,140.0	1,860.0	2,700.0
Investment in affiliates - beginning balance	-	1,200.0	1,300.0	1,410.0
Add: Equity in earnings of affiliates from Income statement		100.0	110.0	121.0
Investment in affiliates - ending balance	1,200.0	1,300.0	1,410.0	1,531.0

Cash Flows				
Net income	540.0	700.0	830.0	961.0
Less: Equity in earnings of affiliates	-	100.0	110.0	121.0
Cash from operations	540.0	600.0	720.0	840.0

Modeling Affiliate Growth Rates

Note that the examples allow the growth rate of the equity investment in affiliates to be specified separately from that of Investor. This is a subtlety that becomes more important for investments less closely related to Investor's core business. If Investor is a brewer and the equity investment is a beer can manufacturer, then it may be acceptable to assume that Investor and Investee's incomes might grow at the same rate. If Investee is in an unrelated industry (or a portfolio of unrelated firms), then a separate growth rate (or growth rates) is probably more appropriate. The analyst must decide the approach to use based on the facts, circumstances, and materiality of the investments, but when deciding, should also remember that sometimes an important refinement is modeling the growth rate for the equity investment.

Accounting for Affiliates in Valuation

The question when treating equity investments for valuation is whether to aggregate the results together for the discounted cash flow valuation or to value Investor and Investee separately.

The ideal case is a firm making equity investments only in publicly traded companies. In these situations the best results are obtained by reversing the results

FIGURE 1·7

Investor's Actual and Projected Financial Statements for Years 20X0 Through 20X3, Modeling an Equity Method Investment Including Deferred Tax Effects

Investor's Financial Statements - Equity method with deferred tax effects

Income Statement	20X0	20X1	20X2	20X3
Gross profit	900.0	1,000.0	1,200.0	1,400.0
Tax rate on earnings	40.0%	40.0%	40.0%	40.0%
Less: Taxes @ 40%	360.0	400.0	480.0	560.0
Tax rate on equity in earnings of affiliates	8.0%	8.0%	8.0%	8.0%
Less: Deferred taxes on earnings of affiliates @ 8%	-	8.0	8.8	9.7
After-tax earnings	540.0	592.0	711.2	830.3
Equity in earnings of affiliate	-	100.0	110.0	121.0
year-over-year growth percent			*10.0%*	*10.0%*
Net income	540.0	692.0	822.2	951.3

Balance Sheet				
Assets				
Cash	540.0	1,140.0	1,860.0	2,700.0
Investment in affiliates - beginning balance	-	1,200.0	1,300.0	1,410.0
Add: Equity in earnings of affiliates from Income statement		100.0	110.0	121.0
Investment in affiliates - ending balance	1,200.0	1,300.0	1,410.0	1,531.0
Liabilities				
Deferred tax liability - beginning	-	-	8.0	16.8
Add: Deferred tax expense	-	8.0	8.8	9.7
Deferred tax liability - ending	-	8.0	16.8	26.5

Cash Flows				
Net income	540.0	692.0	822.2	951.3
Less: Equity in earnings of affiliates	-	100.0	110.0	121.0
Add: Deferred tax expense	-	8.0	8.8	9.7
Cash flows from operations	540.0	600.0	720.0	840.0

of the equity investments from Investor's projected future cash flows and adding Investee's current market valuation to Investor's valuation.

Usually firms do not make equity investment only in publicly traded affiliates. It becomes a matter of the analyst's judgment, based in part on the information available, whether to simply project Investee's results together with Investor's or to disaggregate them and attempt to value Investor and Investee separately.

CHAPTER SUMMARY

Conceptually, it is important to remember that the equity method is a *consolidation* method and that the bottom-line results for Investor are the same as if Investee had

FIGURE 1·8

Investor's Actual and Projected Financial Statements for Years 20X0 Through 20X3, Modeling an Equity Method Investment Paying Dividends

Investor's Financial Statements Equity method with dividends

Income Statement	20X0	20X1	20X2	20X3
Gross profit	900.0	1,000.0	1,200.0	1,400.0
Tax rate on earnings	40.0%	40.0%	40.0%	40.0%
Less: Taxes @ 40%	360.0	400.0	480.0	560.0
Tax rate on equity in earnings of affiliates	8.0%	8.0%	8.0%	8.0%
Less: Deferred taxes on earnings of affiliates @ 8%	-	8.0	8.8	9.7
Tax rate on equity in earnings of affiliates	8.0%	8.0%	8.0%	8.0%
Less: Cash taxes on dividends received @ 8%	-	1.6	1.6	1.6
After-tax earnings	540.0	590.4	709.6	828.7
Equity in earnings of affiliate	-	100.0	110.0	121.0
year-over-year growth percent			*10.0%*	*10.0%*
Net income	540.0	690.4	819.6	949.7

Balance Sheet				
Assets				
Cash	540.0	1,158.4	1,896.8	2,755.2
Investment in affiliates - beginning balance	-	1,200.0	1,300.0	1,410.0
Add: Equity in earnings of affiliates	-	100.0	110.0	121.0
Investment in affiliates - ending balance	1,200.0	1,300.0	1,410.0	1,531.0
Liabilities				
Deferred tax liability - beginning	-	-	6.4	13.6
Add: Deferred tax expense	-	8.0	8.8	9.7
Less: Deferred tax benefit	-	1.6	1.6	1.6
Deferred tax liability - ending	-	6.4	13.6	21.7

Cash Flows				
Net income	540.0	690.4	819.6	949.7
Less: Equity in earnings of affiliates	-	100.0	110.0	121.0
Add: Deferred tax expense	-	8.0	8.8	9.7
Add: Dividends received	-	20.0	20.0	20.0
Cash flows from operations	540.0	618.4	738.4	858.4

actually been consolidated. The difference being that Investee's items of income and net assets are grouped into one line each on Investor's income statement and balance sheet.

Ideally, firms acquiring equity positions in affiliates account for them based on whether they have significant influence or control. Each relationship is unique, and the guidance to use the equity method for investments between 20 and 50 percent is applied on a case-by-case basis. For example, an investor owning 15 percent of a large company, such as General Electric, probably has the ability to exert significant influence. Contrarily, an investor holding 40 percent of a large company where the other stockholders were allied in a voting block, may not be able to effectively exert any influence. In other situations, firms may find it advantageous to divorce their *economic interest* and *controlling interest* through contractual or other arrangements. In these situations, a firm holding a 90-percent interest may avoid full consolidation and consolidate the investment using the equity method by granting a controlling proxy to a third party, while retaining a full 90-percent economic interest.

Investors also have significant latitude regarding taxation of the equity investment *based on how they anticipate ultimately recovering their investment*. These assumptions are key to determining the appropriate rate for calculating the deferred tax effects of the equity investment, dividends received, and the correct cash flows for the firm. Understanding all of assumptions used in the firm's accounting for their equity investments and accurately projecting them is one of the discriminators between a mediocre and a superior credit or equity analysis.

CHAPTER 2

Minority Interests

INTRODUCTION

Accounting for minority interests is a seemingly straightforward topic, but remembering some of the basic misconceptions that I have encountered, I begin by reviewing minority interests and their accounting. Following are some more specialized topics: how to treat minority interests when valuing a firm, forecasting minority interests, what happens to minority interests in M&A transactions, and how to model minority interests in projection valuation models.

MINORITY INTERESTS

Misconceptions about minority interests sometimes exist more with regard to defining what they are, rather than how to account for them. There are three aspects of an accounting relationship that must be present simultaneously for a minority interest to exist. There must be:

1. A parent company that controls a
2. Subsidiary that is
3. Not wholly owned

Although control can exist by other means, for the sake of simplicity, consider it as meaning ownership of more than 50 percent of the voting control. The financial statements of controlled subsidiaries are generally not published separately but, instead, are consolidated together with the parent's financial statements. Because the subsidiary is not wholly owned, meaning that investors other than the parent own less than 50 percent of the subsidiary, a Minority interests account is presented on Parent Company's consolidated financial statements. The Minority interests account represents the proportionate shares of Subsidiary

Company's earnings and net assets that are owned by these other investors. Figure 2-1 shows the Minority interests account when a majority-controlled subsidiary is fully consolidated by Parent Company.

OVERVIEW OF ACCOUNTING FOR MINORITY INTERESTS

The general approach to accounting for minority interests is to first consolidate all of the subsidiary as if it were 100 percent owned, and then to account for the outside interests' proportionate share of periodic earnings and equity in the subsidiary as single line items. To make it clear exactly who does what, I create three entities for the discussion in this chapter; Parent Company who owns 75 percent of the common stock of Subsidiary Company and a third group called Outsiders who represent the one or more other investors that hold the remaining 25 percent of Subsidiary Company's common stock.

Parent Company owns 75 percent of Subsidiary Company and because Parent Company controls Subsidiary Company, it consolidates the results and financial position of Subsidiary Company with its own. It does this by first adding 100 percent of each of Subsidiary Company's separate income statement and balance sheet accounts to Parent Company's own results and arriving at the consolidated income and financial position. This first step results in consolidated financial statements that would be correct only if Parent Company owned 100 percent of Subsidiary Company, which it does not. Instead it only owns 75 percent of Subsidiary Company, and consequently, at the end of this first step, each consolidated account is overstated by Outsiders' percentage of the Subsidiary Company accounts.

The second step corrects for this misstatement to accurately reflect Parent Company's consolidated earnings results and financial position. In the first reporting period after acquiring its 75-percent ownership of Subsidiary Company, Parent

FIGURE 2·1

Minority Interests

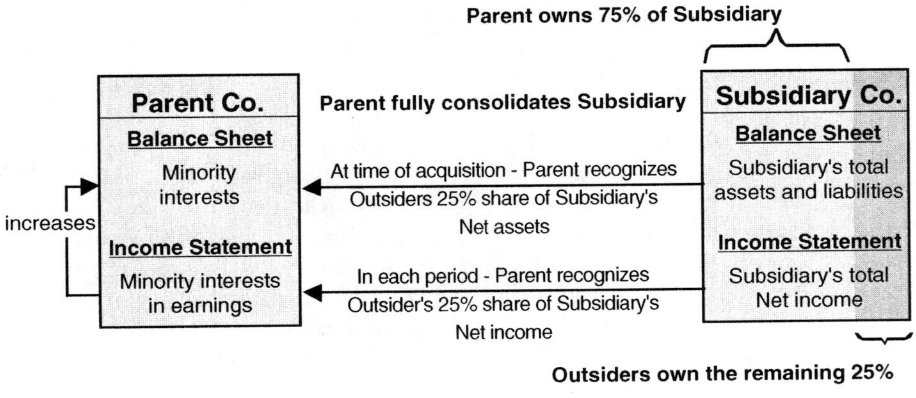

Outsiders own the remaining 25%

Company funds a balance sheet account titled Minority interests, equal to Outsiders' proportionate share of Subsidiary Company's net assets. In each subsequent period, Parent Company recognizes an amount equal to Outsiders' proportionate share of Subsidiary Company's Net income as a reduction to the consolidated income statement earnings, as Minority interests in earnings, which corrects the overstatement of the consolidated earnings. In the last step, Parent Company increases the balance sheet Minority interests account by the amount of the Minority interests in earnings, accounting for the increase in Outsiders' portion of Subsidiary's Owner's equity.

EXAMPLE 2-1. Recording a Purchase of a Partial, Controlling Interest

Subsidiary Company is a publicly traded corporation having assets of 200 and common equity and liabilities of 100 each. It trades in the market at its par value. On 31-Dec-20X0, Parent Company acquires 75 percent of the common stock of Subsidiary Company at par value for cash. The remaining 25 percent of Subsidiary Company is acquired by Outsiders. Because Parent Company owns a controlling interest in Subsidiary Company, Parent Company consolidates Subsidiary Company's results and accounts for the effects of Outsiders' ownership of Subsidiary Company as a minority interest. As a simplification, also assume that the fair value and of each of Subsidiary Company's assets and liabilities is equal to its book value at the time the transaction takes place. The three entities account for this transaction in year 20X0 financial statements as follows:

Subsidiary Company

Neither the 75 percent of the stock acquired by Parent Company nor the 25 percent acquired by Outsiders affects Subsidiary Company's financial statements. Both Parent Company's and Outsiders' purchases occurred in the secondary market (the stock was purchased from existing shareholders). Because Subsidiary Company did not issue or retire any shares, its balance sheet is unaffected, the 100 of equity already represented there has merely changed ownership.

Outsiders

dr:	Investment in affiliates	25.0	
	cr: Cash		25.0
memo:	Outsiders accounts for its 25-percent ownership of Subsidiary Company under the equity method and records it at cost. It increases the Investment in affiliates account by an amount equal to the cash used to purchase the stock.		

Parent Company

dr:	Subsidiary Company assets	200.0	
	cr: Subsidiary Company liabilities		100.0
	cr: Cash (paid out in transaction)		75.0
	cr: Minority interests (created in transaction)		25.0
memo:	Parent Company consolidates its 75-percent investment in Subsidiary Company It adds 100 percent of Subsidiary Company's 200 in assets and 100 in liabilities to its balance sheet. It reduces cash by the 75 it used to pay for the stock. Finally, it records the 25 percent of Subsidiary Company's net assets ($200 - 100 = 100 \times 25\% = 25$) belonging to Outsiders as Minority interests.		

Subsequent Recording of a Partially Owned Subsidiary's Income

In each reporting period following the initial recording of Subsidiary Company's assets and liabilities on the transaction date, Parent Company consolidates 100 percent of each component of the partially-owned subsidiary's income, even though 25 percent of those earnings can be characterized as "belonging" to Outsiders. To recognize the economic effects of Outsiders' ownership in Subsidiary Company, Parent Company subtracts Outsiders' proportionate share of Subsidiary's net income, as Minority interests in earnings, from Parent Company's consolidated after-tax earnings. The Minority interests in earnings, representing Outsiders' proportionate share of Subsidiary Company's net income, is also added to the Minority interests balance sheet account beginning balance. This estimates the change in the value of Outsiders' interest in Subsidiary Company from period to period, much the same way that the Investment in affiliates account estimates an investor's economic interest.

EXAMPLE **2-2. Recording the Minority Interest's Share of Subsidiary Company's Net Income**

Continuing from Example 2-1, in the first year following the acquisition, 20X1, and prior to consolidating the financial statements, Parent Company has Gross income of 800 and taxes of 300. For the same period, 20X1, Subsidiary Company has Gross income of 140 and taxes of 40. Their separate income statements are:

20X1	Parent Co.	Subsidiary Co.
Gross income	800.0	140.0
less: taxes	300.0	40.0
After-tax earnings	500.0	100.0

Since Parent Company owns 75 percent of Subsidiary Company, when their financial results are consolidated, Parent Company's reporting objective is to "split" Subsidiary Company's net income between itself and Outsiders. Accomplishing this, 75 percent of Subsidiary Company's after-tax earnings ($100 \times 75\% = 75$) is treated as "belonging" to Parent. Similarly, the remaining 25 percent ($100 \times 25\% = 25$) is treated as "belonging" to Outsiders. After consolidation, Parent Company's income statement combines the separate results and presents the minority interest's proportionate share of Subsidiary Company's net income:

20X1	*Separately Stated Results* Parent Co.	Subsidiary Co.	*Consolidated Results*	Parent Co.
Gross income	800.0	140.0		940.0
less: Tax	300.0	40.0		340.0
After-tax earnings	500.0	100.0		600.0
less: Minority interests in earnings			25.0	25.0
Net income	500.0	100.0	75.0	575.0

On Parent Company's consolidated balance sheet the Minority interests account is increased by exactly the amount of the Minority interests in earnings from the income statement. This has the effect of "splitting up" the Net income of Subsidiary Company between the Parent Company and the minority interest shareholders. At the end of 20X1, the consolidated balance sheet shows Parent Company's Retained earnings increased by 575 and Minority interests increased by 25.

Minority interests–beginning balance at 1-Jan-20X1	25.0
add: 20X1 Minority interests in earnings	25.0
Minority interests—ending balance at 31-Dec-20X1	50.0
Retained earnings—beginning balance at 1-Jan-20X1	500.0
add: 20X1 Net income	575.0
Retained earnings—ending balance at 31-Dec-20X1	1075.0

Subsequent Recording of a Partially Owned Subsidiary's Loss

In the case where the consolidated subsidiary produces a loss, the accounting treatment is essentially the same as for income. The proportionate share of Subsidiary Company's net loss is added to the consolidated Parent Company's after-tax income and subtracted from the Minority interests account. This is the same treatment that we afforded Subsidiary Company's net income with the signs reversed. An important distinction occurs when the balance sheet Minority interests account is reduced to zero. Generally, once the Minority interests account is reduced to zero, any additional minority interests losses are applied to reduce Parent Company's retained earnings. This occurs because a negative Minority interests account balance implies that Outsiders is compelled to pay in the amount of the deficient equity. This is usually not the case due to the limited liability of common equity investors. It is sometimes desirable to model any amount of minority interest's losses used to reduce Parent Company's equity as a separate component of Owner's equity. Minority interests in earnings in subsequent periods are first applied to offset any losses charged against Parent Company's Owner's equity before being used to increase the Minority interests balance sheet account above zero.

EXAMPLE 2-3. Recording the Minority Interest's Share of a Subsidiary Company's Net Loss

Continuing from Example 2-1, in year 20X1, before consolidating their results, Parent Company has Gross income of 800 and taxes of 300. Subsidiary Company has Gross loss of 140 and a tax benefit of 40. Their separate income statements are:

20X1	Parent Co.	Subsidiary Co.
Gross income (loss)	800.0	(140.0)
less: tax expense (benefit)	300.0	(40.0)
After-tax earnings (loss)	500.0	(100.0)

As before, because Parent Company owns 75 percent of Subsidiary Company, we treat 75 percent of Subsidiary Company's after-tax loss $(100 \times 75\%) = 75$ as "belonging" to Parent Company and the remaining 25 percent $(100 \times 25\%) = 25$ as "belonging" to Outsiders. After consolidation, consolidated Parent Company's income statement combines the separate results and presents the minority interest's proportionate share of Subsidiary Company's net loss:

	Separately Stated Results		Consolidated Results	
20X1	Parent Co.	Subsidiary Co.		Consolidated Parent Co.
Gross income (loss)	800.0	(140.0)		660.0
less: Tax expense (benefit)	300.0	(40.0)		260.0
After-tax earnings (loss)	500.0	(100.0)		400.0
less: Min. int. in earnings (loss)			(25.0)	(25.0)
Net income	500.0	(100.0)	(75.0)	425.0

On Parent Company's consolidated balance sheet, the Minority interests account is decreased by exactly the amount of the Minority interests in earnings (loss) from the income statement. In some instances, the consolidated subsidiary may produce sustained losses sufficient to eliminate the outside investor's equity completely. Usually, the Minority interests account on the balance sheet is not reduced below zero unless the outside investors are obligated to pay in any deficit. Instead, the proportionate share of losses only flows through the consolidated income statement to the point where they bring the Minority interests balance sheet account to zero balance. The minority interest's portion of any additional losses is ignored, and no increase to consolidated net income is made. The simple way of looking at this is after the outside investor's share of losses totally eliminates their equity, any additional losses are taken against the consolidated company's retained earnings.

Minority interests – beginning balance at 1-Jan-20X1	25.0
add: 20X1 Minority interests in earnings	(25.0)
Minority interests – ending balance at 31-Dec-20X1	0.0

Retained earnings – beginning balance at 1-Jan-20X1	500.0
add: 20X1 Net income	425.0
Retained earnings – ending balance at 31-Dec-20X1	925.0

EXAMPLE 2-4. Recording Subsidiary Company's Net Loss with a Zero Minority Interests Balance

Continuing from Example 2-3, assume that in the following year, 20X2, both Parent Company and Subsidiary Company achieve exactly the same operating results as they did in 20X1. All of the losses would go to reduce Parent Company's Retained earnings account because the Minority interests account was already reduced to zero at the end of 20X1.

Retained earnings – beginning balance at 1-Jan-20X2	925.0
add: 20X2 Minority interests in earnings	(25.0)
add: 20X2 Net income	425.0
Retained earnings – ending balance at 31-Dec-20X2	1,325.0

Balance Sheet Classification of Minority Interests

Authoritative sources of U.S. Generally Accepted Accounting Principle (GAAP) sometimes conflict when discussing the balance sheet presentation of minority interests. Alternate treatments are to include it as a long-term liability, a separate component of owner's equity, or in its own realm, between liabilities and equity. Conceptually, it is an equity investment but in the consolidated subsidiary and not the parent company, which speaks to stating it as a separate component of owner's equity. Some analyses are simplified if the Minority interests account is treated as a long-term liability instead of a component of equity, which is likely the reason for the popularity of that approach.

BALANCE SHEET PRESENTATION OF MINORITY INTERESTS MAY CHANGE

In October of 2002, the Financial Accounting Standards Board (FASB) reached a decision that "Noncontrolling (minority) interests in the net assets of consolidated subsidiaries should be identified and presented in the consolidated balance sheet within equity separately from the parent shareholders' equity."[1] This decision was based, in part, on converging U.S. GAAP with the proposed changes to International Accounting Standards (IAS). Under the proposed changes, IAS 27, *Consolidated Financial Statements and Accounting for Investments in Subsidiaries,* would require separate presentation in equity as well.

Another issue that is infrequently encountered relates to investments in the preferred equity of the consolidated subsidiary. In the case of preferred equity, it is presented separately on the consolidated balance sheet as Minority interests in preferred equity and in the case of PIK (payment-in-kind) equity, increased each period to reflect the accretion of dividends.

TREATMENT OF MINORITY INTERESTS FOR ENTERPRISE VALUATION

There are generally two methods of treating the minority interests when valuing the enterprise. The first method is to reduce the free cash flows to the firm by the amount of the projected minority interests in earnings and to use the resulting cash flows to determine the value of the parent shareholder's equity. Although, at first glance, this seems like a reasonable approach, it suffers from two serious flaws:

1. There is rarely enough information available to an outside analyst to allow projecting the operating results of the subsidiary separately and to then project the minority interests in earnings with any expectation of accuracy.

2. The minority interests in earnings is a noncash item not affecting the free cash flows to the enterprise.

The more common and superior treatment of minority interests is to approach them in the same fashion as long-term debt, for analysis but not financial reporting purposes. Simply stated, when performing discounted cash flow analysis, first determine the present value of the entire enterprise and then reduce it by the last reported book value of the minority interests. This resolves both of the issues raised above because it eliminates the need to forecast minority interests with any accuracy and eliminates any need for reducing the enterprise free cash flows.

FORECASTING MINORITY INTERESTS

A common forecasting error that sometimes appears is the simplifying and projecting of both the Minority interests in earnings and Minority interests accounts "flat," or at a constant value through all future periods. This approach is conceptually flawed in two respects and produces errors that, while often insignificant, are easily avoidable. The first issue is projecting no-growth or "flat" minority interests in earnings on the income statement. In reality, we usually expect the earnings of consolidated subsidiaries to grow over time, at least at the long-term inflation rate, so that flat projections understate future period's minority interests in earnings. Because minority interests in earnings is a subtraction before the Net income to common line, understating minority interests in earnings in this manner overstates the parent company's net income and accordingly, earnings per share. The second issue occurs on the balance sheet. Regardless of the income statement treatment, the balance sheet Minority interests account cannot remain "flat" unless the consolidating subsidiary is either dividending an amount exactly equal to its earnings or the holders of the minority interests are adjusting their positions by the exact amount of the dividend. The consistent effect of this error is understating the minority interests of income-producing subsidiaries or understating the minority interests of loss-producing subsidiaries. Its materiality can vary significantly depending on the analysis that is being performed, how it is modeled, and how the debt and equity ratios are constructed. The unavoidable result is that something, somewhere will not balance because failing to capture the minority interests in earnings understates the firm's total capitalization. This may sometimes make the enterprise appear to have less cash than actually available or appear to require unnecessary financing.

TREATMENT OF MINORITY INTERESTS IN M&A TRANSACTIONS

Minority interests positions are changed during M&A transactions in one of three principal ways. The first is the creation of a new minority interest when Parent Company initially acquires less than 100 percent of the outstanding common equity of Subsidiary Company. The second is the purchase, by Parent Company, of all or part of Outsider's interest in Subsidiary Company independent of any other transaction. Lastly is the purchase of all or part of Outsider's interest in Subsidiary Company as a part of Acquiror Company's acquisition of Parent Company.

Creating a Minority Interest In a Partial Acquisition

In a partial acquisition of Subsidiary Company by Parent Company, the portion of Subsidiary Company's common equity that remains outstanding is recognized by Parent Company as a minority interest. Under current U.S. GAAP purchase accounting rules, the portion of Subsidiary's net assets that are purchased are revalued to fair value at the time of the transaction, and the portion that is left outstanding is recorded at book value. While this approach is premised on the establishment of fair market values in arm's-length transactions, it is neither intuitive nor entirely practical.

RECOGNITON OF GOODWILL IN MINORITY INTERESTS TRANSACTIONS MAY CHANGE

FASB decided in late 2002 that "The full goodwill method should be used to recognize goodwill in the acquisition of less than 100 percent controlling interest in the acquired entity."[2] Although FASB board decisions are not considered part of GAAP until the underlying Financial Accounting Standards are formally modified, it is likely that this decision will stand and analysts involved with partial acquisitions should contact their accounting advisors to determine the status of this item. For comparison, an example of each approach is provided.

EXAMPLE 2-5. Recording an Acquisition of Less Than 100 Percent Controlling Interest— Partial Goodwill Method

Subsidiary Company is a publicly traded corporation having assets with a book value of 200 and fair value of 300, common equity of 100, and liabilities whose book values equal their fair values of 100. On 31-Dec-20X0, Parent Company acquires 75 percent of the common stock of Subsidiary Company in the open market for 250 cash. The remaining 25 percent of Subsidiary Company remains in the hands of Outsiders. Parent records the transaction on 31-Dec-20X0 as follows:

dr:	Subsidiary Company assets	275.0		(1)
dr:	Goodwill (created in transaction)	150.0		(4)
	cr: Subsidiary Company liabilities		100.0	(2)
	cr: Cash (paid out in transaction)		300.0	(2)
	cr: Minority interests (created in transaction)		25.0	(3)

memo:
(1) 75 percent of Subsidiary Company assets purchased are written up to fair value.
$(300 - 200) \times 75\% = 75 + 200 = 275$
(2) Subsidiary Company liabilities and cash paid in the transaction are recorded at book / fair value.
(3) 25 percent of Subsidiary Company net assets are recorded as Minority interests at book value.
$(200 - 100) \times 25\% = 25$
(4) Transaction goodwill is recorded as the excess of the purchase price over the fair value of the net identifiable assets.
$300 - (275 - 100) - 25 = 150$

EXAMPLE 2-6. Recording an Acquisition of Less Than 100 Percent Controlling Interest—Full Goodwill Method

Assume the same fact pattern as Example 2-5, except the transaction is recorded using the full goodwill method.

dr:	Subsidiary Company assets		300.0	(1)
dr:	Goodwill (created in transaction)		150.0	(4)
	cr:	Subsidiary Company liabilities	100.0	(2)
	cr:	Cash (paid out in transaction)	300.0	(2)
	cr:	Minority interests (created in transaction)	50.0	(3)

memo:
- (1) 100 percent of Subsidiary Company assets purchased are written up to fair value of 300.
- (2) Subsidiary Company liabilities and cash paid in the transaction are recorded at fair value.
- (3) 25 percent of Subsidiary Company net assets are recorded as Minority interests at fair value.
  $(300 - 100) \times 25\% = 50$
- (4) Transaction goodwill is recorded as the excess of the purchase price over the fair value of the net identifiable assets.
  $300 - (300 - 100) - 50 = 150$

Creating a Minority Interest in Preferred Equity

A seldom encountered transaction that creates a special type of minority interest occurs when Parent Company purchases a controlling interest in Subsidiary Company but leaves some of Subsidiary Company's preferred equity in the hands of Outsiders.

EXAMPLE 2-7. Recording an Acquisition of a Controlling Interest—Preferred Stock Remains Outstanding

Assume that on 31-Dec-20X0, publicly traded Subsidiary Company has assets having both a book and fair value of 200, liabilities having both book and fair values of 100, common equity of 75 and preferred equity of 25. On 1-Jan-20X1, Parent Company purchases 100 percent of the common equity of Subsidiary Company for 75. Parent Company records the transaction as:

dr:	Subsidiary Company assets		200.0	(1)
	cr:	Subsidiary Company liabilities	100.0	(1)
	cr:	Cash (paid out in transaction)	75.0	(1)
	cr:	Minority interests in preferred equity (created in transaction)	25.0	(2)

memo:
- (1) Subsidiary Company's assets and liabilities and cash paid in the transaction are all recorded at fair value.
- (2) 25 of Subsidiary Company preferred equity that is still outstanding is recorded at book value as Minority interests in preferred equity.

Parent Company's Purchase of an Existing Minority Interest

In the second instance, Parent Company "buys in" some or all of Outsider's interest in Subsidiary Company. While not considered to be a business combination, *FAS-141, Business Combinations*, requires that the transaction still be accounted for under purchase accounting even if Outsider's interest were to be purchased by Subsidiary Company directly instead of by Parent Company.[3] Often when firms purchase or "buy in" minority interests in their consolidated subsidiaries, the transaction occurs at a significant premium over the recorded value.

EXAMPLE **2-8. Elimination of a Minority Interest by Parent Company's Purchase of Outstanding Subsidiary Shares**

Following the fact pattern of Example 2-1, Parent Company initially acquires 75 percent of the common stock of Subsidiary Company for cash of 75 and records minority interests of 25 on 31-Dec-20X0. Assume that two years later, on 31-Dec-20X2 the balance of the Minority interests account has grown to 80 due to recognition of minority interests in earnings in 20X1 and 20X2. As a further simplification, assume that the fair value of each of Subsidiary Company's assets and liabilities equals its book value on the transaction date. On 1-Jan-20X3, Parent Company purchases all of the outstanding interest in Subsidiary Company from Outsiders at a 25-percent premium for 100. Parent Company records this transaction on 1-Jan-20X3 as follows:

dr:	Minority interest	80.0	
dr:	Goodwill (created in transaction)	20.0	
	cr: Cash (paid out in transaction)		100.0

MODELING MINORITY INTERESTS

Modeling the accounting for minority interests is fairly straightforward once you resolve the challenges of projecting the minority interests in earnings. If the minority interest is in a single, publicly traded company, then projecting the separate subsidiary earnings may be a relatively simple task. At the other end of the spectrum, minority interests in privately-held subsidiaries may be projected based on industry expectations or even at the long-term inflation rate. The latter may also provide a simplified approximation if multiple minority interests exist in diversified subsidiaries.

EXAMPLE **2-9. Modeling the Minority Interest in a Consolidated Subsidiary**

Assume that Parent Company owns a 75-percent controlling interest in Subsidiary Company which it acquired under the same fact pattern shown in Example 2-1. Subsidiary Company has earnings of 100 in 20X1 and companies comparable to Subsidiary Company expect 3-year average forward earnings growth of 8 percent. Figure 2-2 illustrates Parent Company's consolidated financial statements modeling the minority interests.

FIGURE 2·2

Parent Company's Consolidated Financial Statements for Years 20X0 Through 20X3, Modeling Minority Interests

Parent's consolidated financial statements

Income Statement	20X0	20X1	20X2	20X3
After-tax earnings	500.0	600.0	660.0	726.0
Minority interests in earnings	-	25.0	27.0	29.2
Minority interests in earnings growth			8.0%	8.0%
Net income	500.0	575.0	633.0	696.8

Balance Sheet				
Minority interests - beginning balance	-	25.0	50.0	77.0
Add: Minority interests in earnings		25.0	27.0	29.0
Investment in affiliates - ending balance	25.0	50.0	77.0	106.2

Cash Flows				
Net income	500.0	575.0	633.0	696.8
Add: Minority interests in earnings	-	25.0	27.0	29.2
Cash from operations	500.0	600.0	660.0	726.0

Notice that the forward Minority interests in earnings is projected using the same rate as the consolidated subsidiary's expected growth. This is not always a readily available number and sometimes must be estimated based on expectations for the subsidiary's peer group. If the firm has several partially owned consolidated subsidiaries, it may be appropriate to disaggregate the earnings projections to allow the use of different forward earnings growth rates.

CHAPTER SUMMARY

A minority interest exists whenever a consolidated subsidiary is not wholly owned. The amount of the consolidated subsidiary's earnings that is proportional to the outside owners' interests is reported on the parent's consolidated income statement as Minority interests in earnings. This is a reduction from the parent's after-tax earnings. If the consolidated subsidiary has an operating loss (negative earnings), the effect is to increase the parent company's earnings. The amount of the consolidated subsidiary's net assets that is proportional to the outside owners' interests is reported on the parent's consolidated balance sheet as Minority interests. The balance sheet account increases (or decreases) each period by the amount of the Minority interests in earnings (or losses) from the income statement. The correct balance sheet classification of Minority interests is as an equity account, although it is often treated as a liability when performing credit analyses.

Minority interests should be forecast in line with the expected growth rate of the consolidated subsidiary. If the practice of forecasting minority interests as "flat" or at zero growth is followed, then the parent company's earnings and retained earnings will usually be overstated. To facilitate the proper projection of the minority interests in earnings, projection/valuation models should include the ability to input the consolidated subsidiary's (or peer group's) expected future growth rate. Valuation can be simplified by projecting full financial data forward, performing the discounted cash flow analysis for the entire firm, and then subtracting the current balance sheet amount for minority interests from the present value of the firm.

In M&A transactions, any piece of the target company's equity, either common or preferred, that is not bought in is classified on the parent's (acquirer's) balance sheet as Minority interest. Current guidance is to record the portion of the target that is purchased at fair value and then record the unpurchased portion as a minority interest at historic value. In all probability this treatment will change in the near term, and analysts facing this situation should discuss the facts and circumstances of the transaction with their internal accounting advisory.

CHAPTER 3

Deferred Income Taxes and Income Tax Reporting

INTRODUCTION

A complete understanding of income taxes requires a good understanding of both the financial reporting rules and the federal income tax regulations. Throughout the chapter keep in mind that firms maintain two different sets of financial records, one for financial reporting purposes, which we refer to as the "book" records, and one for federal taxation purposes or "tax" records. Book accounting for the majority of firms is done under the accrual method, and tax accounting is accomplished using a cash method. Other "disconnects" exist between book and tax accounting that are reconciled through the mechanism of deferred income taxes. Without a proper understanding of the relationship between book taxes, cash taxes, and deferred income taxes, it is not possible to accurately analyze or project a firm's cash flows.

I begin the chapter with the U.S. GAAP tax reporting principles and a brief discussion of how deferred income taxes are treated in some M&A transactions. This really sets the groundwork for what follows, how to calculate, model, and project the provision for taxes and separate it into its cash and deferred components.

BASIC PRINCIPLES OF TAX REPORTING

Financial reporting of income taxes under U.S. Generally Accepted Accounting Principles (GAAP) primarily conforms to the requirements of *Statement of Financial Accounting Standards No. 109, Accounting for Income Taxes (FAS-109)*. *FAS-109* presents four basic principles for reporting income taxes:[1]

1. A tax expense or benefit is recognized for the estimated taxes payable or refundable on tax returns for the current year (cash taxes).

2. A deferred income tax liability or asset is recognized for the estimated future tax effects attributable to temporary differences and carryforwards.

3. The measurement of deferred income tax liabilities and assets is based on provisions of the enacted tax law, not on anticipated future tax law.

4. The measurement of deferred income tax assets is reduced, if necessary, by the amount of any tax benefits that, based on currently available evidence, are not expected to be realized.

THE FIRST PRINCIPLE

The first principle is often the point of greatest interest for analysts, particularly credit analysts, because it describes the component of income tax expense (also presented on the income statement as the Provision for income taxes) that is either paid to or refunded from the taxing authorities in cash. The next three items are the additions and subtractions to the first item that are necessary to calculate the appropriate book or GAAP income tax expense or benefit. The next three items address the noncash effects encompassing the differences between the calculation of taxes for financial reporting and federal and state reporting purposes.

THE SECOND PRINCIPLE

Before proceeding to a discussion of the second principle, the tax meanings of two terms, temporary differences and permanent differences must be introduced.

Temporary Differences

Conceptually, temporary differences are what occur when an item of income (expense) or gain (loss) is reported for financial reporting purposes but is deferred to (or from) a different period for the calculation of cash income taxes. Remember that one of the objectives of financial reporting is to group items of income and the expenses incurred in generating that income in the same reporting period. This is true even if the Internal Revenue Service (IRS) is willing to wait until the next year or the year after to collect the taxes due for those earnings. The relevant issue of temporary differences is that the taxes will eventually be paid or the refund will eventually be received, but not in the current reporting period.

FAS-109 lists two general instances that may result in temporary differences:[2]

1. When there is a difference between the amount of taxable income and pretax financial income in a year or

2. When there are differences between the tax bases of assets or liabilities and their reported amounts in financial statements (book bases).

Differences Between Taxable Income and Pretax Financial Income

Differences arise between taxable income (for tax purposes) and pretax financial income (for book purposes) because of the different objectives of tax and book reporting. Financial reporting focuses on recognizing revenues, and the expenses needed to generate those revenues, in the period when they are earned. Income is generally reportable in the period that it is received, without regard to the earnings process being complete. Also, some items of income (or expense) may not be taxable (or tax deductible).

EXAMPLE 3-1. Effects of Differences Between Taxable Income and Pretax Financial Income

An example illustrating the difference between taxable income and pretax financial income is Taxpayer Company selling a prepaid two-year monthly-service subscription for 200. By the end of the first year, it has earned only half the revenue because it has delivered only half of the promised services. For financial reporting, the company recognizes 20X1 revenues of 100; the other 100 of revenues are deferred until the earnings process is complete. However, for tax reporting, the entire 200 received in Year 1 is treated as taxable income. The difference between the taxable income of 200 and pretax financial income of 100 is treated as temporary because Taxpayer Company eventually recognizes the entire 200 for both financial (book) reporting (100 in 20X1 and 100 in 20X2) and tax reporting (200 in 20X1 and 0 in 20X2). The temporary difference of 100 gives rise to a deferred income tax asset in 20X1 that reverses in 20X2. Assume that all earnings of Taxpayer Company are taxable using a 40-percent tax rate.

Taxpayer Company's 20X1 Income Statement

Tax Year 20X1	Book Reporting		Tax Reporting
Pretax financial income	100.0	Taxable income	200.0
Income tax expense	40.0	Cash taxes	80.0
Net income	60.0		

The financial reporting entry recording Year 20X1 taxes is:

dr:	Income tax expense	40.0	
dr:	Deferred income tax asset	40.0	
	cr: Cash		80.0

Note three items: First, the deferred income tax asset is increased to reflect the future tax benefit (for financial reporting purposes) that Taxpayer Company expects to realize in 20X2 because it has paid the full 80 tax obligation in 20X1. Secondly, net income is determined using income tax expense calculated for book purposes, not using current income tax expense (cash taxes). Lastly, if a difference is permanent, such as the difference caused by recognizing nontaxable income, then there is no deferred income tax effect.

Taxpayer Company's 20X2 Income Statement

Tax Year 20X2	Book Reporting		Tax Reporting
Pretax financial income	100.0	Taxable income	0.0
Income tax expense	40.0	Cash taxes	0.0
Net income	60.0		

The financial reporting entry recording 20X2 taxes is:

dr:	Income tax expense	40.0	
	cr: Deferred income tax asset		40.0

In 20X2, we note two items. First, Taxpayer Company pays no cash taxes and secondly, the temporary difference arising from the revenue recognition reverses. Again, note that net income is determined using income tax expense and not current tax expense (cash taxes). The tax rate remains the same, 40 percent.

Differences Between Book and Tax Bases

Differences between the book bases and tax bases of assets and liabilities result in taxable (deductible) amounts in future years when the reported amounts of assets are settled and the reported amounts of liabilities are settled. Some examples are:

- Differences between the assigned values and tax bases of the assets and liabilities recognized in a business combination accounted for as a purchase
- Equity in earnings of affiliates, as discussed in Chapter 1, that are recognized for book purposes before being realized through future dividend income or gains on sales
- A reduction of the tax bases of depreciable assets because of tax credits
- Expenses (such as accelerated depreciation) or losses that are deductible for tax reporting before they are recognized in financial income
- Revenues (such as some subscriptions received in advance) or gains that are taxable before they are recognized in financial income
- Recognition of a liability for an asset retirement obligation and the capitalization of the initial recognition amount into the underlying asset

The temporary differences described in *FAS109* as those between the book bases and the tax bases of assets or liabilities, generally occur for the following reasons. Assets are depreciated at different rates for book and tax purposes, the tax bases of the assets are adjusted to reflect investment credits, or the book bases are written up (down) to fair value (usually as a result of purchase accounting). Figure 3-1 shows how the book basis and tax basis of an individual asset varies over time due to differences between the Modified Accelerated Cost Recovery System (MACRS) and the financial reporting depreciation rates. The figure assumes that an asset with a cost basis of 1000 is placed into service on 30-June-20X0. 30-June is assumed for simplicity because the midyear convention required by MACRS only allows a half-year of depreciation in the first year of service. Note that the only times the book and tax bases are equal is at the beginning and end of life due to the accelerated depreciation allowed for tax purposes.

Two Rules Regarding Differences Between Book and Tax Bases:

1. If goodwill is not deductible for tax purposes, then regardless of any difference between its book and tax bases, it has no deferred income tax effect.

FIGURE 3·1

Comparison of an Asset's Book and Tax Bases Over its Useful Life

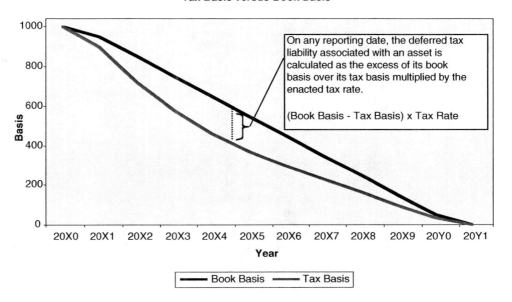

Tax Basis versus Book Basis

On any reporting date, the deferred tax liability associated with an asset is calculated as the excess of its book basis over its tax basis multiplied by the enacted tax rate.

(Book Basis - Tax Basis) x Tax Rate

2. For other assets, including tax-deductible goodwill, an excess (deficit) of book basis over tax basis gives rise to a deferred income tax liability (asset) equal to the difference multiplied by the enacted statutory tax rate. For liabilities, an excess (deficit) of book basis over tax basis gives rise to a deferred income tax asset (liability) equal to the difference times the enacted statutory tax rate.

EXAMPLE 3-2. Deferred Income Tax Effects From Temporary Differences in Book and Tax Bases

This example illustrates the commonly encountered effect of temporary differences in an asset's basis arising from different depreciation rates. Assume that on 30-June-20X1, Taxpayer Company purchases and places in service an asset costing 100. At the time of purchase, they record both the book basis and tax basis as 100. The asset is depreciated over three years using the straight-line method for book purposes and the Modified Accelerated Cost Recovery System (MACRS) method for tax purposes. For book purposes, 20X1 depreciation is 16.7, equal to 100 divided by 3 (3-year expected life) divided by 2 (because the asset was only in service for one-half of 20X1). Tax depreciation of 33.3 is calculated as 66.7 (using the double-declining balance method) divided by 2 to reflect one-half of one year's depreciation.

Taxpayer Company's 20X1 Financial Statements

Tax Year 20X1	Book Reporting		Tax Reporting
Revenues	100.0	Revenues	100.0
Depreciation	16.7	MACRS Depreciation	33.3
Pretax financial income	83.3	Taxable income	66.7
Income tax expense @ 40%	33.3	Cash taxes @ 40%	26.7
Net income	50.0		

Asset Basis	Book Reporting	Tax Reporting
Beginning 30-Jun-20X1	100.0	100.0
Less: 20X1 depreciation	16.7	33.3
Ending 31-Dec-20X1	83.3	66.7

The financial reporting entry recording 20X1 taxes is:

dr:	Income tax expense	33.3	
	cr: Deferred income tax liability		6.6
	cr: Cash		26.7

The 6.6 increase to the deferred income tax liability account is determined by calculating the expected account balance as the excess of the book basis over the tax basis times the tax rate $(83.3 - 66.7) \times 40\% = 6.6$ and then subtracting any existing deferred income tax liability already recorded for this asset. Continuing in 20X2, Taxpayer Company recognizes a full-year of straight-line depreciation (33.3 = 100 divided by 3) for book purposes and for tax purposes (44.4 using MACRS double-declining balance).

Taxpayer Company's 20X2 Financial Statements

Tax Year 20X2	Book Reporting		Tax Reporting
Revenues	100.0	Revenues	100.0
Depreciation	33.3	MACRS Depreciation	44.4
Pretax financial income	66.7	Taxable income	55.6
Income tax expense @ 40%	26.7	Cash taxes @ 40%	22.2
Net income	40.0		

Asset Basis	Book Reporting	Tax Reporting
Beginning 30-Jun-20X1	100.0	100.0
Less: 20X1 depreciation	16.7	33.3
Ending 31-Dec-20X1	83.3	66.7
Less: 20X2 depreciation	33.3	44.4
Ending 31-Dec-20X2	50.0	22.3

The financial reporting entry recording 20X2 taxes is:

dr:	Income tax expense	26.7	
	cr: Deferred income tax liability		4.5
	cr: Cash		22.2

The 4.5 increase to the deferred income tax liability account is determined by calculating the expected Deferred income tax liability balance sheet account balance as the excess of the book basis over the tax basis times the tax rate $(50.0 - 22.3) \times 40\% = 11.1$. The existing deferred income tax liability already recorded for this asset is subtracted to arrive at the 20X2 contribution $(11.1 - 6.6 = 4.5)$. Continuing in 20X3, Taxpayer Company recognizes a full year of straight-line depreciation $(33.3 = 100$ divided by 3) for book purposes and for tax purposes (14.8 using the MACRS double-declining balance method).

Taxpayer Company's 20X3 Financial Statements

Tax Year 20X3	Book Reporting		Tax Reporting
Revenues	100.0	Revenues	100.0
Depreciation	33.3	MACRS Depreciation	14.8
Pretax financial income	66.7	Taxable income	85.2
Income tax expense @ 40%	26.7	Cash taxes @ 40%	34.1
Net income	40.0		

Asset Basis	Book Reporting		Tax Reporting
Beginning 30-Jun-20X1	100.0		100.0
Less: 20X1 depreciation	16.7		33.3
Ending 31-Dec-20X1	83.3		66.7
Less: 20X2 depreciation	33.3		44.4
Ending 31-Dec-20X2	50.0		22.3
Less: 20X3 depreciation	33.3		14.8
Ending 31-Dec-20X3	16.7		7.5

The financial reporting entry recording 20X3 taxes is:

dr:	Income tax expense	26.7	
dr:	Deferred income tax liability	7.4	
	cr: Cash		34.1

Note that the temporary difference begins reversing in this year, reducing (debiting) the deferred income tax liability account by 7.4. $(16.7 - 7.5) \times 40\% = 3.7 - 6.6 - 4.5 = -7.4$

Finally in 20X4 (because the asset was in service for only six months in 20X1) the temporary difference reverses completely (the asset is depreciated to zero for both book and tax) and the associated deferred income tax liability account reduces to zero.

Taxpayer Company's 20X4 Financial Statements

Tax Year 20X4	Book Reporting		Tax Reporting
Revenues	100.0	Revenues	100.0
Depreciation	16.7	MACRS Depreciation	7.5
Pretax financial income	83.3	Taxable income	92.5
Income tax expense @ 40%	33.3	Cash taxes @ 40%	37.0
Net income	50.0		

Asset Basis	Book Reporting	Tax Reporting
Beginning 30-Jun-20X1	100.0	100.0
Less: 20X1 depreciation	16.7	33.3
Ending 31-Dec-20X1	83.3	66.7
Less: 20X2 depreciation	33.3	44.4
Ending 31-Dec-20X2	50.0	22.3
Less: 20X3 depreciation	33.3	14.8
Ending 31-Dec-20X3	16.7	7.5
Less: 20X4 depreciation	16.7	7.5
Ending 31-Dec-20X4	0.0	0.0

The financial reporting entry recording 20X4 taxes is:

dr:	Income tax expense	33.3	
dr:	Deferred income tax liability	3.7	
	cr: Cash		37.0

Note that the temporary difference fully reverses in this year, reducing the deferred income tax liability account by 3.7. $(0.0 - 0.0) \times 40\% = 0.0 - 6.6 - 4.5 - (7.4) = -3.7$.

Carryforwards

The second principle also includes the effects of items that occur in the present for financial reporting purposes but whose effect for federal tax purposes may be carried forward into one or more future periods. Three of the more common items of this nature are net operating loss (NOLs) carryforwards, capital loss carryovers, and income tax credit carryovers. For our understanding here, it is sufficient to focus primarily on the treatment of NOLs and only briefly discuss the other two.

Net Operating Loss Carryforwards

Net operating losses are generally first applied against the last two years (the *Job Creation and Worker Assistance Act of 2002* increased this to five years for losses occurring in 2001 or 2002) of prior earnings, generating a cash tax refund in the current period. If the losses are greater than the earnings in those prior periods, or if the taxpayer elects only to apply the operating losses against future periods, the difference is carried forward and applied against future earnings for up to 20 years. Losses remaining unused after 20 years expire without providing any tax benefit. The amount of the estimated future tax benefits from the carryforwards is recorded as a deferred income tax asset.

EXAMPLE 3-3. Future Tax Benefits of a Net Operating Loss (NOL) Carryforward

Assume that Taxpayer Company suffers an operating loss of 1000 in tax year 20X0. The company elects to treat this loss as a carryforward and to use it to offset taxable income in future periods, expecting that the currently enacted statutory tax rate of (35 percent federal rate + assumed 5 percent state rate) = 40 percent applies. Comparing the treatment of this event for both book and tax reporting, we see:

Taxpayer Company's 20X0 Income Statement

Tax Year 20X0	Book Reporting		Tax Reporting
Pretax financial loss	(1,000.0)	Taxable income	0.0
Income tax benefit	400.0	Cash taxes	0.0
Net income	(600.0)	Loss carryforward	1,000.0

The financial reporting entry recording Year 20X0 taxes is:

dr:	Deferred income tax asset	400.0	
cr:	Income tax benefit		400.0
memo:	To record deferred income tax asset (1,000.0 × 40.0%)		

If Taxpayer Company realizes the results shown in Figure 3-2 for tax years 20X1 through 20X2, then it also realizes the tax benefit shown for each of those years. The total amount of the expected benefit is reported as a deferred income tax asset in 20X0, the year when the loss occurs, and that asset account is reduced by the amount of the tax benefit realized in each future period.

There are several notable items in Figure 3-2, the first being that in 20X0, the entire operating loss is recorded as a net operating loss carryforward in Taxpayer

FIGURE 3-2

Taxpayer Company's Operating Results and Tax Treatment for Years 20X0 through 20X3

Taxpayer Company's Financial Statements

Income Statement	20X0	20X1	20X2	20X3
Earnings before taxes	(1,000.0)	300.0	400.0	500.0
Income tax expense (benefit) @ 40%	(400.0)	120.0	160.0	200.0
Net income	(600.0)	180.0	240.0	300.0

Balance Sheet				
Cash	600.0	900.0	1,300.0	1,720.0
Deferred tax asset	400.0	280.0	120.0	-
Owner's equity	1,000.0	1,180.0	1,420.0	1,720.0

Net Operating Loss Carryforward	20X0	20X1	20X2	20X3
Net operating loss carryforward - beginning	-	1,000.0	700.0	300.0
Net operating loss added (used)	1,000.0	(300.0)	(400.0)	(300.0)
Net operating loss carryforward - ending	1,000.0	700.0	300.0	-

Reconciliation of GAAP Income Tax Expense	20X0	20X1	20X2	20X3
Cash taxes payable (refundable)	-	-	-	80.0
(Increase) decrease in deferred tax asset account	(400.0)	120.0	160.0	120.0
Income tax expense (benefit) @ 40%	(400.0)	120.0	160.0	200.0

Company's working papers. Even though Taxpayer Company reports an income tax benefit of 400 in 20X0, that is a noncash item, as seen from the Reconciliation of GAAP Income Tax Expense, expected to be realized as a cash refund in future periods. Consequently, Taxpayer Company recognizes a deferred income tax asset of 400 reflecting that expectation. Secondly, in year 20X1, Taxpayer Company realizes earnings before taxes of 300 but since the net operating loss carryforward of 1000 is greater, the 300 is completely offset and no cash taxes are paid. This reduces the net operating loss carryforward to (1,000 – 300) = 700, reflecting its use to offset taxable income. Lastly, notice that the Deferred income tax asset account is reduced each period by an amount equal to the enacted statutory tax rate of 40 percent times the amount of earnings before taxes that are offset by using the NOL carryforward. The mechanics of loss carryforwards are discussed in more detail in Chapter 12, Net Operating Loss Deductions.

Capital Loss Carryovers

The accounting and results for capital loss carryovers are very similar to those for net operating loss carryforwards subject to three important distinctions. The first is that capital losses only arise from transactions involving capital assets. Simply stated, for a corporate or business taxpayer, the Internal Revenue Code defines capital assets (by exception) as all assets except:

- Inventory
- Depreciable assets
- Real property
- Accounts or notes receivable
- Supplies
- Commodities contracts held by commodities dealers
- Properly identified hedges

Secondly, losses incurred on the sale of capital assets may only be used to offset capital gains. In periods where Taxpayer Company generates a net capital loss, the capital loss may be carried back into each of the three prior years provided it does not increase or create a net operating loss in any year. The last important difference is that capital loss carryovers have a much shorter life than net operating losses (20 years). After being carried back for three years, any remaining capital losses may subsequently be carried over and applied as short-term capital losses in each of the next *five* years. After the fifth tax year, any unused portion of the capital loss carryover expires.

Income Tax Credits

Income tax credits produce income tax benefits by directly reducing tax liability. One dollar of applicable income tax credits results in a direct one dollar reduction of cash income taxes payable. There are two main types of income tax credits. Refundable income tax credits can be used to offset income tax liability, and if they exceed the tax liability, result in Taxpayer Company receiving an income tax refund. Nonrefundable income tax credits, like refundable income tax credits, may be used to directly offset income tax liability, but unlike refundable income tax credits cannot result in Taxpayer Company receiving an income tax refund. Some nonrefundable income tax credits may be carried over into future periods. When they are carried over, Taxpayer Company recognizes a deferred tax asset equal to the full amount of the tax credit. Remember that income tax credits offset income tax liabilities on a one-for-one basis so one dollar of income-tax-credit carryover produces one dollar of future cash income tax benefit. Table 3-1 shows the

TABLE 3·1

Abbreviated Summary of Carryback and Carryforward Items

Deduction or credit	Carryback Period	Carryforward Period
Net operating loss (all – default)	By default, companies may carry a net operating loss deduction back to each of the 2 taxable years preceding the loss period.	By default, companies may carry any net operating loss deductions remaining after carryback forward to each of the 20 taxable years following the loss period.
Net operating loss (all – waiver of carryback)	Companies may elect to waive the entire carryback period. Such elections are made separately for net operating losses arising in each taxable year and the election is irrevocable.	Companies waiving carryback simply carry the entire net operating loss deduction for a loss year forward to each of the 20 taxable years following the loss year.
Net operating loss (tax years 2001 and 2002 – default)	Under special provisions of the *Job Creation and Worker Assistance Act of 2002*, by default companies may carry a net operating loss deduction arising in tax years 2001 or 2002 back to each of the 5 taxable years preceding the loss period.	By default, companies may carry any net operating loss deductions remaining after carryback forward to each of the 20 taxable years following the loss period.
Net operating loss (tax years 2001 and 2002 – forgoing special provision)	Companies may elect to forgo the special 5-year carryback period. Companies choosing to forgo the special provision treat the losses as if the provision was never enacted.	Companies may carry any net operating loss deductions remaining after carryback (unless waived) forward to each of the 20 taxable years following the loss period.
Net capital loss	Corporations carry a net capital loss deduction back to each of the 3 taxable years preceding the loss period provided the loss does not create or increase a net operating loss in a carryback period.	Corporations may carry any net operating loss deductions remaining after carryback forward to each of the 5 taxable years following the loss period.
Net passive activity credit	Taxpayers may not carry back net passive activity credits.	Taxpayers may carry any unused passive activity credits forward indefinitely.
AMT liability credit	Taxpayers may not carry back AMT liability.	Taxpayers may carry AMT liability credits forward indefinitely and apply them in taxable years that they are not subject to the AMT.

carryback and carryforward periods for net operating losses, capital losses, and tax credits. The table is an abbreviated summary and should not be viewed as a definitive or complete reference.

Permanent Differences

Differences between tax and book reporting that are not temporary are considered permanent. This might include some items such as the nontaxable receipt of certain insurance payments or receipt of tax-exempt interest income. Generally, the effects of permanent differences are excluded when calculating taxes for both financial and tax reporting purposes. Because they are excluded for both, they do not cause recognition of deferred income tax items.

THE THIRD PRINCIPLE

Deferred income taxes are calculated using the currently enacted statutory tax rates. This provides more comparable estimates from period to period and eliminates the need for reporting firms to continually recalculate deferred income tax effects in response to proposed or announced changes in the tax laws. Because tax legislation or rulemaking is rarely enacted exactly as proposed and when imposed often "grandfathers" or exempts prior events, this approach eliminates a considerable amount of unintentional misreporting of deferred income tax items. A reasonable estimate of the enacted statutory tax rate is to take the current federal tax rate of 35 percent and assume a state rate of 5 percent for a total enacted statutory tax rate for calculating deferred income tax items of 40 percent.

THE FOURTH PRINCIPLE

The fourth principle focuses on how the firm should report expected future tax benefits that it feels may not be realized. Recall from Example 3-1 that deferred income tax assets are recorded to reflect future tax benefits that the firm expects to realize. Those benefits may stem from operating losses in the current or prior periods or from other factors such as the result of differences in the financial and tax amortization periods of intangible assets. Because deferred income tax items are reflective of expected future events, they may exhibit varying degrees of uncertainty of realization. This brings to light an aspect of deferred income tax items that is not always apparent from a reading of a firm's disclosures, which is, "all deferred income tax items are not created equal."

As an illustration, consider the certainty of Taxpayer Company realizing a deferred income tax asset recorded due to temporary differences between the book and tax bases of an intangible asset. The majority of tax-deductible intangible assets are assigned a 15-year recovery period under *Internal Revenue Code (IRC) Section 197, Amortization of goodwill and certain other intangibles,* regardless of their actual useful life. This can result in cases where intangible assets are amortized over a shorter period for financial reporting purposes than for income tax purposes. This situation, where at the end of a reporting period an intangible asset's tax basis is higher than its book basis, results in the recognition of a deferred income tax asset. Generally, firms realize the benefits associated with this type of deferred income tax asset because, either through abandonment or continued tax amortization, the book and tax bases of the asset eventually reach zero and, at that point, equal each other. When the book and tax bases of an asset are equal, then the zero difference between the bases produces a zero-deferred income tax effect. Realization of deferred income tax assets due to an excess of the tax basis of an asset over the book basis of the asset are fairly certain events.

Secondly, consider the certainty of Taxpayer Company recovering a deferred income tax asset associated with NOL carryforwards. The company must be capable of using the NOL carryforwards before the 20-year carryforward period (discussed earlier) passes and the NOLs expire. It is unlikely that Taxpayer Company could continue generating losses for that period of time, never realizing any of the tax benefit from the NOL carryforwards. However, it is probable that if Taxpayer Company experiences only one or two years of heavy losses and slowly returns to profitability, they might not be able to realize all of the future tax benefits. Additionally, certain transactions create events triggering sections of the Internal Revenue Code that further restrict the amount of NOLs that may be utilized in each period. The future tax benefits of the NOL carryforwards may or may not be realized and are less certain than the future tax benefits associated with the intangible assets (discussed above). Consequently, the portion of the deferred income tax asset associated with the NOL carryforwards is more likely to be overstated. The fourth principle provides a means for firms to identify the portion of the deferred income tax asset that may not be recovered by recognizing a valuation allowance to reduce the deferred income tax asset account.

Valuation Allowance

If the company believes that it is not likely to realize future benefits relating to some or all of the deferred income tax asset, then it creates a valuation allowance (a contra-asset account) equal to the unrealizable portion. As previously discussed, this may be appropriate in situations where future earnings are highly uncertain. When a valuation allowance is created, it increases income tax expense in the current period. The deferred income tax asset on the balance sheet is shown net of the valuation allowance. The final effect is that the valuation allowance reduces the deferred income tax asset account and increases current period income tax expense (GAAP taxes).

Potential Financial Reporting Abuses

Valuation allowances are sometimes viewed as an area of potential abuse in financial reporting. This arises when the circumstances leading to the creation of the allowance change such that the deferred income tax asset is now considered realizable. When this occurs, the valuation allowance is released, reducing the current period income tax expense. Potential areas of abuse are the:

- Amount of the initial valuation allowance—Booking an excessive allowance "banks" future earnings.
- Timing of any release of allowance—The timing is a judgment area, providing a method of "boosting" selected period earnings.
- Amount of the allowance release—The amount is also a judgment area, providing a method of "boosting" selected period earnings.

TREATMENT OF DEFERRED INCOME TAX ITEMS IN M&A TRANSACTIONS

Treatment of deferred income tax items is significant in nontaxable business combinations using the purchase method. As part of the fair valuation of Target Company's assets and liabilities, deferred income tax assets (together with any associated valuation allowances) and deferred income tax liabilities on Target Company's books are eliminated and then recalculated to reflect the difference between the new book bases and the carryover tax bases of the other assets and liabilities. This requires a detailed knowledge of their carryover tax bases that is often not available, particularly in the early stages of a deal.

Step-Up Transactions

If the nature of the transaction is taxable, such as an *Internal Revenue Code Section 338* or other step-up transaction, then no deferred income tax assets or liabilities are recognized for differences between book and tax bases. This is because the bases of the assets and liabilities are "stepped up" in a taxable transaction so that tax bases equals book bases on the transaction date. Chapter 13 contains more discussion of asset basis step-ups.

Estimating Tax Bases

As a practicality, you may obtain reasonable estimates by assuming that Target Company's existing deferred income tax assets and liabilities were correct at the statement date (reasonable because Target Company knew both the book and tax basis of the assets and liabilities when it calculated the deferred income tax items). Increase or decrease those amounts to reflect the change in book basis resulting from any write-ups (downs) of assets and liabilities to fair value. Another adjustment to the deferred income tax asset may be required if part of that asset reflects the future benefit of net operating loss carryforwards or income tax credit carryforwards. First you must find, from the company's filings, the amount of the deferred income tax asset attributable to the net operating loss carryforwards and to the income tax credit carryforwards. Secondly estimate, based on your projections, the future benefit of the net operating loss carryforwards after considering the limitations of *Internal Revenue Code Section 382* and reduce (or increase) that portion of the deferred income tax asset accordingly. Then adjust the deferred income tax asset to account for the expected future benefit of the income tax credit carryforwards (on a dollar-for-dollar basis).

Purchase Accounting Transactions

Under purchase accounting rules for stock purchases (no step-up), the recalculated deferred income tax asset and liability are also included in the calculation of goodwill. Typically, the net effect is that every 100 write-up of purchased assets reduces goodwill by 60, assuming the use of an enacted 40-percent tax rate. This occurs because the purchased asset write-up (to the book basis) creates a temporary difference equal to the amount of the write-up. This requires the recognition of a deferred income tax liability calculated as the amount of the write-up multiplied by the enacted tax rate $(100.0 \times 40.0\%) = 40.0$. The increase in the book value of the asset of 100 reduces goodwill, but the increase in the book basis of the deferred income tax liability of 40 increases goodwill, resulting in a net reduction to goodwill of $(100 - 40) = 60$. Because the asset write-up is not tax deductible (the write-up is only to the book basis and not the tax basis), as it is amortized in future periods, the associated deferred income tax liability reverses over time.

EXAMPLE **3-4. Deferred Income Tax Effects of Fair Value Adjustments**

Assume that Acquiror Company acquires an asset as part of a no step-up transaction accounted for under purchase accounting. The book basis of the asset is written up to fair value of 100 above its existing book value of 0. Prior to the transaction on the first day of 20X1, the asset was fully depreciated for both book and tax purposes, meaning that both book and tax bases were equal to zero. The estimated remaining life of the asset after the transaction is two years.

Acquiror Company's financial reporting entry to record the write-up at the transaction date is:

dr:	Asset account		100.0
	cr:	Goodwill	60.0
	cr:	Deferred income tax liability	40.0

Acquiror Company's 20X1 Financial Statements

Tax Year 20X1	Book Reporting		Tax Reporting
Revenues	100.0	Revenues	100.0
Amortization of write-up	50.0	MACRS Depreciation	0.0
Pretax financial income	50.0	Taxable income	100.0
Income tax expense @ 40%	20.0	Cash taxes @ 40%	40.0
Net income	30.0		

Asset Basis	Book Reporting	Tax Reporting
Beginning 1-Jan-20X1	100.0	0.0
Less: 20X1 amortization of:	50.0	0.0
Ending 31-Dec-20X1	50.0	0.0

The financial reporting entry recording 20X1 taxes is:

dr:	Income tax expense	20.0	
dr:	Deferred income tax liability	20.0	
	cr: Cash		40.0

At the end of 20X1, the balance in the Asset account is a net of 50 (100 write-up less amortization of 50). The Deferred income tax liability account balance is reduced to 20, reflecting an excess of book basis over tax basis times the tax rate $(50 - 0) \times 40\% = 20$. The 20X2 effects are identical, reducing both the Asset account and Deferred income tax liability account balances to zero.

MODELING INCOME TAXES IN PROJECTION MODELS

When modeling income taxes in a projection model, the analyst's true interest often does not lie in accurately projecting the income taxes of an entity but rather on forecasting the *cash* income taxes of an entity. However, the objectives of financial reporting do not include a direct calculation of cash income taxes or a cash income tax rate. There are three general amounts that analysts attempt to estimate. Knowing any two allows the calculation of the third because, as shown in Figure 3-3, book income tax expense is generally calculated as the sum of the general current and deferred income tax expenses.

Estimating Income Tax Expense Using an Effective Tax Rate

Income tax expense is often estimated by multiplying earnings before taxes by an empirically-derived *effective tax rate*. Effective tax rates are generally reported by firms as part of the income tax footnote to the financial statements or estimated by the analyst using historic reported results. Typically, three years of data are examined,

FIGURE 3·3

Current, Deferred, and Income Tax Relationship

Current tax expense (benefit) + Deferred tax expense (benefit) = Income tax expense (benefit)

Or another way of saying the same thing is:

Cash taxes   +   Deferred taxes   =   Book taxes but probably more importantly than the number of years examined is the quality of the analyst's examination. The appropriateness of using past results as a basis for forecasting future results really hinges on how closely what has been done before parallels what will be done. In the case of projecting a firm's effective tax rate, the analyst must examine the tax structure in the historic years and compare and adjust it before using it to estimate future years. Items that are particularly sensitive when comparing past and future effective tax rates include:

- Net operating loss carrybacks, carryforwards, and other tax credits.
- Changes in enacted tax rates. Although it is not usually desirable to include the effects of *proposed* changes, often enacted changes *phase-in* in future periods. If the phase-ins are defined under current law, their effects should be captured in the projection model.
- The effects of atypical accounting periods having higher or lower than normal taxable income resulting from assets sales, acquisitions, changes in accounting estimates, or other "one-time" effects.

After adjusting data for past events not seen as being representative of future operations, the effective tax rate is often estimated as a three- to five-year average of:

$$\frac{\text{Provision for income taxes (GAAP taxes)}}{\text{Earnings before taxes}}$$

The three- to five-year average is not an industry norm or standard and the real intent is using sufficient data to derive a *representative* effective tax rate. Each of the years used for the estimate should be examined for infrequent or anomalous events and included (or excluded) from the average as the analyst's professional judgment determines. This method of calculating the effective rate also captures the effects of permanent differences without requiring them to be calculated directly because such differences act to lower the effective rate. Here again, the presumption is that any permanent differences will produce a similar taxable outcome in future periods as they did in historic periods. Once calculated, the effective tax rate is applied as the rate for the calculation of the income tax expense in future periods such that:

Forecast earnings before taxes × Effective tax rate = Income tax expense

The forecast income tax expense is subsequently adjusted as needed to account for the effects for any "one-time" events expected to occur in future periods. Figure 3-4 illustrates how to derive the effective tax rate from historical information and apply the result in the projected periods.

Cash Tax Rate

The cash tax rate is not an element of financial or income tax reporting. Instead, it is an analyst-derived metric that assumes, based on historic results, an equivalent

FIGURE 3·4

Derivation and Application of an Effective Tax Rate

Taxpayer Co.'s Financial Statements - Estimating and applying an effective tax rate						
	Historical			Projected		
Income Statement	**20W8**	**20W9**	**20X0**	**20X1**	**20X2**	**20X3**
Earnings before taxes	955.0	990.0	1,150.0	1,225.0	1,375.0	1,410.0
Tax rate on earnings				39.3%	39.3%	39.3%
Less: Income tax expense	365.0	395.0	455.0	481.4	540.4	554.1
After-tax earnings	540.0	592.0	711.2	743.6	834.6	855.9
Implied effective tax rate	38.2%	39.9%	39.6%			

Estimation of the effective tax rate using historical data

$$\frac{\text{Sum of historical income tax expense}}{\text{Sum of historical earnings before taxes}} = \frac{365.0 + 395.0 + 455.0}{955.0 + 990.0 + 1,150.0} = \frac{1,215.0}{3,095.0} = \boxed{39.3\%}$$

"cash tax rate" that the entity can be expected to pay in the future. Obviously this is a "rough justice" type of estimate which, in the face of operating stability, can produce very acceptable estimates. In estimating the cash tax rate, the analyst considers the same items as for the effective tax rate plus the additional fact that corporate income taxes are normally paid in cash on the fifteenth day of the fourth month following the end of the taxable period. Thus the historic cash taxes may lag the associated book taxes by two quarters and sometimes longer if the taxpayer extends their filing. This produces a small effect for entities that have fairly consistent histories but must be considered when adjusting for the cash tax effect of large "one-time" events.

The basic approach to estimating the effective cash tax rate is the same as for the effective tax rate, historical cash taxes are taken from the cash flow statement or as the difference between Income tax expense and the increase (decrease) in net deferred income tax liabilities. After adjusting data to reflect both past events not seen as being representative of future operations (as in the estimation of effective tax rate) and the lag time between the financial reporting period and cash outflow for tax payment, the effective tax rate is estimated as a three- to five-year average of:

$$\frac{\text{Current tax expense (cash taxes)}}{\text{Earnings before taxes}}$$

This effective cash tax rate is then applied for the estimation of cash taxes in the projected periods. The differential between the estimated effective and cash taxes is also usable for estimating the net changes to the deferred income tax accounts. Once calculated, the effective and cash tax rates are used to develop the full financial statements in the projected period as illustrated in Figure 3-5.

FIGURE 3·5

Development of Projected Financial Statements Using Derived Effective and Cash Tax Rates

Taxpayer Co.'s Financial Statements - Estimating and applying an effective tax rate

Income Statement	Historical			Projected		
	20W8	20W9	20X0	20X1	20X2	20X3
Earnings before taxes (EBT)	955.0	990.0	1,150.0	1,225.0	1,375.0	1,410.0
Tax rate on earnings				39.3%	39.3%	39.3%
Less: Income tax expense	365.0	395.0	455.0	481.4	540.4	554.1
After-tax earnings	540.0	592.0	711.2	743.6	834.6	855.9
Implied effective tax rate	38.2%	39.9%	39.6%			

Estimation of the cash tax rate

	20W8	20W9	20X0
Reported income tax expense	365.0	395.0	455.0
Increase in net deferred tax liability	25.0	30.0	45.0
Cash tax expense	340.0	365.0	410.0
Implied cash tax rate	35.6%	36.9%	35.7%

$$\frac{\text{Sum of historic cash tax expense}}{\text{Sum of historic earnings before taxes}} = \frac{340.0 + 365.0 + 410.0}{955.0 + 990.0 + 1,150.0} = \frac{1,115.0}{3,095.0} = 36.0\%$$

Calculation of projected taxes

	20X1	20X2	20X3
Income tax expense (Earnings before taxes x effective tax rate)	481.4	540.4	554.1
Cash tax rate	36.0%	36.0%	36.0%
Less: Cash tax expense (Earnings before taxes x cash tax)	441.0	495.0	507.6
Increase in net deferred tax liability	40.4	45.4	46.5

Income Statement	Historical			Projected		
	20W8	20W9	20X0	20X1	20X2	20X3
Increase in deferred tax liability	25.0	30.0	45.0	40.4	45.4	46.5
Deferred tax liability	325.0	355.0	400.0	440.4	485.8	532.3

CALCULATING THE PROVISION FOR TAXES— DETAILED CALCULATION

Quite often the tax effects of a firm's operations and transactions do not lend themselves to be estimated using the effective and/or cash tax rates. If that is the case, it becomes incumbent upon the analyst to build up the calculation of income tax expense using the information that is available. This is a difficult task and requires a certain degree of professional judgment coupled with diligent investigation because several of the pieces needed to calculate the book income tax expense are not known with certainty outside of the firm's working papers. In some instances the company may provide these to the analyst, but in others they must be inferred from an intimate knowledge of the company. The basic calculation of GAAP taxes is developed in the following manner from the company's reporting perspective:

> Current income tax expense (benefit) [cash taxes]
> + Increase (decrease) in deferred income tax liability account
> + (Increase) decrease in deferred income tax asset account
> + Increase (decrease) in deferred income tax asset valuation allowance
> Income tax expense (benefit) [GAAP taxes]

Or alternately, this might be solved for cash taxes as:

> Income tax expense (benefit) [GAAP taxes]
> − Increase (decrease) in deferred income tax liability account
> − (Increase) decrease in deferred income tax asset account
> − Increase (decrease) in deferred income tax asset valuation allowance
> Current income tax expense (benefit) [cash taxes]

It is important to separate the deferred income tax assets and deferred income tax liabilities when projecting the financial results of a firm. Beyond the reasons stated earlier, disaggregating the two items in your model enhances the transparency of what is sometimes a confusing topic. As an example, an increase in the Deferred income tax liability (balance sheet) account results in an increase in the Deferred income tax expense (income statement) account, increasing income tax expense (GAAP taxes). Because this is the same outcome that occurs from increasing the Deferred income tax asset account, leaving all of the deferred income tax items aggregated adds challenges to understanding the model.

Directly Estimating Deferred Income Tax Expense— Changes in Deferred Income Tax Liabilities

Deferred income tax liabilities are generally driven by differences in the depreciation rates used for tax and book purposes. It follows then that for firms investing in assets having a particular recovery period, it is reasonable to estimate the deferred income tax expense using the change in the asset account. Because of the peculiarities of MACRS depreciation, estimates of deferred income tax expense as a percentage of capital expenditures or property, plant, and equipment are often suboptimal compared to a detailed book versus tax depreciation schedule.

Directly Estimating Deferred Income Tax Expense— Changes in Deferred Income Tax Assets

Attempting to directly estimate the deferred income tax effects stemming from changes in the Deferred income tax asset account also suffers from problems making direct estimation impractical. Deferred income tax assets are often associated with tax-deductible intangible assets having useful lives for financial reporting purposes that are shorter than the statutory 15-year recovery period required under the Internal Revenue Code. The estimation of deferred income tax assets is further complicated when some or all of them are associated with the recovery of net operating loss carryforwards or are subject to partial reversal from a valuation account. Figure 3-6 shows that the 15-year statutory amortization period for tax-deductible intangibles results in an excess of the tax basis over the book basis when the useful life of the intangible asset is less than 15 years.

CHAPTER SUMMARY

If you asked me what one thing you should remember about this chapter, I would tell you to remember this: *The excess of an asset's book basis over its tax basis creates a deferred income tax liability equal to the enacted statutory tax rate times the amount of the excess.* The perturbations of the statement are also true, i.e., the excess of a liability's book basis over its tax basis creates a deferred income tax asset, as does the

FIGURE 3·6

Tax Basis versus Book Basis of an Intangible Asset Having a 10-Year Useful Life

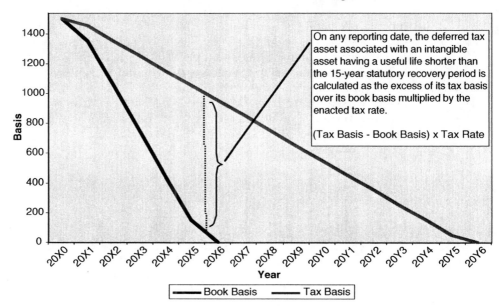

excess of an asset's tax basis over its book basis. But do not try to commit all of the perturbations to memory, just the sentence in italics: that and a piece of paper will get you through all of the other possible outcomes.

If you feel the need to remember two important things about taxes, then the second should be this: You change the tax basis of an asset by buying it. This is a radical simplification, so pay attention. If I buy all of the outstanding stock of Acme Corporation, I own it and I control all of its assets. The tax bases of the assets did not change, however, because I bought the stock and not the assets. Consider a second case: I arrange with Acme Corporation to buy all of their assets, but not the stock of the company. In this case the tax bases of the assets increases to whatever price I paid for them. It is likely that you will encounter many exceptions to this, but it is a key point to remember because, conceptually, it is the starting point.

One common exception is a Section 338(h)(10) or deemed asset sale transaction, also called a "step-up sale." Under 338(h)(10), the stock of a company is purchased but, for federal income tax purposes, it is treated as if the assets of the company were sold. Because the transaction acts as if the assets are being bought, their bases are increased to reflect the sales price. Although this is an exception, it is still true to the rule that you change the tax basis of an asset by buying it because, under 338(h)(10), the asset is deemed to be bought.

The third item that I think useful to commit to memory is that the GAAP provision for taxes is equal to the sum of the cash taxes plus the net increase in deferred income tax liabilities and the net decrease in deferred income tax assets. Again, this information and a piece of paper will provide you with everything that you need to work through most problems that you will encounter in practice.

Lastly, *always* analyze a firm's deferred income tax assets and deferred income tax liabilities separately. In most cases they arise from totally different events and cannot be analyzed or projected in the aggregate. Anecdotally, the reality of deferred income taxes is that the liabilities are almost always settled in cash, but the assets often are written down as being unrealizable. Although firms generally report either a net deferred income tax liability or a net deferred income tax asset, we see in the following chapter that a great deal of important reporting information is lost unless the disaggregated data in the deferred income tax footnote are incorporated into our projection models.

CHAPTER 4

Deciphering the Deferred
Tax Footnote

INTRODUCTION

When companies report their deferred tax assets and deferred tax liabilities, they generally appear netted as two lines on the balance sheet: a long-term and a current position. In the United States, the tax laws tend to encourage capital spending by offering companies accelerated depreciation deductions, so the netted amounts usually appear as net deferred tax liabilities. This level of disclosure is not adequate for sophisticated users of financial statements such as analysts attempting to forecast the company's future operating results, cash flows, and balance sheet positions.

In order to extract the information necessary to make the best possible forecasts and estimates the one- or two-line disclosure on the face of the balance sheet has to be reconstructed into its several parts. This is found within the deferred tax footnote, and from there we can analyze the company's deferred tax items to draw inferences and conclusions that are useful in better understanding the company's financial position and expected future tax burdens and benefits. We can also use the footnote disclosure to estimate the tax basis of the firm's assets to determine gains on taxable assets sales and to estimate a target company's deferred tax balance sheet accounts for business combinations under purchase accounting.

FINANCIAL STATEMENT DISCLOSURE FOR INCOME TAXES

Statement of Financial Accounting Standards No. 109, Accounting for Income Taxes (FAS109), requires companies to disclose specific information concerning the components of the net deferred tax asset or liability. Public enterprises are required to disclose the following five items:

1. The total deferred tax liabilities for temporary differences

2. The total deferred tax assets for temporary differences, net operating loss (NOL) carryforwards, and tax credit carryforwards

3. Any valuation allowance recognized for deferred tax assets

4. The net change in the valuation allowance for the year

5. The approximate tax effects of each type of temporary difference that is a significant part of the deferred tax items

Some public companies are not subject to direct taxation but are pass-through entities such as Subchapter S corporations, real estate investment trusts (REITs), publicly traded partnerships, or trusts. Those companies must disclose the net difference between the tax and book bases of their assets and liabilities.

There is no accepted standard for the disclosure format, and it varies significantly among reporting companies. Depending on the complexity of the reporting firm and their particular view to disclosure, information regarding deferred income taxes may be discussed solely with the *Income taxes* footnote to the financial statements, explained within a separate *Deferred income taxes* footnote, or spread between the two. This seems an appropriate place to pass along good advice I was given in graduate school concerning financial statements in general: Read the footnotes first! The footnotes tell what to watch for when you review the face of the financial statements and this is particularly true for deferred taxes.

Deferred Tax Liabilities for Temporary Differences

Deferred tax liabilities for temporary differences generally arise because depreciation rates for tax purposes are accelerated for many classes of property. This allows firms to recognize depreciation deductions for tax purposes before they recognize depreciation expense for financial reporting purposes.

Another type of temporary difference occurs when an item is depreciable or amortizable for tax purposes but not for financial reporting purposes. This is the case when tax-deductible goodwill is recognized in a transaction and amortized for tax purposes over its statutory 15-year recovery period. All goodwill, deductible and nondeductible, and some classes of intangible assets are not amortized for financial reporting purposes under U.S. GAAP but are carried at their historical costs and periodically tested for impairment. Figure 4-1 illustrates Taxpayer Company's deferred tax disclosure footnote to their 20X1 financial statements showing how the deferred tax liability for temporary differences may be disclosed.

Deferred tax liabilities frequently occur because of temporary differences between book and tax values (bases) for such items as:

- Tax depreciation that exceeds book depreciation
- Expenses recognized for tax reporting before they are for book reporting
- Amortization of intangible assets for tax reporting but not for book reporting
- Unrealized gains on investments

FIGURE 4·1

Taxpayer Company's Deferred Tax Liability Disclosure for Temporary Differences

Notes to the Financial Statements

Note 6: Deferred income taxes

Deferred income taxes are recorded as the result of temporary differences between asset and liability values reported for financial and tax purposes. The Company provides a valuation allowance reducing the portion of its deferred tax assets consisting of net operating loss carryforwards that it doubts it will realize. The increase in the valuation was $160 thousand in 20X1 and $80 thousand in 20X0.

in thousands	20X0	20X1
Deferred tax assets relating to		
Net operating losses and tax credits	1,649	2,021
Assets held for investment	875	535
Valuation allowance	(160)	(320)
Deferred income tax assets	2,364	2,236
Deferred tax liabilities relating to:		
Depreciation and amortization	1,946	1,918
Unrealized gain on investments	1,551	1,303
Deferred income tax liabilities	3,497	3,221

- Earnings of foreign subsidiaries
- Prepaid pension assets

Deferred Tax Assets for Temporary Differences

Deferred tax assets for temporary differences usually are associated with intangible assets having useful lives for financial reporting purposes that are shorter than the 15-year statutory tax recovery period. Under the Internal Revenue Code (IRC), nearly all intangible assets are amortized for tax purposes over a 15-year recovery period (asset lifetime). Many types of intangible assets such as covenants to not compete, licenses, client or customer lists, and high-tech patents have relatively short useful lives. These classes of intangibles are amortized faster for financial reporting purposes than they are for income tax reporting, creating a deferred tax asset. Figure 4-2 illustrates Taxpayer Company's deferred tax disclosure footnote to their 20X1 financial statements showing how the deferred tax assets for temporary differences may be disclosed.

Deferred tax assets frequently occur because of temporary differences between book and tax values (bases) for such items as:

- Tax amortization of intangible assets that exceeds book amortization
- Derivatives qualifying as hedges under FAS133

FIGURE 4·2

Taxpayer Company's Deferred Tax Asset Disclosure for Temporary Differences

Notes to the Financial Statements

Note 6: Deferred income taxes

Deferred income taxes are recorded as the result of temporary differences between asset and liability values reported for financial and tax purposes. The Company provides a valuation allowance reducing the portion of its deferred tax assets consisting of net operating loss carryforwards that it doubts it will realize. The increase in the valuation was $160 thousand in 20X1 and $80 thousand in 20X0.

in thousands	20X0	20X1
Deferred tax assets relating to		
Net operating losses and tax credits	1,649	2,021
Assets held for investment	875	535
Valuation allowance	(160)	(320)
Deferred income tax assets	2,364	2,236
Deferred tax liabilities relating to		
Depreciation and amortization	1,946	1,918
Unrealized gain on investments	1,551	1,303
Deferred income tax liabilities	3,497	3,221

- Inventories
- Pension and postretirement benefit plans
- Impaired investments (book basis written down before tax basis)
- Revenues recognized for tax purposes before they are recognized for book purposes
- Unrealized foreign exchange losses
- Restructuring reserves

Deferred Income Tax Assets for NOLs and Tax Credits

If Taxpayer Company realizes a net operating loss (NOL) for financial reporting purposes, the company recognizes an income tax benefit (for book purposes) in the period that they realize the loss. Under current U.S. tax law, Taxpayer Company does not realize a direct income tax benefit in loss periods but may apply the losses to offset taxable income in other tax years. The Internal Revenue Code (IRC) allows two different schemes for applying the losses as a deduction. The first is called "carryback," where losses in the current accounting period are carried back to offset earnings from prior periods. The second is "carryforward," where losses from the current period are carried forward to reduce taxable income in future periods. Carryback results in an immediate income tax benefit (tax refund) and no deferred tax effect. Carryforward produces no income tax benefit in the loss period but results in benefits being realized in future periods. Taxpayer Company recognizes deferred tax assets when it carries forward NOLs because the NOLs produce income tax benefits (deductions to taxable income) in future periods. Deferred tax assets for NOL carryforwards are estimated using the enacted tax rates and may be adjusted if the enacted tax rates are changed.

Other items resulting in Taxpayer Company recording deferred tax assets are income tax credits. Income tax credits also produce an income tax benefit, but unlike NOL carryforward deductions that reduce taxable income, income tax credits directly reduce tax liability. One dollar of applicable income tax credits results in a direct one dollar reduction of cash income taxes payable. One dollar of applicable NOL carryforwards results in only about a 40-cent reduction in cash income taxes payable.

There are different types of income tax credits. Some result in recognizing deferred tax assets and some do not. Two of the principal distinctions are between refundable income tax credits and nonrefundable income tax credits. As the name implies, refundable income tax credits can be used to offset income tax liability, and if they are greater than the income tax liability also result in Taxpayer Company receiving an income tax refund. Like refundable income tax credits, nonrefundable income tax credits may be used to directly offset income tax liability. Unlike refundable income tax credits, if the nonrefundable income tax credits exceed the income tax liability, they do *not* result in Taxpayer Company receiving an income tax refund. Some nonrefundable income tax credits may be carried over into future periods. When they are carried over, Taxpayer Company recognizes a deferred tax asset equal to the full amount of the tax credit. Remember that income tax credits offset income tax liabilities on a one-for-one basis, so one dollar of income-tax-credit carryover produces one dollar of future cash income tax benefit. Companies are required to disclose the full amount of the deferred tax asset recognized for NOL and income tax credit carryforwards. Figure 4-3 illustrates Taxpayer Company's deferred tax disclosure footnote to their 20X1 financial statements showing how the deferred tax asset for net operating loss carryforwards and tax credits may be disclosed.

Deferred tax assets frequently occur because of NOL and capital loss carryforwards and income tax credits such as:

- AMT credits
- Foreign tax credits
- General business tax credits

Valuation Allowances

Taxpayer Company recognizes deferred tax assets for temporary differences and also for the expected future benefit of net operating loss carryforwards, capital loss carryforwards, and tax credit carryforwards. It is possible to limit Taxpayer Company's ability to realize the future income tax benefits underlying the deferred tax assets due to various situations. When Taxpayer Company believes that "…based on the

FIGURE 4·3

Taxpayer Company's Deferred Tax Asset Disclosure for NOLs and Tax Credits

Notes to the Financial Statements

Note 6: Deferred income taxes

Deferred income taxes are recorded as the result of temporary differences between asset and liability value reported for financial and tax purposes. The Company provides a valuation allowance reducing the portion of its deferred tax assets consisting of net operating loss carryforwards that it doubts it will realize. The increase in the valuation was $160 thousand in 20X1 and $80 thousand in 20X0.

in thousands	20X0	20X1
Deferred tax assets relating to:		
Net operating losses and tax credits	1,649	2,021
Assets held for investment	875	535
Valuation allowance	(160)	(320)
Deferred income tax assets	2,364	2,236
Deferred tax liabilities relating to		
Depreciation and amortization	1,946	1,918
Unrealized gain on investments	1,551	1,303
Deferred income tax liabilities	3,497	3,221

weight of available evidence, it is *more likely than not* (a likelihood of more than 50 percent) that some portion or all of the deferred tax assets will not be realized..."[1] then Taxpayer Company must recognize a valuation allowance account "...sufficient to reduce the deferred tax asset to the amount that is more likely than not to be realized."[2] Essentially the intent of FAS109 is to show all of the potential deferred tax assets yet still have a method to prevent overstating the value of the assets on the balance sheet. The valuation allowance is a contra-asset account that only appears in the deferred income tax footnote to the financial statements and rarely, if ever, on the face of the balance sheet. Figure 4-4 illustrates Taxpayer Company's deferred tax disclosure footnote to their 20X1 financial statements showing how the deferred tax asset valuation allowance may be disclosed.

Changes In the Valuation Allowance

Changes in the valuation allowance are usually disclosed within the text of the income taxes footnote to the financial statement or the deferred income taxes footnote. The footnote shown for Taxpayer Company's financial statements is a fairly typical presentation of the required disclosure for changes in the valuation allowance. Figure 4-5 illustrates Taxpayer Company's deferred tax disclosure footnote to their 20X1 financial statements showing how changes to the deferred tax asset valuation allowance may be disclosed.

FIGURE 4·4

Taxpayer Company's Deferred Tax Asset Disclosure for the Valuation Allowance

Notes to the Financial Statements

Note 6: Deferred income taxes

Deferred income taxes are recorded as the result of temporary differences between asset and liability value reported for financial and tax purposes. The Company provides a valuation allowance reducing the portion of its deferred tax assets consisting of net operating loss carryforwards that it doubts it will realize. The increase in the valuation was $160 thousand in 20X1 and $80 thousand in 20X0.

in thousands	20X0	20X1
Deferred tax assets relating to:		
Net operating losses and tax credits	1,649	2,021
Assets held for investment	875	535
Valuation allowance	(160)	(320)
Deferred income tax assets	2,364	2,236
Deferred tax liabilities relating to:		
Depreciation and amortization	1,946	1,918
Unrealized gain on investments	1,551	1,303
Deferred income tax liabilities	3,497	3,221

FIGURE 4·5

Taxpayer Company's Deferred Tax Disclosure for Changes to the Valuation Allowance

Notes to the Financial Statements

Note 6: Deferred income taxes

Deferred income taxes are recorded as the result of temporary differences between asset and liability values reported for financial and tax purposes. The Company provides a valuation allowance reducing the portion of its deferred tax assets consisting of net operating loss carryforwards that it doubts it will realize. The increase in the valuation was $160 thousand in 20X1 and $80 thousand in 20X0.

Deferred income tax asset valuation allowances are sometimes areas of earnings management, particularly for firms prone to aggressive accounting. The basic scenario unfolds when the circumstances requiring the creation of the valuation allowance change such that the deferred tax asset is now considered realizable. The firm releases the valuation allowance, which reduces the current period income tax expense and increases earnings. Potential areas of concern are the:

- Amount of the initial valuation allowance because recording an overly conservative (excessive) allowance "banks" future earnings
- Timing of any release of allowance because the timing of the decision that the deferred income tax assets are now realizable is a judgment area, meaning it can be made preferentially in periods of weak earnings

■ Amount of the allowance release, which is also a judgment area providing a method of increasing selected period earnings

The footnote disclosure for changes to the deferred income tax asset valuation allowance should be examined and evaluated in light of other known information, particularly when a very large valuation allowance is created or when portions of an existing valuation allowance are released. Is there a material effect on earnings in either case?

RECONSTRUCTING DEFERRED TAXES ON THE FINANCIAL STATEMENTS

FAS109 requires some practices and allows others that cloud our view of deferred taxes, particularly when we examine Taxpayer Company's financial statements prior to a business combination or leveraged buyout transaction. For example, companies are required to separate deferred income tax assets and liabilities to show their current and noncurrent portions. They are also allowed to present a net current and a net noncurrent item, which is also misleading because generally, deferred income tax liabilities are not subject to the same limitations in a change-of-ownership transaction as are deferred income tax assets.

Internal Revenue Code (IRC) Section 382 Limitations

IRC Section 382 places important limitations on a company's recorded deferred income tax assets relating to their net operating loss (NOL) carryforwards. Companies record deferred income tax assets for the future tax benefits they expect to realize from offsetting taxable income by the NOL carryforwards in future periods. When firms having NOL carryforwards undergo changes of ownership, such as in acquisitions, the IRC may significantly limit the rate at which those carryforwards can be utilized in future periods. IRC Section 382 determines the maximum amount of the existing company's NOL carryforwards applicable in any future period as the product of the *long-term tax exempt rate* times the stock value on the date that ownership changed. Example 4-1 illustrates how IRC Section 382 affects the recorded deferred income tax asset by limiting NOL carryforwards following a change of ownership.

EXAMPLE 4-1. IRC Section 382 Limitations Following a Change of Ownership

Taxpayer Company is a 40-percent taxpayer with 5052.5 of net operating loss carryforwards expiring in three years. In its 20X1 financial statements Taxpayer Company presents (5052.5 × 40%) = 2021 in deferred income tax assets from the NOL carryforwards. The company forecasts total combined taxable income of 4252.5 for the next three years, which is only adequate to realize an income tax benefit of (4252.5 × 40%) = 1701 from the carryforwards. Consequently, Taxpayer Company records a (2021 − 1701) = 320 valuation allowance for the unrealizable portion of the deferred income tax assets. Investor, who holds 75 percent of Taxpayer Company's outstanding stock, sells her position for 12,000. This implies that the stock value on the date that ownership changed is (12,000 / 75%) = 16,000. The long-term tax exempt rate on the transaction date is 4.25 percent.

Under IRC Section 382 the utilization of Taxpayer Company's NOL carryforwards posttransaction is limited to no more than $(16,000 \times 4.25\%) = 680.0$ in each of the three periods remaining before the NOL carryforwards expire. Taxpayer Company is limited to only utilizing $(680 \times 3 = 2040)$ of its NOL carryforwards and consequently can only realize a $(2040 \times 40\% = 816)$ income tax benefit. At the transaction date, Taxpayer Company recognizes an additional $(1701 - 816) = 885$ valuation allowance bringing the account total to $(320 + 885) = 1205$. The difference between the recorded deferred income tax asset (2021) and the valuation allowance (1205) is the portion of the deferred tax asset Taxpayer Company believes is realizable after the Section 382 limitation $(2021 - 1205) = 816$.

dr:	Retained earnings	885.0	
	cr: Deferred tax asset		885.0

Adjusting the Financial Statements

To model transactions or even to forecast probable future scenarios requires first "undoing" some of the work that went into the preparation of the company's financial statements. Specifically, disaggregate the net current deferred income tax item into its asset and liability components, and then do the same for the net noncurrent deferred income tax item. Following that, recombine the current and noncurrent deferred income tax assets and the current and noncurrent deferred income tax liabilities. Figure 4-6 shows Taxpayer Company's abbreviated financial statements and footnotes as they were reported.

Note that we are also interested in the note detailing the Prepaid expenses and other current assets account. It provides us with information necessary to adjust the Prepaid expenses and other current asset account and also is useful for reconciling the deferred income tax position presented on the face of the balance sheet with the detailed positions disclosed in the deferred tax asset footnote. If Taxpayer Company had a net current deferred income tax liability instead of a net deferred income tax asset, our interest would be the other current liabilities footnote.

Beginning with the Prepaid expenses and other current assets account, we find that Taxpayer Company has net current deferred income tax assets of 153 in 20X0 and 207 in 20X1. We eliminate these amounts from the current asset, reducing the Prepaid expenses and other current asset account to $(399 - 153) = 246$ in 20X0 and $(565 - 207) = 358$ in 20X1. Simultaneously, we create a Deferred income tax asset account on the balance sheet and fund it (temporarily) with the amount of the net deferred income tax assets we remove from prepaid expenses and other current assets. Figure 4-7 shows Taxpayer Company's abbreviated financial statements and the "corrected" prepaid expenses and other current assets balance sheet presentation and footnote. In practice we would not actually correct the footnote, but it is shown here as an aid to understanding the process of adjusting Taxpayer Company's financial statements.

FIGURE 4-6

Taxpayer Company's As-Reported Financial Statements (Abbreviated)

Taxpayer Company's Financial Statements (unadjusted)		
Balance Sheet	**20X0**	**20X1**
Assets		
Cash and cash equivalents	2,000	2,261
Prepaid expenses and other current assets	399	565
Total current assets	2,399	2,826
Property, plant and equipment - net of accumulated depreciation	7,281	8,044
Total assets	9,680	10,870
Liabilities		
Long-term debt	2,847	4,630
Deferred income taxes	1,286	1,192
Total liabilities	4,133	5,822
Owner's equity	5,547	5,048

Notes to the Financial Statements

Note 6: Deferred income taxes

Deferred income taxes are recorded as the result of temporary differences between asset and liability values reported for financial and tax purposes. The Company provides a valuation allowance reducing the portion of its deferred tax assets consisting of net operating loss carryforwards that it doubts it will realize. The increase in the valuation was $160 thousand in 20X1 and $80 thousand in 20X0.

in thousands	20X0	20X1
Deferred tax assets relating to:		
Net operating losses	1,649	2,021
Assets held for investment	875	535
Valuation allowance	(160)	(320)
Deferred income tax assets	2,364	2,236
Deferred tax liabilities relating to:		
Depreciation and amortization	1,946	1,918
Unrealized gain on investments	1,551	1,303
Deferred income tax liabilities	3,497	3,221

Note 11: Prepaid expenses and other current assets

in thousands	20X0	20X1
Prepaid expenses	123	236
Deferred tax assets	153	207
Other receivables	123	122
Total prepaid expenses and other current assets	399	565

FIGURE 4·7

Taxpayer Company's Financial Statements (Abbreviated) After Adjusting the Current Portion of the Deferred Taxes

Taxpayer Company's Financial Statements (adjusted)

Balance Sheet	20X0	20X1
Assets		
Cash and cash equivalents	2,000	2,261
Prepaid expenses and other current assets	246	358
Total current assets	2,246	2,619
Deferred tax assets temporary adjustment ⟶	153	207
Property, plant and equipment - net of accumulated depreciation	7,281	8,044
Total assets	9,680	10,870
Liabilities		
Long-term debt	2,847	4,630
Deferred income tax liabilities	1,286	1,192
Total liabilities	4,133	5,822
Owner's equity	5,547	5,048

Notes to the Financial Statements

Note 11: Prepaid expenses and other current assets

in thousands	20X0	20X1
Prepaid expenses	123	236
Deferred tax assets eliminated ⟶	-	-
Other receivables	123	122
Total prepaid expenses and other current assets	246	358

The next step is recognizing the full disclosed amount of the deferred tax assets and deferred tax liabilities on the face of Taxpayer Company's balance sheet. We move the footnote amounts for the deferred income tax assets and deferred income tax liabilities (net of any amounts already moved from the other current assets or other current liabilities) to their respective balance sheet accounts. When we are finished, the amounts presented on the face of the balance sheet for the noncurrent Deferred tax assets and Deferred tax liabilities accounts agree with the account balances disclosed in the footnotes. Figure 4-8 shows Taxpayer Company's abbreviated financial statements after completing the adjustments to the balance sheet presentation.

Although we have done so here, there may be times that it is appropriate to bring the deferred tax asset valuation allowance onto the face of the balance sheet. Remembering that the statements we prepare are not for financial accounting purposes, but are for analytical and presentation purposes. In that context there may

FIGURE 4·8

Taxpayer Company's Financial Statements (Abbreviated)–Fully Adjusted

Taxpayer Company's Financial Statements (adjusted)

Balance Sheet	20X0	20X1
Assets		
Cash and cash equivalents	2,000	2,261
Prepaid expenses and other current assets	246	358
Total current assets	2,246	2,619
Deferred income tax assets	2,364	2,236
Property, plant and equipment - net of accumulated depreciation	7,281	8,044
Total assets	11,891	12,899
Liabilities		
Long-term debt	2,847	4,630
Deferred income tax liabilities	3,497	3,221
Total liabilities	6,344	7,851
Owner's equity	5,547	5,048

Notes to the Financial Statements

Note 6: Deferred income taxes
Deferred income taxes are recorded as the result of temporary differences between asset and liability values reported for financial and tax purposes. The Company provides a valuation allowance reducing the portion of its deferred tax assets consisting of net operating loss carryforwards that it doubts it will realize. The increase in the valuation was $160 thousand in 20X1 and $80 thousand in 20X0.

in thousands	20X0	20X1
Deferred tax assets relating to:		
Net operating losses	1,649	2,021
Assets held for investment	875	535
Valuation allowance	(160)	(320)
Deferred income tax assets	2,364	2,236
Deferred tax liabilities relating to:		
Depreciation and amortization	1,946	1,918
Unrealized gain on investments	1,551	1,303
Deferred income tax liabilities	3,497	3,221

be situations where showing the effect of the valuation allowance on the recorded deferred income tax asset is very informative. One example might be when the firm's expectations for realizing future tax benefits change. Presenting the valuation allowance on the face of the balance sheet explains why there is sudden decrease in the Deferred tax asset account.

PROBLEMS WITH RATIO ANALYSIS

Another important effect of reconstructing the balance sheet for analytical purposes is on analytic ratios. Financial accounting standards require firms to present net deferred income tax positions. Leaving the deferred tax items in the "as presented" form for ratio analysis is inadequate from two different perspectives.

Offsetting Deferred Income Tax Items

The first issue is that financial accounting offsets (nets) the deferred income tax asset directly against the deferred income tax liability. Typically the only asset that is netted against liabilities is cash and cash equivalents. That is done under the premise that the decision to either hold cash and an equal amount of debt, or to use the cash to pay down the debt, is entirely in the hands of the firm's management. With other assets, that is generally not the case. The other assets may either lack liquidity or management may not have sufficient operating freedom to make those types of trade-offs. Deferred income tax assets are more the latter, being largely illiquid and not entirely within management's control. (A change to the income tax law could eliminate them entirely and irrevocably with a single stoke of the legislative pen.)

Recorded Values Versus Fair Value

The second issue with netting deferred income tax assets directly against liabilities is that the assets are not recorded strictly at fair value. A deferred income tax item that Taxpayer Company will not realize for 20 years is recorded at the same value as an item that is realizable next year. Because the exact timing of the deferred income tax asset realization is generally not known with certainty, it is reasonable to record them in this fashion, and the valuation issues all eventually resolve themselves. But note that financial reporting never intended for the recorded value of deferred income tax items to have a cash equivalence for analytic purposes.

Effects On Ratio Analysis

Disaggregating the deferred income tax item usually results in an increase in total liabilities because any portion of the deferred income tax liability that was previously offset is fully recognized on the balance sheet. This results in higher, more conservative debt-to-equity ratios. When you use these ratios comparatively, it is important that all of the ratios are developed using the same methodology.

Similarly deferred income tax assets also increase for the same reason as liabilities. This causes ratios such as the asset turnover ratio and return on assets to be more conservatively stated. Again, when using these ratios for comparables, adjust the data as necessary to standardize the approach used for all of the companies being compared.

VALUATION OF DEFERRED TAX ITEMS

When valuing companies having NOL carryforwards, it is often easier to find the present value of the deferred tax asset recorded for the NOL carryforwards separately. This is then added to the present value to the firm value calculated without the effects of applying NOL carryforwards in future periods. The three advantages to this approach are alleviating the need to estimate the earnings before interest and taxes (EBIT) tax rate correctly when reflecting the effects of the NOL carryforwards; providing a clear valuation of the NOL carryforward benefits beyond the explicit forecast period (i.e., a 5-year forecast with NOLs requiring 10 years to recover); and allowing valuation of the tax benefits using a discount rate separate from the cost of capital. The reality of these cash flows is that they are often less risky (in some cases almost bondlike) than other free cash flows. It is common to use a lower discount rate for the NOL cash flows, sometimes even as low as the after-tax cost of debt.

CHAPTER SUMMARY

U.S. GAAP generally requires deferred income tax assets and liabilities to be offset (netted) when presented on the face of the balance sheet. It also requires separation of the current and noncurrent portions of the deferred tax item. While this approach may be convenient for financial reporting purposes, it is sometimes obscure and cumbersome for analytic purposes. The most versatile and informative presentation of deferred income taxes requires reverse engineering of the deferred income tax footnote to the financial statements.

The deferred income tax footnote needs diligent examination, especially the deferred income tax assets because generally, the certainty of realizing a deferred income tax asset is less than the certainty for needing to satisfy a deferred income tax liability. That occurs because realizing a deferred income tax asset is frequently contingent on future events. For example, in order to realize an income tax benefit for NOL carryforwards in future periods, there must be taxable income to offset. Otherwise the NOL carryforward provides no benefit. When a firm believes that a portion of its deferred income tax asset is unrealizable, it recognizes a valuation allowance for the unrealizable amount.

Valuation allowances are sometimes abused when companies use them as an earnings management tool to move earnings from one period to another. Whenever companies recognize valuation allowances in periods having poor earnings results, it is possible that they are "hiding" some of their earnings (which are poor to begin with) in the valuation allowance. These may then be reversed in future periods to boost the latter period's earnings. You should always view changes to the deferred income tax valuation allowance with an air of professional skepticism especially for firms consistently meeting or slightly exceeding analyst's earnings estimates.

Another important use of the deferred income tax footnote is for estimating the tax bases of a company's assets. When companies sell assets in straight asset sales or sell subsidiaries in deemed asset sales, it is difficult for the purchasing company to estimate the income tax liability from the asset sale. Most companies are not required to directly disclose the income tax bases of their assets, which sometimes gives the selling company a bargaining advantage in the transactions. In the next chapter we look at using the deferred income tax footnote to the financial statements to estimate the income tax bases of a company's assets.

CHAPTER 5

Estimating the Tax Basis of a Firm's Assets

INTRODUCTION

Companies selling either assets in straight asset sales or subsidiaries, such as Target Company, in deemed asset sales have a bargaining advantage in the transactions. Because they are not required to directly disclose the income tax bases of Target Company's assets, Seller Company enjoys a knowledge advantage over Buyer Company because only Seller Company can correctly estimate the income tax liability from the sale.

When Target Company's financial statements are available, the deferred income tax footnote provides some information for making an informed estimate of the tax bases of Target Company's assets. When Target Company's financial statements are unavailable, as in the case of a privately held company, the task becomes significantly more challenging and the results of the estimate may be wide of the mark. To fully understand how to estimate Target Company's tax bases in its assets, we need to first develop a good understanding of how book-to-tax bases differentials occur and the factors causing them to change.

Following that discussion we look at two different approaches to estimating the tax bases of Target Company's assets. The first method is more useful for publicly traded companies and relies on Target Company's disclosed (through the deferred income tax footnote) knowledge of the tax bases of its own assets. The second method applies more to cases where little can be learned about Target Company's balance sheet requiring us to develop estimates using assumptions based known on industry norms.

FACTORS AFFECTING DIFFERENCES BETWEEN ASSET'S BOOK AND TAX BASES

There are four principal factors that affect the differences between an asset's book and tax bases: depreciating the asset using different schedules for book and tax depreciation; writing down only the book basis (value) of the asset due to recognizing an impairment; writing down or writing up only the book basis of the asset to reflect fair valuation in a stock purchase transaction; and writing up or writing down both the book basis and the tax basis of the asset to reflect fair valuation in an asset sale or deemed asset sale transaction.

DEPRECIATION (OR AMORTIZATION) USING DIFFERENT SCHEDULES

When Taxpayer Company makes a capital expenditure by acquiring a piece of manufacturing equipment, the company recognizes the transaction in both the financial accounting and income tax books at the equipment's historical cost. At that point in time, the equipment's book basis and tax basis are equal.

Financial Accounting (Book) Depreciation

In each subsequent period, Taxpayer Company records a depreciation expense to match the utilization of the asset with the revenues that the asset produces. In other words, if Taxpayer Company uses an asset to manufacture products over a three-year period, it depreciates the asset to spread its cost over the same period. The total amount Taxpayer Company depreciates the asset is the difference between the asset's cost and estimated *salvage value*. Salvage value is the amount Taxpayer Company expects to receive when it sells the used asset at the end of three years. The downward-sloping line on Figure 5-1 illustrates how a three-year asset's value, originally purchased and recorded for 1000 on 1-January-20X1, decreases over its life as Taxpayer Company records periodic depreciation expense. Note that for financial reporting purposes, depreciation is usually expensed equally over the three years. This is commonly referred to as *straight-line depreciation* and results in the graph of an asset's value drawing a straight line from its cost to its salvage value over the asset's lifetime (the downward-sloping line on Figure 5-1 is a straight line).

Income Tax (Tax) Depreciation

When an asset is placed in service, the Internal Revenue Code (IRC) also allows its cost to be recovered through tax depreciation. However, the regulations surrounding tax depreciation are themselves shaped by other considerations such as legislative purpose and agency initiative. Legislative purposes are other goals that the Congress accomplishes through the IRC, and paralleling that is agency initiative, or

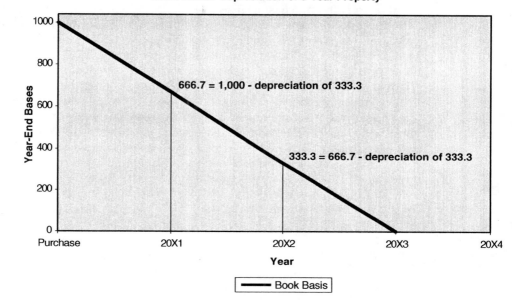

FIGURE 5·1

Book Basis: Depreciation of Three-Year Property

other goals that the Internal Revenue Service (IRS) accomplishes through the IRC and regulations. The IRC and regulations associated with cost recovery (depreciation and amortization) are also written to meet the additional goals of encouraging business capital spending and reduced taxpayer burden through simplification.

Modified Accelerated Cost Recovery System

The IRC encourages businesses to spend by allowing accelerated depreciation schedules for certain classes of property called the Modified Accelerated Cost Recovery System (MACRS). Briefly, MACRS classifies assets into cost-recovery groups based on the number of years over which the assets are depreciated. Cost recovery groups (or classes) of 3, 5, 7, and 10 years are depreciated using the 200-percent declining balance method, and 15- and 20-year assets are depreciated using the 150-percent declining balance method. In addition to the amount of depreciation expense recorded for income tax purposes, MACRS also prescribes the timing of the expense using the *midyear convention*. The midyear convention assumes, with some exceptions, that all assets are placed in service in the middle of the year, so only a half-year's worth of depreciation is allowed in the first year, and the depreciation is spread over one period longer than the asset's cost recovery period. For example, a three-year property depreciates for tax purposes over four fiscal years because it depreciates as: one-half year; one year; one year; and one-half year.

Taxpayer Company recognizes a tax depreciation expense in each subsequent period after purchasing an asset and placing it in service. Instead of recording a tax depreciation expense matching the utilization of the asset with the revenues produced, Taxpayer Company records a tax depreciation expense determined using MACRS. The straight downward-sloping line ending in 20X3 shown on Figure 5-2 illustrates a three-year asset's value, originally purchased and recorded for 1000 on 1-January-20X1, decreasing over its life as Taxpayer Company records the periodic financial reporting (book) depreciation expense. The segmented downward-sloping line ending in 20X4 shows its income tax basis as Taxpayer Company records the periodic income tax depreciation deduction. Note that the segmented line, the tax basis, is actually recovered over four fiscal years because of MACRS's midyear convention, and that the book to tax basis differential can be either positive (book basis exceeds the tax basis) or negative (tax basis exceeds the book basis).

Figure 5-3 shows the same relationship between the book and tax basis of a seven-year MACRS asset. Again, like the three-year asset, it is purchased and

FIGURE 5·2

Book and Tax Basis: Depreciation of Three-Year MACRS Property

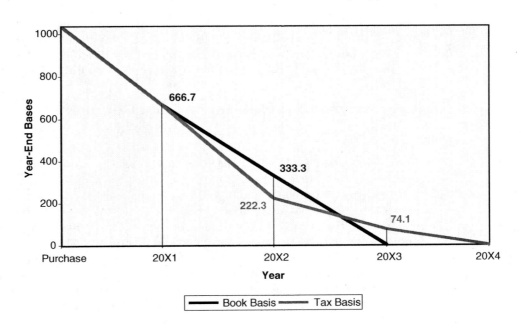

Book and Tax Bases: 3-Year MACRS Property

FIGURE 5·3

Book and Tax Basis: Depreciation of Seven-Year MACRS Property

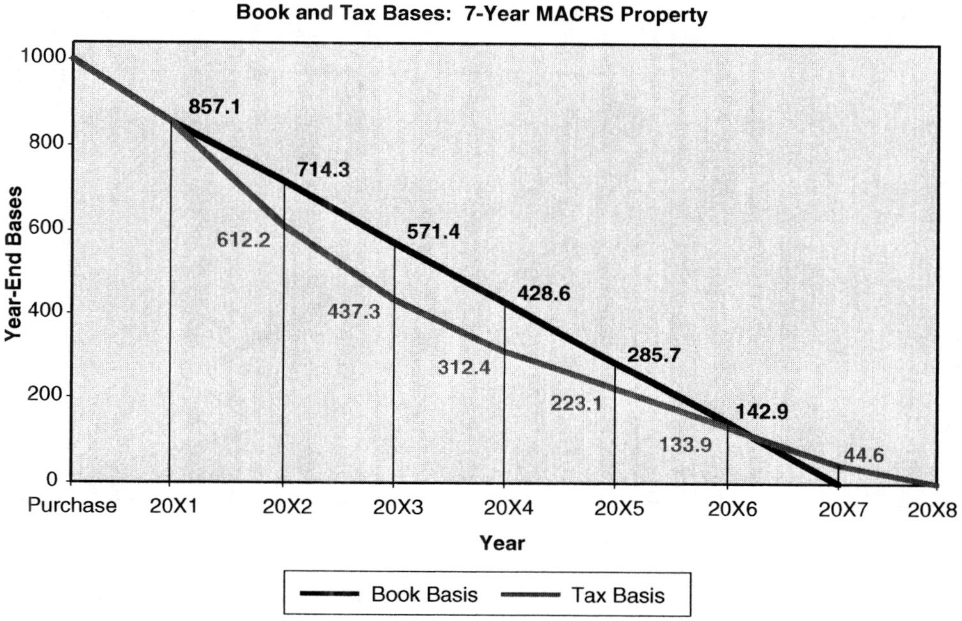

Book and Tax Bases: 7-Year MACRS Property

recorded for 1000 on 1-January-20X1 and subsequently depreciated for book and tax purposes.

Would it make a difference if instead of purchasing and placing the asset in service at the beginning of the year, it actually occurred at the middle of the year? In this new scenario, both financial and income tax reporting would allow a half-year's depreciation in the first fiscal year, and both require four years to fully depreciate the asset. Figure 5-4 illustrates the book and tax bases for a three-year asset purchased and recorded for 1000 on 1-July-20X1 and subsequently depreciated for book and tax purposes. If we assume, similar to the Internal Revenue Code, that a series of asset purchases made over the course of a year is fairly represented by one large purchase made at midyear, then Figure 5-4 gives us the best estimate of how the book to tax differential actually exists for three-year property.

Tax Basis to Book Basis Ratios

Assuming that companies buy assets on an ongoing basis and that the midyear purchase is representative of the timing of asset purchases, we are able to estimate an average book to tax basis differential for each class of asset. Consider that Taxpayer Company purchases and places into service 100 of MACRS three-year assets every

FIGURE 5·4

Book and Tax Basis: Depreciation of Three-Year MACRS Property for a Midyear Asset Purchase

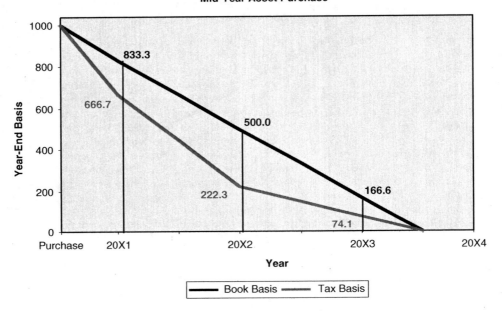

**Book and Tax Bases: 3-Year MACRS Property
Mid-Year Asset Purchase**

year for five years and for the ideal case, there is no mismatch between the book and tax lives of the assets. In other words, a three-year property has a three-year life for both book and for tax purposes. Figure 5-5 shows that after the first year, the higher tax depreciation reduces the tax basis of the asset to 80 percent of its book basis.

In the second year Taxpayer Company adds a second layer by buying another 100 of assets, and the combined effect of the two different depreciation schemes reduces the total tax basis of the assets to 66.7 percent of the total book basis (again remembering that Taxpayer Company is only buying three-year assets). Similarly, in the third year the tax basis reduces to 64.2 percent of the book basis, and from that year onward (because these are three-year assets), as long as Taxpayer Company continues to purchase a level 100 of assets each period, the tax basis of the assets remains as 64.2 percent of their book basis. Table 5-1 summarizes the ideal case ratios for MACRS properties.

There are two important ideas to gain from examining Table 5-1. The first is that by examining the types of assets, we see that many of the assets commonly found in a business environment are five-year and seven-year MACRS properties. The second is that longer-lived assets have higher tax basis to book basis ratios. We will draw on both of these ideas later when we estimate the bases of Taxpayer Company's assets using tax basis to book basis ratios.

FIGURE 5·5

Tax Basis as a Percentage of Book Basis: Three-Year MACRS Property

MACRS 3-year property	Year 1	Year 2	Year 3	Year 4	Year 5	Year 6
Book basis	83.33	50.00	16.67	-		
		83.33	50.00	16.67	-	
			83.33	50.00	16.67	-
				83.33	50.00	16.67
	83.33	133.33	150.00	150.00	————————→	
Tax basis	66.67	22.22	7.41	-		
		66.67	22.22	7.41	-	
			66.67	22.22	7.41	-
				66.67	22.22	7.41
	66.67	88.89	96.30	96.30	————————→	
Tax basis as % of book basis	80.00%	66.67%	64.20%	64.20%	————————→	

TABLE 5·1

MACRS Properties Ideal Case Tax Basis to Book Basis Ratios

MACRS Recovery Period	Partial Classification of Assets	Tax Basis to Book Basis Ratio
3-Year	■ qualified rent-to-own property	64.20%
5-Year	■ automobiles ■ taxis and buses ■ light general purpose trucks ■ semiconductor manufacturing equipment ■ qualified technological equipment ■ computer-based telephone switches ■ computers and peripherals ■ office machinery ■ research and development property	71.94%
7-Year	■ office furniture and fixtures ■ agricultural machinery ■ all otherwise unclassified property	74.88%
10-Year	■ single-purpose agricultural structures ■ single-purpose horticultural structures ■ vessels, barges and tugboats	76.89%
15-Year	■ retail motor fuels outlets (gas stations)	91.24%
20-Year	■ farm buildings	91.67%

In the ideal cases, we determined tax basis to book basis ratios for assets having equal depreciation lives for both tax and book purposes. It is not uncommon that an asset may be depreciated over different periods. Figure 5-6 presents the tax basis to book basis ratios for assets having different tax and book depreciation lives.

Other assets such as rental real estate and business real property are depreciated over longer periods of time using straight-line depreciation. Because the same depreciation scheme is used for book and tax purposes, the tax basis to book basis ratio for real property is usually very close to 100 percent (i.e., book basis and tax basis are equal).

Amortization of Intangible Assets

Under the IRC, intangible assets are amortized for income tax purposes over a statutory 15-year period. This simplification of the tax code, sometimes referred to as "rough justice," alleviates the Internal Revenue Service (IRS) from having to examine every tax return to determine if each intangible asset's amortization period is reasonable. Unfortunately there is no corresponding simplification used for financial accounting purposes, so a tax basis to book basis differential nearly always exists for intangible assets.

RECOGNIZING ASSET IMPAIRMENTS

Another cause of differences between an asset's book and tax bases occurs when Taxpayer Company recognizes an impairment charge for the asset. When the book (carrying) value of an asset exceeds its fair value and is unrecoverable, *Statement of Financial Accounting Standards No. 144, Accounting for the Impairment or Disposal of Long-Lived Assets* (FAS144) requires Taxpayer Company to reduce the asset's carrying value by recognizing an impairment loss. Recognizing an impairment loss reduces the book basis of the asset and the future book depreciation but does not

FIGURE 5·6

Tax basis to Book Basis Ratios for Assets Having Different Tax and Book Depreciation Lives

		Tax Depreciation Periods					
		3 years	5 years	7 years	10 years	15 years	20 years
	3 years	64.20%	104.53%	127.11%	146.40%	171.63%	178.42%
Book	**5 years**	38.52%	71.94%	97.69%	121.02%	155.61%	165.71%
Depreciation	**7 years**	27.51%	51.38%	74.88%	101.42%	141.52%	154.21%
Periods	**10 years**	19.26%	35.97%	52.41%	76.89%	122.09%	138.73%
	15 years	12.84%	23.98%	34.94%	51.26%	91.24%	114.80%
	20 years	9.63%	17.98%	26.21%	38.45%	68.43%	91.67%

affect either the tax basis or the tax depreciation schedule. Example 5-1 shows how recognizing an impairment loss for an asset affects the book basis and book depreciation schedule.

EXAMPLE 5-1. Recognizing an Impairment Loss

On 30-June-20X1, Taxpayer Company purchases for 100 and places into service a five-year MACRS asset also having a five-year financial accounting life. Figure 5-7 shows the asset's book and tax bases without Taxpayer Company recognizing any impairment charge.

One year later, on 30-June-20X2, Taxpayer Company recognizes an impairment loss of 40 for the asset. One-half year's depreciation expense of 10 in 20X1 reduces the initial 100 cost of the asset to (100 – 10) = 90, and an additional one-half year's depreciation expense of 10 in the first half of 20X2 reduces the asset account balance to (90 – 10) = 80 on 30-June-20X2. At that time, Taxpayer Company recognizes an asset impairment loss of 40, reducing the asset account balance to (80 – 40) = 40. The 40 carrying value is depreciated over the remaining 4-year life at 10 per year. The depreciation expense for the second half of the year is one-half of the new annual depreciation expense or (10 / 2) = 5 and reduces the asset account balance to (40 – 5) = 35 at year-end. Figure 5-8 shows the asset's book and tax bases after Taxpayer Company recognizes the impairment charge.

The journal entries to record the asset purchase, depreciation, and asset impairment loss are:

30-June-20X1

dr:	Asset account	100.0	
	cr: Cash		100.0
memo:	To record the purchase of the asset for cash		

31-December-20X1

dr:	Depreciation expense	10.0	
	cr: Accumulated depreciation		10.0
memo:	To record one-half year's depreciation expense (20 / 2 = 10)		

FIGURE 5-7

Book and Tax Bases Without Recognizing an Impairment Charge

Taxpayer Company: 5-Year MACRS Asset - No Impairment Loss					
	20X1	**20X2**	**20X3**	**20X4**	**20X5**
Asset's book basis - beginning	100.0	90.0	70.0	50.0	30.0
Less: depreciation expense	10.0	20.0	20.0	20.0	20.0
Asset's book basis - ending	90.0	70.0	50.0	30.0	10.0
Asset's tax basis - beginning	100.0	80.0	48.0	28.8	17.3
Less: depreciation expense	20.0	32.0	19.2	11.5	11.5
Asset's tax basis - ending	80.0	48.0	28.8	17.3	5.8
Tax basis to book basis ratio	88.9%	68.6%	57.6%	57.6%	57.6%

FIGURE 5·8

Book and Tax Bases after Recognizing an Impairment Charge

Taxpayer Company: 5-Year MACRS Asset - 40.0 Impairment Loss In 20X2					
	20X1	**20X2**	**20X3**	**20X4**	**20X5**
Asset's book basis - beginning	100.0	90.0	35.0	25.0	15.0
Less: impairment loss	-	40.0	-	-	-
Less: depreciation expense	10.0	15.0	10.0	10.0	10.0
Asset's book basis - ending	90.0	35.0	25.0	15.0	5.0
Asset's tax basis - beginning	100.0	80.0	48.0	28.8	17.3
Less: depreciation expense	20.0	32.0	19.2	11.5	11.5
Asset's tax basis - ending	80.0	48.0	28.8	17.3	5.8
Tax basis to book basis ratio	88.9%	137.1%	115.2%	115.2%	115.2%

30-June-20X2

dr:	Depreciation expense	10.0	
	cr: Accumulated depreciation		10.0
memo:	To record one-half year's depreciation expense (20 / 2 = 10)		

30-June-20X2

dr:	Loss on impairment of asset	40.0	
	cr: Accumulated depreciation		40.0
memo:	To record the asset impairment charge of 40		

Note how the tax basis to book basis ratio changes between Figure 5-7 and Figure 5-8 because of the impact of the asset impairment charge on the asset account balance and on the book depreciation schedule.

TRANSACTION FAIR VALUE ADJUSTMENTS

Transaction fair value adjustments in stock purchase transactions affect differences between an asset's book and tax bases in much the same manner as recognizing asset impairments. One important difference is that recognizing an asset impairment may only decrease the book (carrying) value of an asset, whereas adjusting an asset's carrying value to fair value may either increase or decrease its book value. Because the actual item being sold in a stock purchase transaction is the stock of the corporation and not the individual assets, the tax bases of the assets are unaffected. Consequently, adjustments to the book value of assets in a business combination recorded using purchase accounting either diverge or converge the book basis and tax basis, depending on the difference existing prior to the transaction. If the book basis exceeds the tax basis and the asset's book value is written down to fair value, it reduces the difference between the book and tax bases (the book and tax bases converge); if the book basis exceeds the tax basis and the asset's book value is written up to fair value, it increases the difference between the book and tax bases (the book and tax bases diverge).

ASSET SALES OR DEEMED ASSET SALES

Usually, when the stock of Target Company is purchased for cash or other consideration, Seller Company pays taxes on any gain realized from selling the stock (sales price—its adjusted basis). The tax bases of Target Company's underlying assets (inside bases) pass, unchanged, into the hands of Buyer Company, the purchaser. This is sometimes referred to as a "no-step-up" transaction because the tax bases of Target Company's assets and liabilities are the same after the transaction as they were before the transaction, even though the bases for financial reporting purposes (book bases) may change as a result of the transaction.

An asset sale or deemed asset sale under IRC Section 338(h)(10) has the effect of equalizing the book bases and tax bases of the assets. In asset sales or deemed asset sales, Seller Company pays tax on the difference between the deemed (imputed) sale price of the assets and their tax bases. The sales price, which consists of consideration given, liabilities (including the tax liability from the sale) assumed and acquisition costs, becomes the new aggregate basis of the assets being purchased. The Aggregate Grossed-Up Basis (AGUB) is allocated to the assets purchased in class order up to their fair market value. The allocation scheme results in the book (fair market value) bases and tax bases being equal. If the AGUB exceeds the fair values of the assets in classes I through VI, then the residual value of any basis not allocated to assets in classes I through VI is allocated to class VII, goodwill. Goodwill created in an asset or deemed asset sale is deductible for income tax purposes.

ESTIMATING THE TAX BASES OF TARGET COMPANY'S ASSETS—KNOWN BALANCE SHEET

As we discussed earlier, particularly when analyzing an IRC Section 338(h)(10) transaction, Buyer Company can improve its negotiating position if it is able to accurately estimate the tax bases of Target Company's assets. Estimating the tax bases of Target Company's assets is greatly simplified if we have access to their fully disclosed financial statements, but that is generally not the case, particularly in an IRC Section 338(h)(10) transaction where the company being purchased is actually a subsidiary of Seller Company and is consolidated for both book and tax purposes. Occasionally, Target Company is an SEC registrant and files its own audited financial statements (as it might in cases where it issues its own debt) or otherwise makes the statements available to Buyer Company. In those cases, the basic procedure to follow is to first reconstruct the deferred income tax items on the balance sheet (as we did in the previous chapter) and then to isolate the items in the deferred income tax footnote relating to differences between the book and tax bases of the asset. These will generally be items for the temporary differences arising from depreciation and amortization. If Target Company holds a material amount of investment assets, their bases are usually determinable from a separate line disclosure in the footnote. This may be either a deferred income tax asset or liability, depending on the performance of the investments. Example 5-2 describes the methodology for estimating the tax bases of Target Company's assets using its financial statements.

EXAMPLE 5-2. Estimating the Tax Bases of Target Company's Assets Using Its Financial Statements

Buyer Company is considering acquiring Target Company, a wholly owned subsidiary of Seller Company. As part of the analysis, Buyer Company wants to assess the advantages of acquiring Target Company in a deemed asset sale transaction under IRC Section 388(h)(10). Buyer Company obtains Target Company's latest financial statements from Seller Company but cannot obtain any information about the tax bases of Target Company's assets. Figure 5-9 shows Target Company's latest balance sheet and deferred income tax footnote.

Note the three amounts in 20X1 that are circled in the deferred income tax footnote: a deferred income tax asset of 98 for amortization; a deferred income tax liability of 1918 for depreciation; and a deferred income tax liability of 130 for unrealized gain on investments. The example uses a single tax venue (or tax jurisdiction) for illustrating the basic method of estimating the tax bases of Target Company's assets. If Target Company has foreign operating segments, the company is required to disclose both the assets and deferred tax items for each segment separately. This analysis would be repeated for each segment and their individual results totaled to arrive at Target Company's total.

The next step is determining the enacted tax rate that Target Company uses for calculating their deferred income tax items. One common pitfall in this analysis is for analysts to use either a company-disclosed or individually derived *effective tax rate*. Deferred income taxes are calculated using currently *enacted statutory tax rates*. This provides more comparable period-to-period estimates and eliminates the need for Target Company to continually recalculate deferred income tax items as proposed changes in the tax laws are announced. It also alleviates the need for Target Company to predict the future with certainty (unintentional misreporting) and, along that same vein, limits (but does not eliminate) the company's ability to use deferred income tax items as a vehicle for managing future earnings. As mentioned in previous chapters, a reasonable beginning estimate of the enacted statutory tax rate is obtained by taking the current 35 percent federal tax rate and adding an assumed state rate of 5 percent to yield a total 40-percent enacted statutory tax rate for calculating deferred income tax items.

Finally, each of the deferred income tax items would be examined to determine how to properly adjust Target Company's book bases to reflect the tax bases. The first item is the deferred tax liability for the temporary difference relating to depreciation. Because Target Company records a deferred tax liability of 1918 for this item, our inference is that the book basis of the depreciable asset (Property, plant, and equipment account = 8044) exceeds the tax basis of the asset. Estimating the tax basis requires reducing the recorded book basis for the asset by an amount equal to the deferred income tax liability recorded for depreciation (1918) divided by the enacted statutory tax rate (40 percent).

The two formulae we need to consider are:

Tax basis = Book basis + (deferred income tax asset / enacted statutory tax rate); and
Tax basis = Book basis − (deferred income tax liability / enacted statutory tax rate)

FIGURE 5-9

Target Company's Latest Balance Sheet and Deferred Income Tax Footnote

Target Company's Financial Statements

Balance Sheet	20X0	20X1
Assets		
Cash and cash equivalents	2,000	2,261
Prepaid expenses and other current assets	246	358
Total current assets	2,246	2,619
Property, plant and equipment - net of accumulated depreciation	7,281	8,044
Investments	1,322	1,199
Deferred income tax assets	1,600	1,799
Intangible assets	975	866
Total assets	13,424	14,527
Liabilities		
Long-term debt	2,847	4,630
Deferred income tax liabilities	2,101	2,048
Total liabilities	4,948	6,678
Owner's equity	8,476	7,849

Notes to the Financial Statements

Note 6: Deferred income taxes

Deferred income taxes are recorded as the result of temporary differences between asset and liability values reported for financial and tax purposes. The Company provides a valuation allowance reducing the portion of its deferred tax assets consisting of net operating loss carryforwards that it doubts it will realize. The increase in the valuation was $160 thousand in 20X1 and $80 thousand in 20X0.

in thousands	20X0	20X1
Deferred tax assets relating to:		
Net operating losses	1,649	2,021
Amortization	111	98
Valuation allowance	(160)	(320)
Deferred income tax assets	1,600	1,799
Deferred tax liabilities relating to:		
Depreciation	1,946	1,918
Unrealized gain on investments	155	130
Deferred income tax liabilities	2,101	2,048

Figure 5-10 shows the estimation of the tax bases of Target Company's assets. Note that we generally assume the book and tax bases of current assets to be equal. It would seem that approach would not hold true for inventories recorded under the last-in, first out (LIFO) method of valuation. Under the LIFO inventory valuation system, the most recently purchased inventory is considered to be the first inventory

FIGURE 5·10

Calculating the Tax Bases of Assets

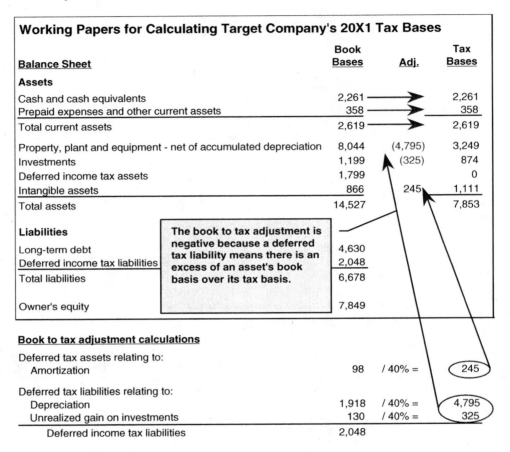

Working Papers for Calculating Target Company's 20X1 Tax Bases

Balance Sheet	Book Bases	Adj.	Tax Bases
Assets			
Cash and cash equivalents	2,261 ⟶		2,261
Prepaid expenses and other current assets	358 ⟶		358
Total current assets	2,619 ⟶		2,619
Property, plant and equipment - net of accumulated depreciation	8,044	(4,795)	3,249
Investments	1,199	(325)	874
Deferred income tax assets	1,799		0
Intangible assets	866	245	1,111
Total assets	14,527		7,853
Liabilities			
Long-term debt	4,630		
Deferred income tax liabilities	2,048		
Total liabilities	6,678		
Owner's equity	7,849		

> The book to tax adjustment is negative because a deferred tax liability means there is an excess of an asset's book basis over its tax basis.

Book to tax adjustment calculations

Deferred tax assets relating to:			
Amortization	98	/ 40% =	245
Deferred tax liabilities relating to:			
Depreciation	1,918	/ 40% =	4,795
Unrealized gain on investments	130	/ 40% =	325
Deferred income tax liabilities	2,048		

item to be sold. This leads to differences between the fair value and book value of the inventory, but the book basis and tax basis are kept fairly closely aligned by the IRC requirement that companies use the same valuation method for book as for income tax reporting.

In our example the tax basis of the Property, plant and equipment asset calculates as:

Tax basis = Book basis – (deferred income tax liability / enacted statutory tax rate)
Tax basis = 8,044 – (1,918 / 40%) = 8,044 – 4,795
Tax basis = 3,249

Similarly, we calculate the tax basis for the Investments account by dividing the recorded deferred income tax liability (130) for the unrealized gain by the enacted statutory tax rate (40 percent) and subtracting the result (325) from the recorded book basis (1199) of the asset.

Tax basis = Book basis – (deferred income tax liability / enacted statutory tax rate)
Tax basis = 1,199 – (130 / 40%) = 1,199 – 325
Tax basis = 874

The last calculation is for the deferred income tax asset recorded for amortization. It is not uncommon for companies to record deferred income tax assets for the amortization of intangible assets because the IRC imposes a statutory 15-year amortization period for all deductible intangible assets. In many sectors, intangible assets such as noncompete agreements, licenses, and even some patents and copyrights may have useful lives for financial accounting purposes that are shorter than 15 years. This means that they amortize more quickly for financial reporting purposes than for income tax purposes, resulting in an *excess of the tax basis over their book basis*. In our example the recorded deferred income tax asset (98) is divided by the enacted statutory tax rate (40 percent) and that result (245) added to the recorded book basis (866) of the asset.

Tax basis = Book basis + (deferred income tax asset / enacted statutory tax rate)
Tax basis = 866 + (98 / 40%) = 866 + 245
Tax basis = 1,111

ESTIMATING THE TAX BASES OF TARGET COMPANY'S ASSETS—UNKNOWN BALANCE SHEET

The more practical case occurs when very little information about the balance sheet of the subsidiary is available. In this situation we need to make a series of estimations based on the information available and to also realize that our estimates may at times be far afield and at others right on the money. The steps to estimating the tax bases of the assets are: first determining Target Company's balance sheet (book bases of the assets); secondly, estimating the asset's useful lives for financial accounting purposes, and the recovery periods for tax accounting purposes, and deriving the tax basis to book basis ratios; and finally applying the tax basis to book basis ratios to estimate the tax bases of the assets.

Target Company's Balance Sheet

Generally there is a balance sheet available for the Target Company in a deemed asset sale under IRC Section 338(h)(10) if for no other reason than hostile deemed asset sales cannot occur since the election for treatment under 338(h)(10) must be made simultaneously by both Seller Company and Buyer Company. Quite often Target Company's full balance sheet is not presented but instead a net assets position showing assets and liabilities (but not owner's equity) is available. Since our interest is determining the tax bases of Target Company's assets a statement of net assets is usually adequate.

Estimating the Asset's Useful Lives

Most companies have a mixture of assets composed of both tangible and intangible assets. Tangible assets having a difference between their book bases and tax bases are usually classified on the balance sheet as property, plant, and equipment. Within the Property, plant, and equipment or Fixed assets accounts are the following: land that is not depreciable for either book or tax purposes and consequently should have equal book and tax bases; other real property assets such as buildings and factories, which, while depreciated using the straight-line method for both book and tax purposes, may have different useful lives for financial reporting purposes than the statutory recovery periods for income tax purposes; and finally the remaining fixed assets that are usually depreciated using a straight-line method for financial purposes but using an accelerated schedule for income tax purposes, often over a different recovery period. As a general view for depreciation versus recovery periods, companies would rather have the shortest possible recovery period for income tax accounting purposes because that provides them with cash tax benefits sooner rather than later; companies would rather have the longest possible depreciation life for financial accounting purposes because that pushes the negative impact of depreciation on the firm's earnings into future periods.

When analyzing Target Company's fixed assets, our information needs are satisfied if we are able to determine:

1. The quantity of fixed assets
2. How they are segregated into different depreciation classes for financial reporting purposes
3. How they are segregated into different cost recovery classes for income tax reporting purposes
4. If any special events have transpired that affect either the book or tax bases directly, such as recent acquisitions as business combinations, asset sales, or recognition of asset impairments

Usually the first item is discernible from Target Company's balance sheet or statement of net assets. The second item is more challenging, and, lacking firm-specific information, we have to look to outside sources to find for a particular sector the average fixed asset depreciation period. Similarly, for the third item we would use firm-specific values when available but, lacking those, substitute industry-average tax recovery periods. Once we have the industry-average book and tax depreciation periods, we are able to construct depreciation schedules and determine the tax basis to book basis ratio as discussed earlier in the chapter. Figure 5-11 shows the tax basis to book basis ratios for different combinations of average book and tax depreciation periods.

Example 5-3 describes the methodology for estimating the tax bases of Target Company's assets using tax basis to book basis ratios.

EXAMPLE 5-3. Estimating the Tax Bases of Target Company's Assets Using Tax Basis to Book Basis Ratios

Buyer Company is considering acquiring Target Company, a wholly owned subsidiary of Seller Company. As part of the analysis, Buyer Company wants to assess the advantages of acquiring Target Company in a deemed asset sale transaction under IRC Section

FIGURE 5·11

Tax Basis to Book Basis Ratios

		Average Recovery Period for Income Tax Reporting									
		3-Year	4-Year	5-Year	6-Year	7-Year	8-Year	9-Year	10-Year	15-Year	20-Year
	3	64.20%	93.75%	119.89%	146.91%	174.71%	201.69%	229.32%	256.31%	456.19%	611.17%
	4	48.15%	70.31%	89.92%	110.19%	131.04%	151.27%	171.99%	192.23%	342.14%	458.38%
Average	5	38.52%	56.25%	71.94%	88.15%	104.83%	121.02%	137.59%	153.78%	273.71%	366.70%
Book	6	32.10%	46.88%	59.95%	73.46%	87.36%	100.85%	114.66%	128.15%	228.09%	305.58%
Depreciation	7	27.51%	40.18%	51.38%	62.96%	74.88%	86.44%	98.28%	109.85%	195.51%	261.93%
Life Time	8	24.08%	35.16%	44.96%	55.09%	65.52%	75.64%	86.00%	96.12%	171.07%	229.19%
in years	9	21.40%	31.25%	39.96%	48.97%	58.24%	67.23%	76.44%	85.44%	152.06%	203.72%
	10	19.26%	28.13%	35.97%	44.07%	52.41%	60.51%	68.80%	76.89%	136.86%	183.35%
	15	12.84%	18.75%	23.98%	29.38%	34.94%	40.34%	45.86%	51.26%	91.24%	122.23%
	20	9.63%	14.06%	17.98%	22.04%	26.21%	30.25%	34.40%	38.45%	68.43%	91.68%

388(h)(10). Buyer Company obtains Target Company's latest financial statements from Seller Company showing fixed assets of 8044 but cannot obtain any information about the tax bases of Target Company's assets or its deferred income tax items. The average book depreciation lifetime for fixed assets in Target Company's industry is 6.9 years, and the average recovery period for income tax reporting is 4.0 years. Interpolating linearly from Figure 5-11, the tax basis to book basis ratio is approximately $40.18 + (46.88 - 40.18)/10 = 40.85$ percent. We estimate the tax bases of Target Company's assets as $(8044 \times 40.85\%) = 3286$.

Intangible assets are estimated using the same technique.

Compensating for Previously Recognized Asset Impairments

The last item to consider is whether recent events may have disrupted the ratio between the tax and book bases of the assets. Assume that two years ago Target Company recognized an asset impairment loss of 250. We adjust for that by calculating what the book bases of the assets would have been if the impairment loss had never been recognized. The 250 had a 6.9-year life, meaning that it would have depreciated by $(250 / 6.9 = 36.2 \times 2) = 72.4$ to $(250 - 72.4) = 178$ by the date of the balance sheet we are examining. Compensating for the impairment charge, we write up the asset balance of 8044 to $(8044 + 178) = 8222$ to calculate the tax bases of the fixed assets as $(8222 \times 40.85\%) = 3359$. Note that the write-up to the book bases is *only* for the calculation of the tax bases of the assets and does not affect Target Company's book bases.

CHAPTER SUMMARY

In some transactions Seller Company possesses a negotiating advantage because it knows with certainty the tax bases of the assets it is selling, either through a direct asset sale or a deemed asset sale under IRC Section 338(h)(10). Buyer Company can infringe upon Seller Company's advantage by estimating the tax bases of the assets being sold by adjusting the reported book bases of the assets by the calculated difference between the book and tax bases.

Differences occur between an asset's book basis and tax basis because of three factors:

- Depreciating the asset using different methods for tax and book purposes (i.e., straight-line versus accelerated depreciation schedules)
- Depreciating the asset based on a different useful lifetime for financial reporting purposes than the recovery period used for income tax reporting
- Adjustments to the book value of the asset for items such as purchase accounting adjustments or asset impairments that do not result in a parallel adjustment for income tax purposes

The book bases of Target Company's assets are generally available either from the company's financial statements or from a statement of net assets. The income tax bases of the assets are almost never available and must be estimated. There are two principal methods for estimating the tax bases of Target Company's assets:

- Isolating the portion of the deferred income tax items associated with temporary differences between the book and tax bases of Target Company's assets, then calculating the tax bases resulting from that difference
- Adjusting the reported amounts of Target Company's assets based on a tax basis to book basis ratio estimated from industry average book and tax depreciation periods

CHAPTER 6

Pension and Other Postretirement Benefits

INTRODUCTION

In early September, 2003 the Pension Benefit Guarantee Corporation, the government agency that insures employer-sponsored pension plans, estimated the total underfunding for all private employer-sponsored pension plans as being in excess of $400 billion.[1] The implications for firms with substantial underfunding are reduced future earnings, reduced future cash flows, higher levels of debt, and possible financial distress. Many believe that the financial accounting standards relating to pensions are at least partly to blame for the current situation where companies facing substantial underfundings are able, for the present, to avoid recognizing significant liabilities on their balance sheets. It follows that a sound grasp of pensions and pension accounting is important for any analyst.

It would be wonderful if there were a definitive work fully and clearly explaining pension accounting in one or two chapters. The many complexities of pension accounting make that a practically unattainable goal, but if we leave the fine and infrequently encountered points to pension specialists, we can concentrate on achieving a degree of understanding how pensions work and how companies report their pension liabilities. Specifically, this chapter focuses on simply and clearly explaining the fundamental concepts of pensions and pension accounting. These are the basics of pension accounting terminology and rules needed in later chapters to decipher the pension footnote and estimate a company's pension position.

When talking about pensions, we are actually discussing two components of postretirement benefits: pension benefits that are cash payments received by retirees; and other postretirement benefits such as health insurance, life insurance, etc. Typically it seems we tend to focus on the costs of pension benefits and to minimize the cost of other postretirement benefits but, in many cases, the costs of other postretirement benefits greatly exceed the costs of pension benefits. Although pension and other postretirement benefits have many similarities, financial accounting addresses them under separate Statements of Financial Accounting Standards. To align our discussion with the standards and to avoid unnecessary confusion in terminology, this chapter begins by discussing pension benefits and then follows with a separate discussion of other postretirement plans.

PENSION VERSUS OTHER POSTRETIREMENT BENEFIT PLANS

Pension plans provide cash income for retirees, whereas postretirement benefit plans provide other forms of value, usually medical, dental, or life insurance. Although the two forms of benefits seem very similar, there are currently significant differences in the legal and accounting requirements for the two different types of benefits. This comes about largely because pension benefits are usually guaranteed by insurance from the Pension Benefit Guarantee Corporation (PBGC), which was created the *Employee Retirement Income Security Act of 1974* (ERISA). ERISA places specific requirements on the administration and funding of pension plans but does not place those same requirements on other postretirement benefit plans.

TYPES OF PENSION PLANS

There are two basic forms of pension plans, defined contribution plans and defined benefit plans. Defined contribution plans are the cleanest and neatest of the two; for each period employees work, they receive some percentage of their wages as an additional contribution to a retirement account. After the contribution is made, the company's liability for the retirement benefit is satisfied and the worker is usually responsible for managing or directing the managing of the retirement funds from that point until the worker retires. The accounting is, as mentioned previously, clean and neat. Employer Company recognizes an additional compensation expense equal to its contribution to the employee's retirement accounts, and that completes Employer Company's involvement with the pension plan. Employer Company does not recognize any pension assets or liabilities in its financial statements, makes no footnote disclosures, and never has to account for any liability relating to any past pension plan contributions. There is generally little, if any, concern with defined contribution pension plans.

Defined Benefit Plans

When we speak of pension plans, we are interested in the second major type, defined benefit plans. With a defined benefit plan, for each period employees work, they receive a claim to some defined amount of future income after they retire. Unlike the defined contribution plan where Employer Company makes one immediate contribution and settles its liability to the employee completely, under the defined benefit plan, Employer Company assumes a liability to give the employee a specified amount each month for as long as the employee lives in retirement. To make the accounting even messier, the "specified amount" is usually specified as a percentage of the employee's highest three-year average, last year's salary, or some other amount that cannot be known until a date far in the future. Our focus in this work is on defined benefit pension plans.

Funded versus Unfunded Plans

Another significant discriminator between plans is whether they are funded or unfunded. In a funded plan, Employer Company makes cash payments into the plan by placing funds with a third-party trustee. The trustee invests the funds, which are usually placed beyond the control of Employer Company. In certain cases where the plan is overfunded, Employer Company may ask for a portion to be returned, but that is an odd case. ERISA requires pension plans to maintain certain minimum levels of funding. Other postretirement benefit plans (other than pension plans) are not addressed by ERISA and consequently do not fall under the act's funding requirements. Many of these other postretirement plans are, in fact, unfunded, even though they represent substantial liabilities for employers.

ECONOMIC OBJECTIVES OF PENSION PLANS

Simply stated, the economic objective of a pension plan is for Employer Company to place enough assets in a pension fund today so that by the time Employee retires, the assets have grown to the point where they are sufficient to pay Employee's pension throughout retirement. The challenges for Employer Company are apparent as we ask the obvious questions arising from this simplified objective, such as:

- What is the future rate of return on money invested in the pension fund?
- How long is it before Employee retires?
- How much will Employee be making when she retires (since the amount of the pension is likely based on final salary)?
- How long will Employee live in retirement?

As obvious as these questions seem, it is equally obvious that they are impossible to answer *for any one individual.* No one has any hope of predicting with certainty when any particular employee will retire, how much they will be making when they retire, or how long they will live after retirement. But if we talk about a *group of individuals,* things change. Actuaries can predict fairly accurately how long the *average individual* in a group will continue working, what the *average individual* in a group will make when retiring, and how long after retiring the *average individual* in a group will continue living and receiving benefits. Similarly, no one can predict with any certainty what the future return on a particular investment over a particular period will be, but it is possible to predict with relative accuracy the long-term return on well-diversified managed portfolios.

Perhaps a more informative statement of the economic objective of pension plans is *estimating* the level of assets that Employer Company must place in a pension fund today so that by the *estimated* time Employee retires the *estimated* asset growth is adequate to pay Employee's pension for the remainder of her *estimated* life. The emphasis is of course on the fact that the pension process relies on estimates. This is not to imply that it is necessarily doomed to error because of that (actuarial science can be frighteningly accurate in its predictions) but to focus on some earlier discussions about accounting estimates, managerial incentives, and professional skepticism. In areas where management has incentives to understate expenses, overstate income, or control more cash, analysts should exercise a reasonable amount of professional skepticism when reviewing accounting estimates made by management because those estimates might be biased. This is especially germane to pension accounting because the size of some pension obligations makes the pension assumptions produce material effects on Employer Company's financial results.

HOW PENSION PLANS WORK

The simplest way to describe how pension plans work is by working through Example 6-1.

EXAMPLE 6-1. Basic Pension Plan Formula.

Assume that you are an employee of my firm, Employer Company and that:

- Today is 1-January-20X2.
- You are 25 years old.
- You were hired two years ago, 1-January-20X0.
- Your current annual salary is $50,000.

At the beginning of last year on 1-January-20X1 (which coincidentally is your twenty-fourth birthday), I announced that Employer Company will begin providing a benefit package including a defined benefit pension plan. The terms of the pension plan provide, beginning when you reach age 65, an annual pension equal to 1 percent of your highest year's salary for each year that you work for me. In other words, if you work for 40 years before retiring at age 65, your annual pension is equal to 40 percent of your highest year's salary. If instead you were now 30 years old and work 35 years before retiring at age 65, your annual pension is equal to 35 percent of your highest year's salary.

Because you are 25 years old, you must wait 40 more years to begin receiving your annual pension (apologies to those readers that in fact are 25, but the insertion of this very cold reality is necessary for demonstrating the point). On 1-January-20X2, Employer Company's liability for the benefit that you have earned since the inception of the pension plan on 1-January-20X1 is the present value of:

$$\text{1 year of service} \times \frac{\text{1 percent of your highest salary}}{\text{for each year of service}} \times \text{your \$50,000 current salary}$$

Although you have worked for me for two years, 20X0 and 20X1, the pension plan did not begin until 1-January-20X1, so 20X1 is your first year of creditable service, and (for the present) your service in the year 20X0 does not contribute to your pension benefits. Under the pension plan your one year of creditable service for 20X1 entitles you, at age 65, to begin receiving an annual pension of:

$$1 \times 1\% \times \$50,000 = \$500$$

Accumulated Benefit Obligation

In reality, you should retire at a considerably higher salary and with many more years of service, but based solely on what you have done to date, $500 is sort of the minimum pension you expect to receive every year from your retirement date until you pass away. Again, no one can predict how long any one individual lives after retiring, but, assuming that you are equivalent to the actuarially average member of your demographic, we expect you to live exactly 12 years after retiring. (I chose 12 years as a convenient representative retirement period, but the PBGC currently estimates an average male's retirement lifetime as 18.1 years).[2] To determine the present actuarial value of the expected stream of pension payments you will receive after retirement, we first determine a discount rate (which should be the rate at which I would borrow to fund the pension payments). Then we use that rate to discount the stream of payments back to an annuity value at your retirement date. Figure 6-1 shows the stream of pension payments discounted at an assumed rate of 8 percent, yielding an annuity value of $3768 at your retirement date.

The $3768 represents the annuity value that settles your pension entitlement as a single up-front payment on your retirement date. On that date an average member of your group would be indifferent between receiving either the single payment of $3768 or a stream of payments of $500 per year for the next 12 years. But that is $3768 forty years in the future, and to find the present value of those payments, we discount the annuity value of $3768 back to the present (still using the 8-percent discount rate) to arrive at the present value of $173. That amount, the $173 is called the *accumulated benefit obligation* (ABO) and is formally defined by

FIGURE 6·1

Present Actuarial Value of a Pension Obligation

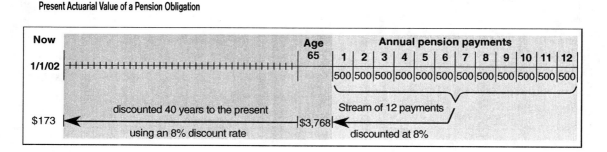

the *Statement of Financial Accounting Standards No. 87, Employers' Accounting for Pensions* (FAS87), as "the actuarial present value of benefits (whether vested or non-vested) attributed by the pension benefit formula to employee service rendered before a specified date and based on employee service and compensation (if applicable) before that date."[3] An important attribute of the ABO is that it does not consider projected future compensation; it is based only on your current salary.

Projected Benefit Obligation

Another way that we could view your pension is more realistically considering that over your 40-year career you will receive pay increases due to cost of living and merit considerations which, as your employer, I forecast will average 4 percent per year. Growing your current salary of $50,000 forward at 4 percent, you should expect to be earning just over $240,000 when you retire. If we base your pension on 1 percent of that final salary, you can expect to receive $2400 each year of your retirement for the year of service you have just completed. Figure 6-2 shows the stream of cash flows, annuity, and discounted present value of your benefits resulting from your higher assumed final salary.

The annuity value to settle your pension entitlement is a significantly higher $18,087 which, when discounted back to the present (still using the 8-percent discount rate), produces a present value of $833. That amount is called the *projected benefit obligation* (PBO), which FAS87 defines as "the actuarial present value as of a date of all benefits attributed by the pension benefit formula to employee service rendered prior to that date. The projected benefit obligation is measured using assumptions as to future compensation levels if the pension benefit formula is based on those future compensation levels (pay-related, final-pay, final-average-pay, or career-average-pay plans)."[4]

Although the ABO is used to determine certain minimum funding levels (remember we said that the ABO was really the absolute minimum benefit that

FIGURE 6-2

Present Actuarial Value of a Pension Obligation Considering Future Compensation Levels

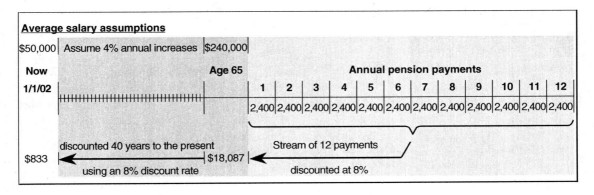

you expect to receive) we find that the PBO is a much more important concept for pension accounting. Intuitively, this makes sense because the PBO is probably much closer to the benefit that you will eventually receive and also much closer to my actual liability as your employer.

In the remainder of this section on pension benefits, the terms ABO and PBO are used for determining some of the components of net periodic pension cost (expense), although the two are conceptually different. PBO assumes that Employer Company continues operating and that you continue working and earning additional pension benefits. That approach equates with the accounting concept of a going-concern, and the resulting PBO is the present value (fair value) of Employer Company's expected liability to you, settled on your retirement date as an annuity. ABO equates with the liquidation or bankruptcy value and represents Employer Company's liability to you based on the present value of the pension benefits that you have actually earned, settled in the present; it is the amount Employer Company owes you today.

As an aside, the standards and regulations concerning pensions and other postretirement benefits are fairly consistent regarding the use of the terms accumulated and projected. Accumulated is used to signify an amount based on current levels of compensation, and projected is used to signify amounts based on future expected levels of compensation.

NET PERIODIC PENSION COST

FAS87 refers to net periodic pension *cost* where we would normally expect to think of net periodic pension *expense*. The Financial Accounting Standards Board (FASB) explains that its rationale for using the terminology is because net periodic pension cost is often capitalized into items such as inventory and that the term cost is more technically correct. Remaining consistent with FAS87, I continue using the word cost but could have just as correctly used the term expense.

The financial accounting objectives for pension plans are attributing the costs of the pension plan to the periods benefited to match revenues with the costs of producing them and reporting to financial statement users the company's financial position regarding the pension plan that it provides its employees. The process begins with the measurement of the *net periodic pension cost,* which FAS87 defines as "The amount recognized in an employer's financial statements as the cost of a pension plan for a period."[5] FAS87 lists six components of net periodic pension cost as:

1. Service cost
2. Interest cost
3. Expected return on plan assets
4. Amortization of unrecognized prior service cost
5. Gain or loss
6. Amortization of the unrecognized net obligation or asset

An important note on the expected return on plan assets: The technical accounting approach to the return on plan assets is somewhat confusing because it initially includes the *actual* return on plan assets as part of net periodic pension cost and then includes a separate adjustment equal to the difference between the expected and actual returns on plan assets. As a simplification, through the rest of the discussion I skip the interim accounting steps and simply use the *expected* return on plan assets when calculating net periodic pension cost. This is a reasonable and common simplification and is the disclosure found in the pension footnote.

Pension Service Cost

The first two items of net periodic pension cost to consider are the service cost and the interest cost. The pension service cost is the present value of the benefits that you earn in a period. In the example that we used before (see Figure 6-2), last year (in 20X1), you earned projected pension benefits with a present value of $833, which is the pension service cost for that period. When you work a second cred-itable year (20X2), you earn an additional 1 percent of your highest annual salary. Looking at Figure 6-3, we see that it is the same analysis as for the previous year (20X1), the difference being that the 20X2 annuity value is discounted back 39 instead of 40 years (because we are one year closer to your retirement). The service cost for 20X2 is the present value ($899) of the additional pension benefit that you earned in your second year of covered employment.

Pension Interest Cost

In addition to the service cost for your second covered year of employment, there is also an interest cost, which is the amount that the present value of your first cov-ered year's PBO increased due to the passage of time. It is equal to the present value of the first covered year's PBO ($833) times the discount rate of 8 percent

FIGURE 6·3

Present Actuarial Value of a Pension Obligation Earned in the 2^d Covered Year – 20X2

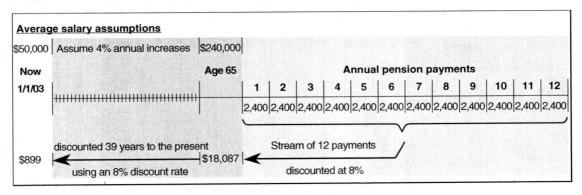

FIGURE 6-4

Present Value of a Pension Benefit Appreciating over Time to Retirement

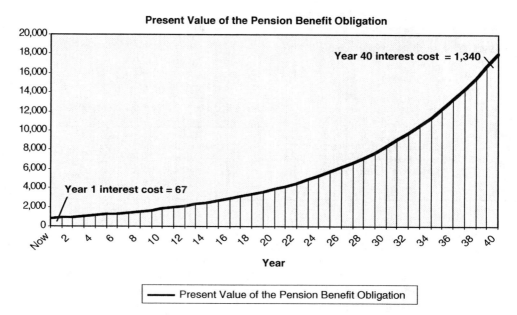

and equals ($833 × 8%) = $67. Figure 6-4 shows the increase in the first covered year's pension benefit obligation appreciating over the 40-year service period from now until retirement. The increase in each period is the interest cost component of the net periodic pension cost. Note two items about pension interest cost. First, it is different than other interest costs and is always a component of net periodic pension cost and never part of gross interest expense. Secondly, due to the compounding effect of the discounting, for a particular stream of cash flows, the pension interest cost increases in each subsequent period. Figure 6-4 shows pension interest cost increasing in each period from Year 1 to Year 40 because of the effect of compounding.

When we calculate the pension cost component for your second covered year of service (20X2), it consists of:

interest cost (20X1 benefit)	$67
Add: service cost for 20X2	$899
periodic pension cost for 20X2	$966

To check that we are calculating this correctly, look at Figure 6-5, where we calculate the total projected benefit obligation at the end of 20X2, your second year of creditable service. You have earned an annual pension retirement benefit equal to 2 percent (1 percent for each of the two years of creditable service you completed, 20X1

FIGURE 6·5

Total Projected Benefit Obligation—at the End of 20X2

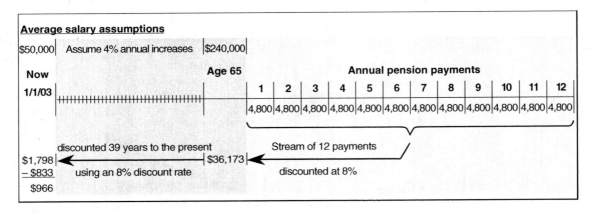

and 20X2) of your highest projected salary level of $240,000, which equals ($240,000 × 2%) = $4800 per year or retirement. The stream of twelve $4800 retirement payments discounts to an annuity value of $36,173 at your retirement date. This amount, discounted again at 8 percent for the 39 years between the end of your second creditable year and your retirement returns a present value of $1798, which is ($1798 − $833) = $966 higher than the PBO at the end of 20X1, your first covered year. So our calculation for the periodic pension cost of $966 exactly accounts (allowing for rounding differences) for the increase in the PBO between 20X1 and 20X2.

Expected Return on Plan Assets

This discussion illustrates the very basic elements of a pension plan—how an employee earns benefits and the costs that the basic benefits impose on the employer: the service cost and the interest cost. There are other types of benefits and costs we discuss later, but for the present, we will try to keep the discussion at the simplest functional level. To complete the study, the next piece to consider is the matter of funding a pension plan.

After your first year of covered service (20X1), I realize that, as your employer, in 40 years I will have to come up with $18,087 to fund the annuity value of your retirement payments and decide that I want to start to fund this retirement plan now. I engage a trustee to administer the plan, who informs me that it expects to earn an average return of 10 percent on plan assets, which is the expected long-term rate of return on plan assets. That means that if I place $400 in the plan at the end of 20X1, your first year of service, by the time you are ready to retire in 40 years, the $400 will have grown at an average 10 percent return into $18,087, enough to fund the annuity value of the pension benefits attributable for your first year's service.

There are three rates that we need to use, but we must keep them mentally separate.

- The first is the *expected rate-of-return on plan assets,* which is the rate I use to make my funding decision. It is the rate at which I expect plan assets to grow over the long-term. The pension fund administrator usually provides estimates of the expected return on plan assets, and it is the rate used to calculate net periodic pension cost.
- The second rate, called the *actual rate-of-return on plan assets,* is the rate at which assets increase (or decrease) in any given period. The actual rate-of-return on plan assets is a useful measure of the plan's investment performance and is derived as the rate of change (positive or negative) in plan assets after adjusting for contributions made by Employer Company and payments to the plan's retirees.
- The third rate used is the *discount rate,* which is the rate at which we discount future obligations to determine the present value of pension obligations. The discount rate usually reflects Employer Company's long-term borrowing costs (weighted average-cost of capital).

The addition of income-producing plan assets adds another layer to the required accounting for your pension under Employer Company's (now funded) pension plan. At the completion of your first year of creditable service, Employer Company recognizes a net periodic pension cost for your 20X1 service cost and a corresponding accrued pension cost. Because this is the first year of the pension plan, the net periodic pension cost has a single component, which is your first year's service cost of 833.

31-December-20X1

dr:	Net periodic pension cost	833.0	
	cr: Accrued pension cost		833.0
memo:	To record the first year's projected benefit obligation (PBO)		

Because Employer Company chooses to fund the pension plan they record the contributions to the plan's administrator as a reduction to the accrued pension cost.

31-December-20X1

dr:	Accrued pension cost	400.0	
	cr: Cash		400.0
memo:	To record a cash payment to the pension plan.		

Employer Company's balance sheet reflects the 20X1 ending accrued pension cost (liability) for your first year of covered service:

Accrued pension cost – beginning 20X1	0.0
Add: Net periodic pension cost – 20X1	833.0
Less: Contributions to plan	(400.0)
Accrued pension cost – ending 20X1	433.0

One year later, on 31-December-20X2, Employer Company records the net periodic pension cost for 20X2 as your second covered year service cost (new projected benefit obligation earned in 20X2) plus the interest cost for the projected benefit obligation from 20X1 minus the expected return on the plan assets (400 × 10%) = 40 at the beginning of 20X2.

31-December-20X2

Service cost component	899.0
Add: Interest cost component	67.0
Less: return on plan assets (400 × 10%)	(40.0)
Net periodic pension cost	926.0

Although the most correct accounting term is Net periodic pension cost, it is common to see this item recorded simply as Pension expense. Employer Company records this as:

dr: Net periodic pension cost (Pension expense)   926.0
    cr: Accrued pension cost   926.0

Employer Company's balance sheet reflects the 20X2 ending accrued pension cost liability:

Accrued pension cost – beginning 20X2	433.0
Add: Net periodic pension cost – 20X2	926.0
Less: Cash payments to plan	0.0
Accrued pension cost – ending 20X2	1,358.0

Reconciling this balance to our calculated 20X2 projected benefit obligation from Figure 6-5, it is the projected benefit obligation of $1798 less $400 cash funding less $40 expected return on plan assets ($1798 – $400 – $40)= $1358.

Prior Service Cost

Figure 6-6 shows all three years of your employment, the prior service period (before the inception date of the pension plan) and the two periods of creditable service since the inception of the plan. As the employer, it is my option when initiating a pension plan to either ignore your prior service or, as is more commonly done, give you credit for your prior service. At the inception date of 1-January-20X1, you have one year of prior service credit. Since that year of service credit equates to your receiving 1 percent of your final salary of $240,000 in each of your 12 retirement years, it produces an annuity value at your retirement date of $18,087 as shown in Figure 6-7.

Rather than immediately recognizing a service cost component for the prior service, FAS87 allows amortizing the prior service cost ratably over the future service period of 41 years. In other words, we treat the prior service cost as if you earn it in equal amounts over each of the remaining years until you retire.

FAS87 also gives employers a choice of methods for amortizing the unrecognized prior service cost using either a straight-line average future service basis or on a service years rendered basis. Companies are more likely to choose the service

FIGURE 6·6

Pension Plan Timeline

Plan inception date
1-Jan-20X1

20X0	20X1	20X2
Prior service period	1st year of creditable service	2d year of creditable service
	31-Dec-20X1	31-Dec-20X2

FIGURE 6·7

Present Actuarial Value of the Projected Benefit Obligation for the Prior Service Period

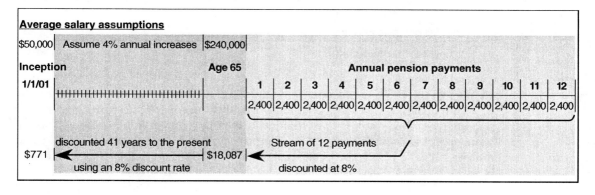

years rendered method because that usually results in the slowest recognition of prior service cost and the least negative earnings impact.

In the inception year Employer Company recognizes prior service cost of ($771 / 41) = $19 and interest cost related to the prior service PBO of ($771 × 8%) = $62. In the second year after inception, Employer Company again recognizes prior service cost of ($771 / 41) = $19 (because the amortization of prior service cost is straight-lined) and interest cost related to the prior service PBO of ($771 + $62 + $19 = $852 × 8%) = $68. Figure 6-8 shows the components of net periodic pension cost, including the amortization and interest cost for the unrecognized prior service cost.

Amortization of Unrecognized Gain or Loss

Now we move into what is sometimes a very controversial area of pension accounting often referred to as the smoothing mechanism. FASB adopted an approach called the corridor method to mitigate or dampen the volatility "noise" (and associated earnings impact) resulting from large stock market swings and/or significant

FIGURE 6·8

Net Periodic Pension Cost with Prior Service Credit

Plan inception date
1-Jan-20X1

20X0	20X1	20X2
Prior service period	1st year of creditable service	2d year of creditable service
	31-Dec-20X1	31-Dec-20X2

	31-Dec-20X1	31-Dec-20X2
Service cost:	833	899
Interest cost:	-	67
Expected return on plan assets:	-	(40)
Prior service cost:	19	19
Prior service cost interest:	62	68
Net periodic pension cost:	914	1,013

changes in the projected benefit obligation. In a perfect world, fund assets and the projected benefit obligation would move exactly as predicted and there would be no impact from market volatility or changes in the PBO from events like layoffs, down-sizings, and early retirements. In an imperfect world, a particularly good or bad return year for a plan could produce a material change in earnings that will reverse over the long run. This is conceptually palatable considering two issues: First, that a diversified, managed portfolio has an estimable long-term return and secondly that while it is important to understand a company's pension position, the results of its pension plan should not mask or obscure its operating results.

The corridor approach begins by measuring the combined, unrecognized gain or loss from the difference between the expected and the actual return on plan assets and from other actuarial changes such as changes in the discount rate. Once that value is quantified, it is compared with 10 percent of the larger of that year's PBO or the plan asset balance. Any amount that is "outside the 10-percent corridor" is amortized as a component of net periodic pension cost. Example 6-2 continues the previous examples and calculates the "corridor" for your defined benefit pension plan.

EXAMPLE **6-2.** The Gain/Loss Corridor

On 1-January-20X1, Employer Company established a defined benefit plan giving you one year of credited prior service. The plan discount rate is 8 percent, the expected return on plan assets is 10 percent, and your $50,000 annual salary is expected to grow at 4 percent per year. All of these estimates turn out to be correct, and over the next five years the PBO increases as shown in Figure 6-9.

To determine if the unrecognized gain or loss is too large to remain unrecognized, a corridor is established as plus and minus 10 percent of the larger of the beginning-of-the-year PBO or plan asset value. Because the only funding for our plan is $400 on 1-January-20X2, the PBO is the larger value and the corridor is based on plus or minus 10 percent of the beginning-of-the-year PBOs, as shown in Figure 6-10.

FIGURE 6-9

Employer Company PBO—Beginning of Plan Years Two through Six

		Age	Years to age 65	Annuity at age 65	Pension service cost	Pension interest cost	Prior service cost	Prior service interest	PBO
Plan initiation	1-Jan-20X1	24	41	-	-	-	$771	-	$771
Begin year 2	1-Jan-20X2	25	40	$18,087	$833	-	$19	$62	$1,684
Begin year 3	1-Jan-20X3	26	39	$36,173	$899	$67	$19	$68	$2,738
Begin year 4	1-Jan-20X4	27	38	$54,260	$971	$139	$19	$75	$3,942
Begin year 5	1-Jan-20X5	28	37	$72,346	$1,049	$216	$19	$83	$5,308
Begin year 6	1-Jan-20X6	29	36	$90,433	$1,133	$300	$19	$91	$6,851

FIGURE 6-10

Unrecognized Gain or Loss Corridor

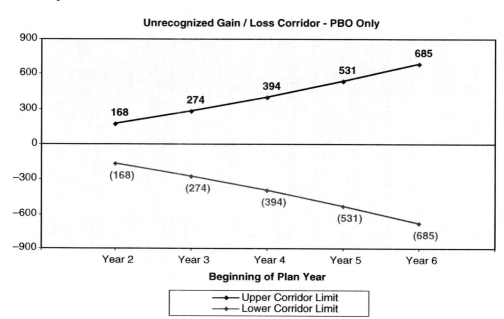

Applying our example, we make a $400 contribution to the plan at the beginning of both 20X2 (the end of 20X1) and 20X3. During 20X2, the plan assets earn 11 percent, and at the beginning of 20X3 the plan balance is ($400 + $400 x 11%) = $444. The expected return on plan assets is 10 percent, so Employer Company recognizes that amount ($400 × 10%) = $40 as a component of periodic pension cost, and the difference between the actual and expected returns ($44 − $40) = $4 is recorded as an unrecognized net gain.

The balance of the unrecognized net gain account ($4) is well within the corridor value of $274 (Figure 6-10). On 1-January-20X3, Employer Company makes the second $400 contribution to the $444 currently in the plan, bringing the 20X3 beginning balance to $844. Note that the gain or loss was calculated before the effects of Employer Company's contribution.

The fund was poorly positioned during 20X3, and when two key market sectors contracted, the fund lost 60 percent ($844 × 60%) = $506, ending the year with a balance of ($844 − $506.4) = $337.6. The expected return for the fund was 10 percent or ($844 × 10%) = $84.4 and the actual return was − $506.4 resulting in a loss for 20X3 of (−$506.4 − $84.4) = −$590.8. Combining the 20X3 result with the existing net unrecognized gain or loss ($4) produces a new net unrecognized gain or loss of (−$590.8 + $4) = −$586.8. Figure 6-11 shows that the unrecognized loss is out of the corridor by ($587 − $394) = $193.

The excess corridor test amount ($193) is recognized by amortizing it as a component of net periodic pension cost over the remaining active employees' average service period, which in our case is 37 years, making the annual recognition ($193 / 37) = $5.2. Net periodic pension cost increases when amortizing a loss and decreases when amortizing a gain.

FIGURE 6·11

Unrecognized Gain or Loss Corridor–Plan Losses

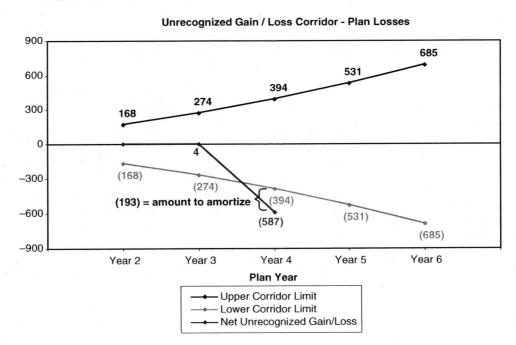

Another commonly encountered unrecognized gain or loss results from changes to the actuarial assumptions used in the plan. A simple example of this type of change would be at the beginning of the year. Figure 6-12 shows the effect of lowering the actuarial discount rate used to compute the PBO of the prior service cost. Because the assumed discount rate is lower, it increases the present value of the pension benefit, which increases Employer Company's liability. This increases the PBO, resulting in an unrecognized loss that is combined with the existing net unrecognized gain or loss. There is no impact on net periodic pension cost unless the net unrecognized gain or loss exceeds the bounds of the unrecognized gain or loss corridor, in which event the amount outside the corridor is amortized over the remaining active employees' average service period.

Note that changes in the plan due to overt actions of Employer Company such as negotiated modifications to the plan, effects of plant closings, or large reductions in force are recognized immediately and are not subject to the corridor test.

Amortization of the Unrecognized Net Obligation or Asset

Unrecognized net obligations or assets arose when FAS87 became effective and employers began accounting under the (then) new standard. This is also referred to as the transition liability or asset and is accounted for similarly to but separately from prior service costs. It is the unrecognized net liability or net asset representing the unrecognized portion of the unfunded *PBO*, and at the plan's inception is amortized using the straight-line method over either the remaining service life of the employees, an elective 15-year period, or the life expectancy of retirees for inactive plans

FIGURE 6·12

Unrecognized Gain or Loss from Actuarial Changes in the Discount Rate

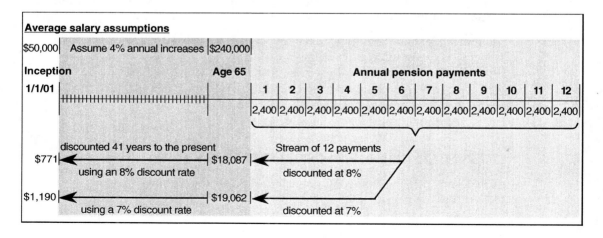

MINIMUM PENSION LIABILITY

When we discussed the projected benefit obligation and the accumulated benefit obligation, we saw that the PBO reflected your expected pension entitlement after you perform what are often significant periods of service. The ABO, on the other hand, was a reasonable approximation of the benefit you had already earned, which equates to a liability that Employer Company has effectively incurred. FAS87 requires that the excess of the ABO over the fair value of plan assets (less any recognized accrued pension liability or plus any recognized accrued pension asset) must be recognized immediately as a minimum pension liability. Think of this as the unfunded portion of the ABO, which should be presented on the balance sheet to the extent that it exceeds any already recognized accrued pension liability. If Employer Company's plan had an ABO of $512 and fair value of plan assets of $400, then Employer Company recognizes a minimum pension liability of ($512 − $400) = $112 by recognizing a pension intangible asset and additional liability in the same amounts. The additional pension liability is usually presented in the financial statements as a component of the Accrued/prepaid pension cost account balance.

dr:	Pension intangible asset	112.0	
	cr: Additional pension liability		112.0
memo:	To adjust the additional liability to reflect the unfunded ABO.		

One limitation imposed when recognizing the pension intangible asset is that the amount recognized may not exceed the amount of any unrecognized prior service cost. Whenever the amount of the minimum pension liability to be recognized exceeds the unrecognized prior service cost, the excess amount is recognized instead as a contra-equity account. Following the case above, assume further that Employer Company had an unrecognized prior service cost of $80. The amount of the minimum pension liability ($112) exceeds unrecognized prior service cost ($80), so Employer Company recognizes a pension intangible asset for the maximum amount ($80) and the excess amount ($112 − $80) = $32 as Excess additional pension liability over unrecognized prior service cost (a contra-equity account):

dr:	Pension intangible asset	80.0	
dr:	Excess add'l pension liab. over unrecognized prior service cost	32.0	
	cr: Additional pension liability		112.0
memo:	To adjust the additional liability to reflect the unfunded portion of ABO.		

PENSION BENEFITS SUMMARY

The term "pension benefits" properly refers to the periodic payments made to retirees from a pension plan and are accounted for separately from other postretirement benefits such as health or life insurance. Pension plans fall within one of two categories as being either defined contribution plans or defined benefit plans. Employer Company's liability arising from a defined contribution plan is readily determined and is periodically settled by payments to a trustee that administers the retirement plan. From that point forward, Employer Company has no further liability, and all of the risk associated with the pension plan is borne by the employees and retirees participating in the plan. The accounting for defined contribution plans is very straightforward and results in Employer Company recognizing a periodic pension cost and a credit to either cash or to an accrued pension cost liability.

Accounting for defined benefit plans is more complex and requires Employer Company to estimate the present values of future liabilities using currently available information. Most of the risk is borne by Employer Company, the guaranteeing agency, which is the Pension Benefit Guarantee Company (PBGC), and Employer Company's creditors. Employer Company's creditors bear additional risk in bankruptcy because the PBGC may exercise a preferential claim of up to 30 percent of Employer Company's assets in cases where part of the ABO is unfunded.

Employer Company recognizes its liability through the net periodic pension cost (expense). The net periodic pension cost has six components, which are:

1. Service cost
2. Interest cost
3. Expected return on plan assets
4. Amortization of unrecognized prior service cost
5. Gain or loss
6. Amortization of the unrecognized net obligation or asset

Net periodic pension cost is measured using the expected return on plan assets, which may vary widely from the actual return on plan assets. To "smooth" net periodic pension expense by removing the short-term effects of plan returns, that difference is recorded in Employer Company's working papers as an unrecognized net gain or loss. If the net unrecognized gain or loss arising from the difference in plan returns and other actuarial changes in plan assumptions exceeds the greater of 10 percent of the PBO or the market value of plan assets, then the excess portion of the net unrecognized gain or loss is amortized over the average remaining service life of the employees as a component of net periodic pension cost.

OTHER POSTRETIREMENT BENEFIT PLANS

Postretirement benefit plans provide retirees benefits other than cash, usually in the form of medical, dental, or life insurance. Accounting for the two forms of benefits are very similar but are defined under different Statements of Financial Accounting Standards. One of the barriers to learning about pension and other postretirement benefits is the similarity in the abbreviations used, which sometimes all tend to dissolve into an alphabet soup of pension accounting. As much as possible, I point out the parallels between pension benefit and other postretirement benefit accounting to try to avoid the common areas of confusion. An important regulatory difference between pension benefits and other postretirement benefit plans is that ERISA places specific requirements on the administration and funding of pension plans but does not apply to other postretirement benefit plans. Accordingly, the Pension Benefit Guarantee Corporation does not guarantee other postretirement plans as it does pension benefit plans.

Accumulated Postretirement Benefit Obligation

The accumulated postretirement benefit obligation (APBO) in a postretirement benefit plan is the parallel to the ABO in a pension benefit plan. One significant difference is that in a pension benefit plan, employees generally continue to earn additional entitlements for each year that they work, causing their ABO to grow every year until retirement. Under many postretirement benefit plans, employees earn additional entitlements for each year that they work up until the *full eligibility date*, which, for example, might be age 55. After the full eligibility date, an employee does not earn any additional level of postretirement benefit by rendering additional service.

Expected Postretirement Benefit Obligation

The expected postretirement benefit obligation (EPBO) in a postretirement benefit plan is the parallel to the PBO in a pension benefit plan. *Statement of Financial Accounting Standards No. 106, Employers' Accounting for Postretirement Benefits Other Than Pensions* (FAS106), is the authority for accounting for postretirement benefits. It defines the EPBO as "The actuarial present value as of a particular date of the benefits expected to be paid to or for an employee, the employee's beneficiaries, and any covered dependents pursuant to the terms of the postretirement benefit plan."[6] Because the types of benefits typically provided by postretirement benefit plans include items such as heath and life insurances, FAS106 includes beneficiaries and dependents as potential recipients of benefits.

NET PERIODIC POSTRETIREMENT BENEFIT COST

Net periodic postretirement cost measured under FAS106 is the postretirement benefit parallel to net periodic pension cost measured under FAS87 for pension benefits. The six components of net periodic postretirement cost are the same as those for net periodic pension cost. We continue to apply the common simplification of using the expected return on plan assets rather then using the actual return and adjusting it for the difference between the expected and actual returns. FAS106 lists six components of net periodic postretirement cost as:

1. Service cost
2. Interest cost
3. Expected return on plan assets
4. Amortization of unrecognized prior service cost

5. Gain or loss
6. Amortization of the unrecognized net obligation or asset

Postretirement Benefit Service Cost

The most commonly encountered difference between the postretirement benefit service cost and the parallel pension benefit component of pension service cost is the attribution method used for the EPBO. Unlike the generally regular attribution used for pension benefit plans (such as 1 percent for each year of service rendered), postretirement benefit plans often attribute a much higher share of the EPBO to the employee's early years of service. Consequently, the service cost associated with these types of plans is correspondingly higher early in an employee's career.

Postretirement Interest Cost

Postretirement interest cost parallels pension interest cost. Just as with pension interest cost, postretirement pension cost differs from other interest costs in that it is always a component of net postretirement pension cost and never part of gross interest expense. Also, due to the compounding effect of the discounting, postretirement interest cost for any stream of future cash flows increases from period to period.

Expected Return on Plan Assets

ERISA requires certain minimum funding levels for pension plans, but these requirements do not apply to other postretirement benefits plans. Many employers still provide no or only token funding for postretirement plans. As the rise in health care costs continues to outpace normal economic growth rates, the issue of unfunded postretirement plans becomes increasingly important for employers, employees, and analysts.

COMPANIES MAY TRY TO LIMIT THEIR POSTRETIREMENT BENEFIT PLAN LIABILITY

Recently lobbyists on behalf of some large employers have tried to influence legislation to exclude postretirement plans from age discrimination statutes. If this legislation is eventually enacted, it would be an important first step to limiting postretirement benefits for older retirees. If you follow companies with material postretirement benefit exposure, then this is an item that you might want to begin tracking because it has the potential to eliminate significant future liabilities for many large companies.

Prior Service Cost

The prior service cost for net periodic postretirement benefit cost parallels that of net periodic pension benefit cost. One subtle difference is the selection of the amortization period of the prior service costs, which is often a much shorter period for postretirement benefit plans.

Amortization of Unrecognized Gain or Loss

FAS106 applies the same 10-percent criterion for determining if Employer Company must recognize and amortize unrecognized gains or losses. It is important to note that although the criterion and methodology are the same, the accounting for the postretirement benefits and pension benefits are separate, and the gains and losses are never netted together. It is entirely likely that Employer Company may have to recognize and amortize an unrecognized gain for pension accounting and not have to recognize any gain or loss when accounting for its postretirement benefits.

Amortization of the Unrecognized Net Obligation or Asset

Just as with pension benefits under FAS87, unrecognized transition obligations or unrecognized transition assets arose when FAS106 became effective and employers began accounting for postretirement benefits under that financial accounting standard. The unrecognized transition obligations or assets are accounted for similar to prior service costs but are generally amortized over longer periods. The unrecognized portion of the unfunded *APBO* at the plan's inception is either recognized immediately or, if Employer Company elects deferred recognition, amortized using the straight-line method over either the remaining service life of the employees or an elective 20-year period.

EFFECTS OF BUSINESS COMBINATIONS

When a pension sponsoring company, such as Target Company, is acquired in a business combination, Acquiror Company recognizes the assets and liabilities of Target Company at fair value, both for calculating transaction goodwill and for consolidating the two entities. In situations where Target Company sponsors a defined benefit pension plan, Acquiror Company must recognize a liability (or asset) for the unfunded (or overfunded) portion of the *projected benefit obligation* for defined benefit pension plans and/or the *accumulated postretirement benefit obligation* for defined benefit postretirement benefit plans existing on the acquisition date. Note that this differs from the minimum liability recognized for the unfunded portion of the *accumulated benefit obligation* for pension benefit plans. Consequently, all of the unrecognized items (unrecognized prior service cost, unrecognized gain or loss, and unrecognized net obligation) are eliminated through recognition. When analyzing the accretion or dilution to earnings resulting from a business combination, it is important to examine Target Company's net periodic pension expense. If the expense is inflated through the amortization of unrecognized items, then recognition of those items on the acquisition date reduces Target Company's expenses going forward and is accretive to the transaction.

TABLE 6-1

Comparison of Pension Benefit and Postretirement Benefit Elements

Pension Benefits – FAS87 §264	Postretirement Benefits – FAS106 §518	Comparison
ABO	**APBO**	
Accumulated Benefit Obligation	**Accumulated Postretirement Benefit Obligation**	Two significant differences exist between the ABO and the APBO: The first is that full eligibility for postretirement benefits is often earned over a short period of time (as little as five years) and at the completion of that period the employee's entitlement no longer increases. The second is that, because employees have a legal claim (under ERISA) to pension benefits, Employer's must recognize a minimum liability for any *unfunded* portion of the ABO but there is no requirement to recognize a minimum liability for any unfunded portion of the APBO.
"The actuarial present value of benefits (whether vested or nonvested) attributed by the pension benefit formula to employee service rendered before a specified date and based on employee service and compensation (if applicable) before that date. The accumulated benefit obligation differs from the projected benefit obligation in that it includes no assumption about future compensation levels."	"The actuarial present value of benefits attributed to employee service rendered to a particular date. Prior to an employee's full eligibility date, the accumulated postretirement benefit obligation as of a particular for an employee is the portion of the expected postretirement benefit obligation attributed to that employee's service rendered to that date; on and after the full eligibility date the accumulated and expected postretirement benefit obligations for an employee are the same."	
PBO	**EPBO**	
Projected Benefit Obligation	**Expected Postretirement Benefit Obligation**	Two significant differences exist between the PBO and the EPBO: The first is that full eligibility for postretirement benefits is often earned over a short period of time (as little as five years) and at the completion of that period the employee's entitlement no longer increases. Consequently after the full eligibility date there is no additional service cost for the postretirement benefit, only interest cost. The second is that, because of the nature of postretirement benefits, the definition explicitly includes the employee's beneficiaries and dependents as stakeholders in the benefits.
"The actuarial present value as of a date of all benefits attributed by the pension benefit formula to employee service rendered prior to that date. The projected benefit obligation is measured using assumptions as to future compensation levels if the pension benefit formula is based on those future compensation levels (pay-related, final-pay, final-average-pay or career-average-pay plans)."	"The actuarial present value as of a particular date of the benefits expected to be paid to or for an employee, the employee's beneficiaries, and any covered dependents pursuant to the terms of the postretirement benefit plan."	
Unfunded accumulated benefit obligation	**Unfunded accumulated postretirement benefit obligation**	A significant difference because ERISA gives employees legal rights to their pension benefits but not to other postretirement benefits. Consequently employers must recognize a minimum liability on their balance sheet for the unfunded accumulated benefit obligation but not for the unfunded accumulated postretirement benefit obligation.
"The excess of the accumulated benefit obligation over [the fair value of] plan assets."	"The accumulated postretirement benefit obligation in excess of the fair value of plan assets."	

117

CHAPTER SUMMARY

There are many parallels between the accounting for pension benefit plans and other postretirement benefit plans and many symmetries in the terminology used when discussing the two types of major benefit plans. Some of the differences arise because ERISA gives employees legal rights to pension benefits but not to other postretirement benefits. Once employees are *vested* in their pension benefits, Employer Company has a liability for, at a minimum, the employee's vested benefits. Table 6-1 compares some of the similar items used when accounting for pension benefit and other postretirement benefit plans.

Two of the more controversial related issues in accounting for both pension benefit and other postretirement benefits are those of unrecognized liabilities and the "smoothing" of net periodic pension and postretirement cost. It is difficult to develop a view of the "right" way to report the effect of plans on Employer Company's financial return. At one extreme, the "smoothing" approach could be eliminated, which reduces the unrecognized items but potentially produces tremendous "noise" in operating earnings, masking Employer Company's true operating results. At the other end, Employer Company reports operating results and a financial position that delays the recognition of the true cost of the pension and postretirement plans and pushes material liabilities into the footnotes to the financial statement. In the next chapter we learn the information that Employer Company is required to disclose, either on the face of the financial statements or in footnotes.

CHAPTER 7

Deciphering the Pension Footnote

INTRODUCTION

The previous chapter presents an overview of pension accounting basics for single-employer defined benefit plans providing pension and other postretirement benefits. Because these are the most frequently encountered, employers are required to disclose specific information concerning their pension and postretirement plans in their financial statements. Originally the disclosure requirements for each of the types of benefit plans were found in their respective Statements of Financial Accounting Standards. In 1998 the Financial Accounting Standards Board (FASB), considering the comments of financial statement users, issued new disclosure requirements in *Statement of Financial Accounting Standards No. 132, Employers' Disclosures about Pensions and Other Postretirement Benefits* (FAS132). The new standard improved the overall disclosure levels, but analysts still find some areas of disclosure about pension and other postretirement benefits to be obtuse and incomplete.

This chapter reviews the required disclosures for pension benefit plans and continues with examples from FAS132 showing example disclosures. As in the previous chapter, the discussion on pension benefits is followed with a parallel discussion on differences between the accounting for pension benefit and other postretirement benefit plans. Since FAS132 requires additional disclosures for other postretirement benefit plans beyond those required for pension benefit plans (primarily in the areas of estimates for future health care costs), those additional disclosures are introduced in the postretirement benefits section. This chapter's objective is becoming familiar with the disclosure requirements and knowing what information about pension and postretirement plans is available in the financial statements.

This chapter follows the convention established in *Statement of Financial Accounting Standards No. 87, Employers' Accounting for Pensions* (FAS87) and *Statement of Financial Accounting Standards No. 106, Employers' Accounting for Postretirement Benefits Other Than Pensions* (FAS106) of referring to the periodic components of pension accounting as costs instead of expenses. While this is consistent with those standards and also with FAS132, it is probably more common outside of strict financial accounting definitions to refer to these items as pension expenses. When discussing items that are common to both pension and other postretirement plans such as net periodic pension benefit cost and net periodic postretirement benefit cost, this chapter simplifies the terminology to just *net periodic benefit cost,* implying that the item is treated the same for either pension or other postretirement benefit plans.

PENSION BENEFIT DISCLOSURE REQUIREMENTS

Many of the disclosure requirements for pension benefit plans are also required for other postretirement benefit plans. In fact, FAS132 allows some of the information to be presented in parallel within the same footnote to the financial statements. That refinement is ignored for the present, allowing a more focused approach to the disclosures. The chapter summary contains examples of parallel disclosures from FAS132.

BENEFIT OBLIGATION RECONCILIATION

Employers reporting in conformance with FAS132 reconcile the beginning and ending balances of their benefit obligations in the pension footnote to the financial statements. The reconciliation must present at least the current and previous year and account for all of the components causing changes in the benefit obligation. Beginning with the prior year's ending balance, the reconciliation includes the components affecting the benefit obligation, which are:

- Service and interest costs
- Actuarial gains and losses and plan amendments
- Contributions by and benefit payments to participants
- Business combinations and divestitures
- Foreign currency rate changes
- Settlements and curtailments

As an aside, the reconciliation in the financial statement's pension footnote traditionally presents the column for the most recent year to the left of the column(s) for the preceding year(s). Because many but not all companies follow this convention I have seen more than one analyst that needed to go back and repeat or correct their work because they failed to check the dates at the top of the columns. Companies also report different parts of the same year's financial statements differently depending on whether it is the front of the statement or a footnote disclosure. The obvious and simple point here is that this is a convention and not a rule so it is always necessary to check the dates at the tops of the columns. This is a particularly good habit for analysts to develop because of the tendency to think in "forecast space," beginning at the left of a spreadsheet and forecasting out to the right. Because I believe it is more natural for this audience (and if the truth be known for me as well), I place the later years to the right as they are normally forecast and not to the left of the preceding years as with the accounting convention.

Large employers, particularly those having grown through acquisition, frequently have multiple pension benefit or postretirement benefit plans. Their footnote disclosures aggregate the components of all of their defined benefit pension benefit plans into one disclosure and similarly, aggregate the components of all of their defined benefit postretirement benefit plans into another. However, only "like" plans may be aggregated, so the balances for defined benefit and defined contribution plans must be disclosed separately.

Changes in the Benefit Obligation from Service Cost

The last chapter explained that pension plans use a pension or postretirement benefit formula to determine the participant's entitlements under the plan. A typical benefit formula increases the employee's postretirement entitlement by a certain amount for each year of service rendered to Employer Company. The particular formula that Employer Company uses depends on the company's objectives and the employee behaviors they are attempting to influence or encourage.

As an example, a "plain vanilla" pension benefit plan formula might credit employees with 1 percent of the average of their highest one-year salary or the average of their highest three year salaries ("high three") for each year of service. Often the pension benefit formula contains a bias favoring employees with long tenures either because Employer Company wishes to encourage employees to stay with the firm or sometimes because the architects of the plan themselves have long tenures and shift benefits from new employees to themselves. An example of a plan formula favoring long-tenure employees is the following. Employees earn 1-⅔ percent of their "high three" average for each year of service, which is retroactively increased to 2 percent for each year of service, for employees staying with Employer Company for more than 20 years, up to a maximum of 30 years of service (60-percent entitlement). Employer Company's apparent objective is providing employees with an economic incentive for remaining with the firm and rewarding employees that have "passed the test of time." Sometimes companies use the promise of higher postretirement benefits as a mechanism to reduce compensation expense in current periods by granting lower pay raises to employees approaching the transition mark (20 years of employment in our example).

As we discussed in the previous chapter, the service cost component of net periodic benefit cost is sensitive to the discount rate. Lower discount rates result in higher service costs but the trade-off is that lower discount rates also result in lower periodic interest costs; higher discount rates result in lower service costs and higher periodic interest costs. Figure 7-1 shows Employer Company's pension footnote to the financial statements reconciling the beginning-of-the-year benefit obligation balance increased by the service cost component with the end-of-the-year benefit obligation balance. This service cost is also a component of the net periodic benefit cost.

Changes in the Benefit Obligation from Interest Cost

The interest cost component of the change in the benefit obligation represents the time value of the benefit obligation "aging" for one year. It should approximately equal the beginning benefit obligation multiplied by the discount rate, allowing for other changes to the benefit obligation from settlements and payments to participants. Lower discount rates result in lower interest costs. Figure 7-2 continues from Figure 7-1 by adding Employer Company's additional change to the benefit obligation from the interest cost. This interest cost is also a component of the net periodic benefit cost.

FIGURE 7·1

Changes in Employer Company's Benefit Obligation from Service Cost [1]

Change in benefit obligation	20X0	20X1
Benefit obligation at 1-January	$1,200	$1,272
Add: service cost	72	76
Benefit obligation at 31-December	$1,272	$1,348

FIGURE 7·2

Changes in Employer Company's Benefit Obligation from Interest Cost

Change in benefit obligation	20X0	20X1
Benefit obligation at 1-January	$1,200	$1,380
Add: service cost	72	76
Add: interest cost	108	114
Benefit obligation at 31-December	$1,380	$1,570

[1] Financial Accounting Standards Board, *Statement of Financial Accounting Standards No. 132, Employers' Disclosures about Pensions and Other Postretirement Benefits*, Financial Accounting Standards Board, Norwalk, CT, February 1998, paragraph 61.

Changes in the Benefit Obligation from Actuarial Gains and Losses and Plan Amendments

Actuarial gains or losses occur as the result of changes to actuarial assumptions such as: mortality rates of retirees; employee longevities and average retirement ages; the plan discount rate; and employee compensation average growth rate. Actuarial gains (losses) increase (decrease) the benefit obligation and are recognized as a component of either net periodic pension cost or postretirement benefit cost.

Plan amendments are generally modifications to a plan that grant employees some form of retroactive benefits. Prior service costs are one type of plan amendment that increase the benefit obligation as they are amortized as a component of net periodic benefit cost. Continuing the footnote disclosure example, Figure 7-3 adds the actuarial gains and losses and plan amendments components of Employer Company's benefit obligation.

Changes in the Benefit Obligation from Payments to or from the Plan's Participants

The benefit obligation represents the actuarial present value of the benefits attributed to the employee's service. In our previous examples, we used the convenient simplification of settling individual employee benefit obligations with a single annuity at their retirement date. In reality many plans make payments to retirees as part of administering the plan. These payments reduce the benefit obligation because they satisfy it with a cash payment.

Some pension and postretirement benefit plans require the employees to partially fund the plan through contributions. These contributions increase the benefit obligation because the employees make the contributions for their own benefit. Figure 7-4 reduces the benefit obligation as a result of payments made *to* plan participants and would have increased the obligation had the employees contributed in either year.

FIGURE 7-3

Changes in Employer Company's Benefit Obligation from Actuarial Gains and Plan Amendments

Change in benefit obligation	20X0	20X1
Benefit obligation at 1-January	$1,200	$1,380
Add: service cost	72	76
Add: interest cost	108	114
Add: amendments	-	100
Less: actuarial gain	-	(25)
Benefit obligation at 31-December	$1,380	$1,645

FIGURE 7·4

Changes in Employer Company's Benefit Obligation from Payments to Plan Participants

Change in benefit obligation	20X0	20X1
Benefit obligation at 1-January	$1,200	$1,266
Add: service cost	72	76
Add: interest cost	108	114
Add: amendments	-	100
Less: actuarial gain	-	(25)
Add: participants' contributions	-	20
Less: benefits paid	(114)	(125)
Benefit obligation at 31-December	$1,266	$1,426

Acquisitions and Other Changes to the Benefit Obligation

Other less frequently encountered components of the benefit obligation include increases for any additional benefit obligation acquired by Employer Company in a business combination and similarly, decreases for the amount of benefit obligation assigned to a segment or subsidiary divested in a sale or exchange. The effects of acquisitions and divestitures are included in the reconciliation in Figure 7-5.

If Employer Company has foreign operations or subsidiaries whose functional currency is not the same as Employer Company's reporting currency (U.S. dollars in our example), then the effect of changes in the foreign currency exchange rate is included for purposes of reconciling the opening and closing balances of the benefit obligation.

Statement of Financial Accounting Standards No. 88, Employers' Accounting for Settlements and Curtailments of Defined Benefit Pension Plans and for Termination Benefits (FAS88) prescribes the recognition and accounting for plan settlements and curtailments. In regard to defined benefit pension plans, settlements occur when Employer Company is irrevocably relieved of its obligation to provide benefits to a plan participant. This is commonly accomplished by either making a cash payment for the benefit or by purchasing a third-party instrument such as an annuity to settle the obligation. Because a settlement reduces Employer Company's liability, it is a reduction to the benefit obligation.

Curtailments are actions reducing or terminating the number of years of creditable service a present employee is expected to earn, usually through actions such as plant closures, terminations, or discontinuing operations. The other method for curtailing benefits is modifying or suspending the plan to reduce or eliminate employees' potential for earning future benefits. Example 7-1 describes the effects of a pension plan curtailment. Curtailments reduce or eliminate the ability of employees to earn future benefits and consequently reduce the benefit obligation.

FIGURE 7·5

Changes in Employer Company's Benefit Obligation from Acquisitions

Change in benefit obligation	20X0	20X1
Benefit obligation at 1-January	$1,200	$1,266
Add: service cost	72	76
Add: interest cost	108	114
Add: amendments	-	100
Less: actuarial gain	-	(25)
Add: participants' contributions	-	20
Less: benefits paid	(114)	(125)
Add: acquisitions and divestitures	-	900
Benefit obligation at 31-December	$1,266	$2,326

EXAMPLE 7-1. Pension Plan Curtailment

For example, you are a 40-year-old worker employed by Employer Company. Your pension plan benefit formula credits you with 1 percent of your "high three" (average of your three highest salary years) salary for each year of rendered creditable service. You expect to earn an additional 25-percent entitlement for the 25 years of future service rendered between now and your retirement at age 65. Employer Company enters Chapter 11 and the bankruptcy court orders, as part of the Plan of Reorganization, that the current defined benefit pension plan terminate in one year and be replaced by a defined contribution benefit plan. Because this action eliminates accrual of defined benefits for a significant number of employees, it is a pension plan curtailment. Your PBO originally included the actuarial present value of the benefits you expected to earn during your remaining 25 years of service. The action of the bankruptcy court in terminating the plan in one year reduces the PBO by the present value of the expected benefits for the other 24 years.

THE BENEFIT OBLIGATION RECONCILIATION MAY BE CHANGING

On September 12, 2003 FASB released an exposure draft entitled *Proposed Statement of Financial Accounting Standards, Employer's Disclosures about Pensions and Other Post Retirement Benefits,* as a proposed replacement to FAS132. The statement requests comment on its proposal eliminating the requirement for firms to reconcile their opening and closing benefit obligation balances. Instead the proposed statement requires only the ending balance of the benefit obligation to be presented along with some, but not all, of the components of the reconciliation, such as benefit payments and participant contributions. When it is finally adopted, the proposed Statement of Financial Accounting Standards supercedes the existing FAS132 and you should review the proposal's final form to determine the changes that FASB actually enacted.

The exposure draft also asks for comment on a proposal requiring companies to disclose the defined benefit plan accumulated benefit obligation (ABO). FASB feels that disclosure of the ABO allows financial statement users to monitor the funded status of plans because ABO is the best currently available measure of the cost of settling the pension obligations in the present. In a distress, it is the amount that Employer Company actually owes employees for the benefits they have already earned (liquidation cost).

PLAN FAIR VALUE RECONCILIATION

FAS132 also requires employers to show the beginning and ending balances of the fair value of plan assets. Like the reconciliation of the benefit obligation the reconciliation of the fair value of plan assets usually covers the current and previous year and shows separately the items causing the balance to change. Beginning with the prior year's ending balance it includes changes resulting from:

- Actual return on plan assets
- Employer and plan participant contributions
- Benefit payments to participants
- Business combinations and divestitures
- Foreign currency rate changes
- Settlements and curtailments

Actual Return on Plan Assets

Employer Company presents the actual return on the plan assets as an increase or decrease, depending on the plan's performance. The plan's assets are separate from Employer Company's assets and are not recognized on the face of Employer Company's balance sheet. Similarly, the gain or loss on the plan assets does not appear directly on Employer Company's income statement. Figure 7-6 begins the reconciliation of the plan's beginning and ending balances by showing the results of the plan's investments as the actual return on plan assets.

Employer and Plan Participant Contributions

Employer Company's contributions to the plan on the behalf of the participants are shown as a separate component of the change in plan assets for years that Employer Company contributes. Some plans either require or allow employees to contribute (particularly true for mandatory contributions to postretirement health care plans), and those contributions are also shown separately from Employer Company's contributions. Separation of the employee and employer contributions aids us later when we attempt to forecast cash flows associated with the benefit plans. Note in Figure 7-7 that the participant's contributions increase both the plan

FIGURE 7·6

Changes from the Actual Return on Plan Assets

Change in benefit obligation	20X0	20X1
Benefit obligation at 1-January	$1,200	$1,266
Add: service cost	72	76
Add: interest cost	108	114
Add: amendments	-	100
Less: actuarial gain	-	(25)
Add: participants' contributions	-	20
Less: benefits paid	(114)	(125)
Add: acquisitions and divestitures	-	900
Benefit obligation at 31-December	$1,266	$2,326
Change in plan assets	**20X0**	**20X1**
Plan assets (fair value) at 1-January	$880	$1,068
Add: actual return on plan assets	188	9
Plan assets (fair value) at 31-December	$1,068	$1,077

asset ending balance and the benefit obligation ending balance because the participants are contributing for their own benefit.

Benefit Payments to Plan Participants

Benefit payments to the participants are made by the plan's administrator from the plan's assets. Consequently payments of benefits result in a dollar-for-dollar reduction to both the benefit obligation and to the plan assets. Note in Figure 7-8 that the benefit payments to the plan participants decrease both the plan assets and the benefit obligation equally.

Acquisitions, Divestitures, and Other Settlements

Just as with the benefit obligation balance, the plan asset balance is increased by the fair value of plan assets acquired in a business combination and reduced for any assets that "go with the employees" of divested segments or subsidiaries.

Any effect of changes in the foreign currency exchange rate is reflected when reconciling the opening and closing balances of the plan assets, but only for Employer Company's foreign subsidiaries or operations that use a functional currency different than Employer Company's reporting currency (usually U.S. dollars).

FIGURE 7·7

Changes from Employer and Plan Participant Contributions

Change in benefit obligation	20X0	20X1
Benefit obligation at 1-January	$1,200	$1,266
Add: service cost	72	76
Add: interest cost	108	114
Add: amendments	-	100
Less: actuarial gain	-	(25)
Add: participants' contributions	-	20
Less: benefits paid	(114)	(125)
Add: acquisitions and divestitures	-	900
Benefit obligation at 31-December	$1,266	$2,326

Change in plan assets	20X0	20X1
Plan assets (fair value) at 1-January	$880	$1,182
Add: actual return on plan assets	188	9
Add: employer contributions	114	75
Add: plan participant contributions	-	20
Plan assets (fair value) at 31-December	$1,182	$1,286

Settlements reduce plan assets because they are payments either as cash or as purchased annuities to settle liabilities to plan participants. Remember that settlements also reduce the benefit obligation balance, and because the fair value of the benefit obligation reduction should very closely equal the cost of the settlement, then the decrease in plan assets and the decrease in benefit obligation should also be equal.

THE PLAN ASSET RECONCILIATION MAY ALSO BE CHANGING

FASB's September 12, 2003 exposure draft also requests comment on its proposal to eliminate the requirement for firms to reconcile their opening and closing plan asset balances. As with the benefit obligation, the proposed standard only requires disclosure of the ending balance of the plan's assets. The proposed standard continues the requirement for companies to disclose only:

- Actual return on plan assets
- Employer and plan participant contributions
- Benefit payments to participants

FIGURE 7·8

Changes from Benefit Payments to Plan Participants

Change in benefit obligation	20X0	20X1
Benefit obligation at 1-January	$1,200	$1,266
Add: service cost	72	76
Add: interest cost	108	114
Add: amendments	-	100
Less: actuarial gain	-	(25)
Add: participants' contributions	-	20
Less: benefits paid	(114)	(125)
Add: acquisitions and divestitures	-	900
Benefit obligation at 31-December	$1,266	$2,326
Change in plan assets	**20X0**	**20X1**
Plan assets (fair value) at 1-January	$880	$1,068
Add: actual return on plan assets	188	9
Add: employer contributions	114	75
Add: plan participant contributions	-	20
Less: benefits paid	(114)	(125)
Plan assets (fair value) at 31-December	$1,068	$1,047

As we discuss in the next chapter, part of our interest in pension and postretirement plan disclosures is obtaining information that we can use to reliably forecast Employer Company's future cash flows relating to the plans. FASB recognizes the changing needs of financial statement users, so the exposure draft is also requesting comments on its proposed new requirement to have employers provide cash flow information in the form of a schedule of their expected future contributions to the plan.

EMPLOYER SECURITIES INCLUDED IN PLAN ASSETS

An important disclosure, particularly for employers facing distress, is the amount and types of plan securities issued by the Employer Company and/or its subsidiaries. Firms like to fund pension liabilities with their own securities or the securities of their subsidiaries because it may sometimes be done with less negative economic impact than making a primary offering to raise an equivalent amount of cash. For the employer, this alleviates the cash flow demands of funding the plan but, in some situations, may set the stage for a "double whammy" if Employer Company's financial position degrades significantly and the value of its securities fall. When that occurs, the fair value of any of Employer Company's or its subsidiaries' securities fall as well, reducing the plan's funding level. This has the potential of creating a funding crisis for Employer Company because the plan may require additional funding, which Employer Company may need to supply by issuing additional securities at an inopportune time because their price is depressed.

NET PERIODIC BENEFIT COST DISCLOSURE

The previous chapter discusses the individual components of net periodic pension cost and net periodic postretirement benefit cost in detail. From a disclosure perspective, FAS132 requires employers to disclose all of the components of their net periodic pension cost and their net periodic postretirement benefit cost. Figure 7-9 shows a typical disclosure indicating how the service cost and interest cost components of net periodic benefit cost directly increase the benefit obligation.

FUNDED STATUS AND UNRECOGNIZED ITEMS

The accounting standard also requires a footnote disclosure of the funded status of the plans. Funded status refers to the net difference between the plan assets and the benefit obligation. If the benefit obligation (PBO or APBO) exceeds the fair value of plan assets, the plan is negatively funded or underfunded. Conversely, if the fair value of plan assets exceeds the benefit obligation, then the plan is positively funded or overfunded. The funded status of the plan is combined with the unrecognized items such as unrecognized service cost; unrecognized gain or loss; and any unamortized, unrecognized net (transition) obligation or asset; net pension or postretirement benefit prepaid assets or accrued liabilities; and any intangible assets recognized for minimum liabilities. Figure 7-10 shows the disclosure of the funded status of the plan.

RATE DISCLOSURES

FAS132 requires Employer Company to disclose in the footnotes the weighted-average discount rate used for discounting future obligations to present values, weighted-average rate of compensation (pay) increases for pay-based plans, and the expected long-term rate of return on plan assets used for determining net periodic pension benefit cost and net periodic postretirement benefit cost. The current standard does not specify a particular format for the disclosure, and consequently it can be found displayed as tabular data or disclosed within a paragraph. Disclosure of the rates is important to anyone evaluating the status of the pension plans because it gives an indication of how Employer Company approaches its pension liability. Above-average expected long-term rates of return on plan assets or below-average rates of expected compensation increases should trigger analysts'

FIGURE 7·9

Net Periodic Benefit Cost Disclosure

Change in benefit obligation	20X0	20X1
Benefit obligation at 1-January	$1,200	$1,266
Add: service cost	72	76
Add: interest cost	108	114
Add: amendments	-	100
Less: actuarial gain	-	(25)
Add: participants' contributions	-	20
Less: benefits paid	(114)	(125)
Add: acquisitions and divestitures	-	900
Benefit obligation at 31-December	$1,266	$2,326

Change in plan assets	20X0	20X1
Plan assets (fair value) at 1-January	$880	$1,068
Add: actual return on plan assets	188	9
Add: employer contributions	114	75
Add: plan participant contributions	-	20
Less: benefits paid	(114)	(125)
Add: acquisitions and divestitures	-	1,000
Plan assets (fair value) at 31-December	$1,068	$2,047

Net periodic benefit cost components		
Service cost	$72	$76
Interest cost	108	114
Expected return on plan assets	(88)	(107)
Amortization of prior service cost	20	20
Amortization of unrecognized gain or loss	2	8
Net periodic benefit cost	$114	$111

professional skepticism, causing them to look more closely at how Employer Company is meeting and reporting its benefit plan obligations. Similarly, changes in the rates should be consistent with changes made by other employers and with the general view of the economy. If not, then Employer Company's motives should be questioned to see if there is a potential that they are using the benefit plans to manage their reported earnings.

FIGURE 7·10

Funded Status Disclosure

Change in benefit obligation	20X0	20X1
Benefit obligation at 1-January	$1,200	$1,266
Add: service cost	72	76
Add: interest cost	108	114
Add: amendments	-	100
Less: actuarial gain	-	(25)
Add: participants' contributions	-	20
Less: benefits paid	(114)	(125)
Add: acquisitions and divestitures	-	900
Benefit obligation at 31-December	$1,266	$2,326
Change in plan assets	**20X0**	**20X1**
Plan assets (fair value) at 1-January	$880	$1,068
Add: actual return on plan assets	188	9
Add: employer contributions	114	75
Add: plan participant contributions	-	20
Less: benefits paid	(114)	(125)
Add: acquisitions and divestitures	-	1,000
Plan assets (fair value) at 31-December	$1,068	$2,047
Funded status	($198)	($279)
Add: unrecognized net actuarial loss	38	83
Add: unrecognized prior service cost	160	260
Prepaid (accrued) benefit cost	$0	$64

The proposed standard replacing FAS132 adds a degree of consistency in the disclosure of the key rate assumptions by requiring them to be presented within the pension footnote specifically in a tabular format.

HEALTH CARE DISCLOSURES

All of the disclosures we have discussed to this point apply equally to either pension benefit or postretirement benefit plans. In fact, a common manner of presentation in the pension footnote to the financial statements is using a parallel presentation with the pension benefit and postretirement benefit information presented side-by-side in the pension footnote. An example of that disclosure method taken from FAS132 is presented in the chapter summary.

FAS132 specifies several disclosures relating only to postretirement health care benefit plans. One is the health care cost trend rate that Employer Company assumes for the upcoming year for benefits being paid out by the plan. This is coupled with a discussion of Employer Company's general view of assumed health care trend rates and the long-term rate assumed to ultimately occur.

Continuing to focus on health care costs, FAS132 also requires Employer Company to discuss the sensitivities of the service and interest cost components of net periodic postretirement health care benefit costs and the accumulated postretirement health care benefit obligation to a 1-percent increase and a 1-percent decrease in the assumed health care cost trend rates.

CHAPTER SUMMARY

The most informative disclosures for pension benefit and postretirement benefit plans are generally found in the financial statements pension footnote. Nearly all of the items discussed in this chapter appear in the footnote. Although FAS132 does not prescribe a specific disclosure format for much of the information, many companies choose to follow the presentation examples found in that accounting standard. This is true for both pension benefit and postretirement benefit plans, which are often shown side by side in the footnote. A common difference between pension and postretirement plans is the reconciliation of plan assets because many postretirement benefit plans are unfunded and consequently have no assets. Figure 7-11 is an example of the disclosure shown in FAS132; note that in this example the columns are presented according to the standard accounting convention of the latest period on the left and not on the right as in the remainder of the figures.

Considering the complexity ascribed to pension and other postretirement benefit plan accounting, the disclosures are relatively simple and many would argue not exhaustive enough to accurately determine Employer Company's pension position. In the last chapter we reviewed how pension plans worked and how employers accounted for the pension assets and liabilities. In this chapter we looked at the disclosure requirements for the pension footnote. In the next chapter we determine our objectives for analyzing the firm's pension position, the information we need to make the analysis, and how we can derive or estimate that information from the required disclosures.

FIGURE 7·11

Example Footnote Disclosure for Pension and Postretirement Benefit Plans[2]

	Pension Benefits		Other Benefits	
Change in benefit obligation	**20X2**	**20X1**	**20X2**	**20X1**
Benefit obligation at beginning of year	$1,266	$1,200	$738	$700
Service cost	76	72	36	32
Interest cost	114	108	65	63
Plan participants' contributions	-	-	20	13
Amendments	(20)	-	-	-
Actuarial gain	(25)	-	(24)	-
Benefits paid	(125)	(114)	(90)	(70)
Benefit obligation at end of year	$1,286	$1,266	$745	$738
Change in plan assets				
Fair value of plan assets at beginning of year	$1,156	$968	$206	$87
Actual return on plan assets	29	188	(3)	24
Employer contribution	139	114	171	152
Plan participants' contributions	-	-	20	13
Benefits paid	(125)	(114)	(90)	(70)
Fair value of plan assets at end of year	$1,199	$1,156	$304	$206
Funded status	($87)	($110)	($441)	($532)
Add: unrecognized net actuarial loss	83	38	59	60
Add: unrecognized prior service cost	170	225	510	540
Net amount recognized	$166	$153	$128	$68
Recognized balance sheet amounts				
Prepaid benefit cost	$255	$227	$128	$68
Accrued benefit liability	(153)	(127)	-	-
Intangible asset	50	53	-	-
Accumulated other comprehensive income	14	-	-	-
Net amount recognized	$166	$153	$128	$68

[2] Financial Accounting Standards Board, *Statement of Financial Accounting Standards No. 132, Employers' Disclosures about Pensions and Other Postretirement Benefits*, Financial Accounting Standards Board, Norwalk, CT, February 1998, paragraph 61.

CHAPTER 8

Analyzing the Firm's Pension Cash Flows

INTRODUCTION

To analyze a company's pension position, we must first decide what aspect of the benefit plan has our real interest. Generally, the three principal areas of interest are the future cash flows that Employer Company must make into the plan, the impact of the plan's overfunded or underfunded status on Employer Company's net identifiable assets if it should become the target in an acquisition or other business combination, and the effect of net periodic pension benefit cost and net periodic postretirement benefit cost on Employer Company's future reported earnings. There is a large body of literature addressing the last point, so this chapter focuses only on the first two items: estimating Employer Company's short-term cash flows for credit analysis and estimating the impact of Employer Company's plan funded status as an acquisition or takeover target.

Because of the complexities of pension and other postretirement plans, it is difficult to forecast items with great certainty. Disclosures in the pension footnote are insufficiently detailed to project forward or to even provide a good basis for projections. The analyst's task becomes making the best possible estimates with the available information and remaining flexible and diligent to adjust those estimates as more timely information becomes available.

On September 12, 2003 the Financial Accounting Standards Board (FASB) released an exposure draft entitled *Proposed Statement of Financial Accounting Standards, Employer's Disclosures about Pensions and Other Post Retirement Benefits,* as a proposed replacement to FAS132. Some of the items that the exposure draft addresses include requirements for companies to disclose estimates of Employer Company's expected plan contributions during the next year, discriminating between mandatory and discretionary contributions, increased disclosure of cash flow items in interim financial statements, disclosure of the distribution of plan assets in major assets categories, and disclosure of the accumulated benefit oblig-ation (ABO). The last chapter discussed some of the items that the proposed stan-dard no longer requires employers to report. Because of the level of dissatisfaction with the current state of pension and postretirement benefit reporting and the sig-nificant impact these plans can have on companies, it seems likely that FASB will eventually impose reporting standards allowing analysts better access to the com-pany's information.

For the present this chapter discusses how to use the information currently reported to estimate the three interests previously identified:

- Projected future cash flows from Employer Company into the plan (mandatory plan funding)
- The effect of net periodic pension benefit cost and net periodic postretire-ment benefit cost on Employer Company's future reported earning
- The impact of the plan's overfunded or underfunded status on Employer Company's net identifiable assets if the company should become the target in an acquisition or other business combination

ESTIMATING FUTURE FUNDING CASH FLOWS

Estimating future cash flows to fund pension benefit obligations and postretire-ment benefit obligations is necessary for credit analysis but, as previously mentioned, is difficult to perform with high certainty. This is one area where a lack of disclo-sure sometimes provides better information than detailed disclosure, specifically in the case of postretirement benefit plans. We look at estimating cash flows to Employer Company's postretirement benefit plans and then to their pension benefit plan.

Cash Flows for Postretirement Benefit Plans

Because many employers do not maintain funded postretirement benefit plans and there is no legally-defined minimum level of funding for them to maintain, they operate in the "pay-as-you-go" mode and fund the plan only to meet current levels of plan expenses.

This sometimes provides us with surprisingly clear information about periodic cash requirements for funding for the postretirement benefit plans. Coupling this with Employer Company's disclosed one-year forward health care cost trend rate allows us to estimate the next year's expected cash flows for the postretirement healthcare costs. In most plans the postretirement health care costs account for the major part of the postretirement costs. Although it intro-duces some inaccuracy, it is generally acceptable to assume that all postretire-ment costs grow at the estimated health care cost trend for the next forecast year.

Estimating Funding of a Postretirement Benefit Plan— Unfunded Plan

The next matter is attempting to determine the growth of the health care cost trend. This can be accomplished by trending back through several years of financial statements to determine if Employer Company's health care cost increases are accelerating or if they are remaining relatively constant. Example 8-1 describes a method for estimating Employer Company's cash funding of its postretirement benefit plan. Note that the example presents the postretirement benefit plan disclosure following the accounting convention of latest period to the left.

EXAMPLE **8-1. Estimating Funding of a Postretirement Benefit Plan—Unfunded Plan**

Figure 8-1 shows Employer Company's disclosures of the following information in its 20X2 financial statements.

For measurement purposes, a 10-percent annual rate of increase in the per capita cost of health care was assumed for 20X3. The rate is assumed to decrease gradually to 4 percent in 20X9 and remain at that level thereafter.

Because this is an unfunded plan, we start by assuming that the contributions of the participants and the employer are adequate to meet the cash funding needs for the periods disclosed. That means that in 20X1 the cash needs of the plan were equal to the participant's contributions plus the employer's contributions or $(70 - 13) = 57$. For 20X2, the cash needs were $(90 - 20) = 70$. Comparing the increases to Employer Company's estimate of 10 percent, we find the following true for 20X1 to 20X2:

Participant's cash cost increase 20X1 to 20X2:	$(20 - 13) / 13 = 53.9\%$
Employer's cash cost increase 20X1 to 20X2:	$(70 - 57) / 57 = 22.8\%$
Total plan cash cost increase 20X1 to 20X2:	$(90 - 70) / 70 = 28.6\%$

Based on these values, Employer Company's estimate of a 10-percent increase in health care costs seems to understate the plan's funding requirement. Looking back we find that the cost increases were:

	3 years ago	2 years ago	last year
Total plan cash cost increase:	41.1%	38.4%	33.1%
Employer's cash cost increase:	33.2%	29.3%	25.4%

More reasonable estimates for the increase in Employer's costs over the next three years might be: 20X3 – 20%; 20X4 – 15%, and 20X5 – 10%, making Employer Company's projected cash contributions to the plan ($90 \times 1.20 = 108 \times 1.15 = 124.2 \times 1.10 = 136.6$):

	20X3	20X4	20X5
Employer's projected cash contributions:	108.0	124.2	136.6
Assuming 100% deductibility, after-tax:	64.8	74.5	82.0

FIGURE 8·1

Change Benefit Obligation—Unfunded Plan[1]

Change in benefit obligation - unfunded plan	20X2	20X1
Benefit obligation at beginning of year	$738	$700
Service cost	36	32
Interest cost	65	63
Plan participants' contributions	20	13
Amendments	-	-
Actuarial gain	(24)	-
Benefits paid	(90)	(70)
Benefit obligation at end of year	$745	$738

Estimating Funding of a Postretirement Benefit Plan— Funded Plan

If Employer Company had instead a funded postretirement benefit plan then the new cash flow variable introduced is the return on plan assets. Although prudent fund management would be to allow the plan's returns to average over the long-term, the situation frequently encountered is that in times of strong returns many employers tend to reduce contributions allowing the return on plan funds to provide cash flows for benefit payments. Example 8-2 describes a method for estimating Employer Company's cash funding of its postretirement benefit plan. Again note that the example presents the postretirement benefit plan disclosure following the accounting convention of latest period to the left and that in this example we are able to examine the change in plan assets because this is a funded plan.

EXAMPLE **8-2.** Estimating Funding of a Postretirement Benefit Plan—Funded Plan

Employer Company discloses the following information in its 20X2 financial statements as shown in Figure 8-2.

One significant difference with a funded plan is the additional information about Employer Company's actual contributions. In both 20X1 and 20X2, Employer Company is contributing approximately two-and-one-half times the current cash needs of the plan. For 20X1 the excess is (152 – 70 +13) = 95 excess or 152 = (152 / 57) = 2.7x plan cash needs and for 20X2 the excess is (171 – 90 + 20) = 101 excess or 171 = (171 / 70) = 2.4x plan cash needs.

From purely a short-term cash flow perspective, Employer Company's contributions can be bifurcated into two different streams, a necessary funding to meet the immediate

[1] Financial Accounting Standards Board, *Statement of Financial Accounting Standards No. 132, Employers' Disclosures about Pensions and Other Postretirement Benefits*, Financial Accounting Standards Board, Norwalk, CT, February 1998, paragraph 61.

FIGURE 8·2

Change in Plan Assets—Funded Postretirement Plan

Change in plan assets - funded postretirement plan	20X2	20X1
Fair value of plan assets at beginning of year	$206	$87
Actual return on plan assets	(3)	24
Employer contribution	171	152
Plan participants' contributions	20	13
Benefits paid	(90)	(70)
Fair value of plan assets at end of year	$304	$206

funding requirements of the plan and a discretionary funding, which are contributions apparently in excess of minimum funding needs. For Employer Company the two streams are:

	20X2	20X1
Necessary plan funding:	70	57
Discretionary funding:	101	95

The next step is attempting, through a thorough reading of the pension and the financial statement footnotes to determine Employer Company's motivation for the excess contribution. Generally it is either because there is a contractual obligation or a decision based on overfunding the plan in times of good operating results, an inference being that in times of poor operating results, excess funding would decrease. If Employer Company's past practice (as evidenced in its previous financial statements) indicates a pattern of "on and off" funding, then that weighs for the excess funding to be truly discretionary, and this portion of the funding might be ignored when projecting future cash flow needs for debt capacity analysis. Alternatively, if the funding occurs even when it is disadvantageous for Employer Company to make excess contributions, this indicates a higher likelihood that the funding results from a contractual obligation and should be projected as an expected use of cash in future periods.

CASH FLOWS FOR PENSION BENEFIT PLANS

Unlike most postretirement benefit plans, pension benefit plans are funded. Employer Company's contributions to the plan are disclosed in the reconciliation showing the change in plan assets. Three different funding schemes are reasonable for Employer Company to fund its plan: contributing only enough to fund short-falls between the actual return on plan assets and the benefits paid, contributing enough to fund the cost of plan benefits, or contributing enough to maintain the plan balance equal to or greater than the accumulated benefit obligation (ABO). The first two items are relatively simple to forecast, and either can be sustainable for a three- to five-year horizon. The third, maintaining the ABO, may be difficult to forecast for companies that do not recognize a minimum liability because disclosure of the ABO is not required under current U.S. Generally Accepted Accounting Principles (GAAP).

DISCLOSURE OF ABO MAY BE REQUIRED

On September 12, 2003 FASB released an exposure draft entitled *Proposed Statement of Financial Accounting Standards, Employer's Disclosures about Pensions and Other Post Retirement Benefits*, as a proposed replacement to FAS132. The statement requests comment on a proposal requiring companies to disclose the defined benefit plan accumulated benefit obligation (ABO). FASB feels that disclosure of the ABO allows financial statement users to monitor the funded status of plans because ABO is the best currently available measure of the cost of settling the pension obligations in the present. In a distress it is the amount that Employer Company actually owes employees for the benefits they have already earned (liquidation cost).

Example 8-3 discusses estimating Employer Company's cash funding of its pension benefit plan. The example presents the pension benefit plan disclosure following the accounting convention of latest period to the left, and in this example we are able to examine the change in plan assets because this is a funded plan.

EXAMPLE 8-3. Estimating Funding of a Pension Benefit Plan

Employer Company discloses the information shown in Figure 8-3 for its 20X2 financial statements.

The item of immediate interest is benefits paid of 114 for 20X1 and 125 for 20X2. In the short run, Employer Company can maintain a somewhat healthy plan by contributing

FIGURE 8-3

Change in Plan Assets–Funded Pension Plan[2]

Change in plan assets	20X2	20X1
Fair value of plan assets at beginning of year	$1,068	$880
Actual return on plan assets	29	188
Employer contribution	75	114
Benefits paid	(125)	(114)
Fair value of plan assets at end of year	$1,047	$1,068

[2] Financial Accounting Standards Board, *Statement of Financial Accounting Standards No. 132, Employers' Disclosures about Pensions and Other Postretirement Benefits*, Financial Accounting Standards Board, Norwalk, CT, February 1998, paragraph 61.

only enough to fund any shortfall between the actual return on plan assets and the benefits paid. If Employer Company had used this funding approach in 20X1 and 20X2, then its 20X1 contribution is zero and its 20X2 is the shortfall of (126 – 29) = 96. Pro forma disclosure showing the results of Employer Company funding to only cover the shortfall is shown in Figure 8-4.

Employer could instead choose to contribute enough to fund the benefits paid, in which case the change in plan assets reflects contributions equal to the benefits cash outflow. Figure 8-5 shows the pro forma disclosure for Employer Company contributing to cover only the benefits paid.

For employers not recognizing minimum liabilities for underfunded pension benefit plans, a reasonable short-term estimate of Employer Company's cash contributions is the amount of cash necessary to fund the difference between the expected benefits paid and the return that plan assets would earn from being invested in a risk-free or near risk-free vehicle. Examine prior years' financial statements to develop trend rates for benefits paid and forecast the benefits paid forward at that rate. This is the amount that Employer Company needs to fund if there is no return on the plan assets. Assume plan assets earn a conservative return and then reduce Employer's Company forecast cash contributions by that return.

The last method is applicable for companies recognizing a minimum liability for their pension benefit plan. In this case a reasonable approximation for forecasting

FIGURE 8·4

Change in Plan Assets—Covering Shortfall

Change in plan assets - covering shortfall	20X2	20X1
Fair value of plan assets at beginning of year	$954	$880
Actual return on plan assets	29	188
Employer contribution	96	0
Benefits paid	(125)	(114)
Fair value of plan assets at end of year	$954	$954

FIGURE 8·5

Change in Plan Assets—Covering Benefits Paid

Change in plan assets - covering benefits paid	20X2	20X1
Fair value of plan assets at beginning of year	$1,068	$880
Actual return on plan assets	29	188
Employer contribution	125	114
Benefits paid	(125)	(114)
Fair value of plan assets at end of year	$1,097	$1,068

Employer Company's minimum cash contributions is to choose the larger of the amount necessary to maintain the minimum liability at current levels and continue paying benefits at their forecast levels.

EMPLOYER COMPANY'S PLAN ASSETS AND LIABILITIES IN AN ACQUISITION

One other area that is often the subject of estimation is the status of Employer Company's pension benefit and postretirement benefit plans when Employer Company is acquired in a business combination. *Statement of Financial Accounting Standards No. 141, Business Combinations* (FAS141) requires that the difference between the projected benefit obligation (PBO) and the plan assets be recognized as either an asset (if assets exceed the PBO) or a liability (if the PBO exceeds assets) on Employer Company's (Target Company's) balance sheet at the acquisition date. Example 8-6 explains how Employer Company's balance sheet is adjusted for the calculation of goodwill at the acquisition date.

FIGURE 8·6

Employer Company Plan Status at Acquisition

	Pension Benefits		Other Benefits	
Change in benefit obligation	**20X2**	**20X1**	**20X2**	**20X1**
Benefit obligation at beginning of year	$1,266	$1,200	$738	$700
Service cost	76	72	36	32
Interest cost	114	108	65	63
Plan participants' contributions	-	-	20	13
Amendments	(20)	-	-	-
Actuarial gain	(25)	-	(24)	-
Benefits paid	(125)	(114)	(90)	(70)
Benefit obligation at end of year	$1,286	$1,266	$745	$738
Change in plan assets				
Fair value of plan assets at beginning of year	$1,156	$968	$1,006	$887
Actual return on plan assets	29	188	(3)	24
Employer contribution	139	114	171	152
Plan participants' contributions	-	-	20	13
Benefits paid	(125)	(114)	(90)	(70)
Fair value of plan assets at end of year	$1,199	$1,156	$1,104	$1,006

EXAMPLE **8-6.** Recognition of Postretirement Assets and Liabilities at the Acquisition Date.

On 31-December-20X2 Acquiror Company purchases 100 percent of the outstanding stock of Employer Company in an all-cash transaction. At the transaction date, Acquiror adjusts the items on Employer Company's balance sheet to fair value prior to allocating the purchase price paid to the underlying assets and liabilities. Figure 8-6 shows Employer Company's PBO and plan assets at the transaction date.

Because the PBO of Employer Company's defined benefit pension benefit plan exceeds the fair value of the plan assets, any liability or accrued pension cost already recognized by Employer Company is written up to equal the excess of the PBO over the plan assets (1286 − 1199) = 87. Similarly, any prepaid postretirement benefit cost recognized on Employer Company's balance sheet is written up to equal the excess of the fair value of plan assets over the accumulated postretirement benefit obligation (APBO) (1104 − 745) = 359.

PLAN LIQUIDATION VALUES

Another aspect of Employer Company's pension benefit or postretirement benefit plans that is sometimes of interest is the plan's liquidation or termination values. This may come into play in distress or acquisition scenarios if the plans are to be terminated and settled at their current APBO for postretirement benefit plans or ABO for pension benefit plans. The funding status of plans can also be a source of value to Acquiror Company even if the plan is not terminated because the plan's overfunding reduces or eliminates Acquiror Company's need to make cash payments to the plan in future periods.

APBO for Postretirement Benefit Plans

The APBO for postretirement benefit plans represents the present value of benefits that employees have earned for prior service and approximates the cost of settling the plan for cash. Unlike its equivalent measure in a pension benefit plan, the ABO, the APBO for a postretirement benefit plan is disclosed directly in the pension footnote of Employer Company's financial statements as the benefit obligation.

ABO for Pension Benefit Plans

The ABO for pension benefit plans is not directly disclosed and may be calculated if Employer Company recognizes a minimum liability because the ABO exceeds the funded status of the plan. When a minimum liability is recognized for a pension benefit plan, the ABO can be calculated as:

Accrued benefit liability (from balance sheet)
<u>+ closing plan asset balance (from pension footnote)</u>
Accumulated benefit obligation

When no minimum liability is recognized, there is no direct way of estimating its balance. One method is constructing several historical years of plan asset balances. If in any of the historical years a minimum liability was recognized, calculate the ABO at that period and grow it forward to the present at the stated discount rate (not the expected return on plan assets). If it is less than the present plan asset balance, then use it as the estimate for ABO. Otherwise, if it exceeds the current plan asset balance, then use the current plan asset balance as the estimate for ABO.

If Employer Company did not recognize a minimum liability in any of the historical years, then grow the plan asset balance forward from each historical year using the discount rate (again, not the expected return on plan assets). If the smallest value of any of the projections is less than the current plan asset balance, use the smallest projected amount as the estimate of ABO. Otherwise, use the current plan asset balance as the estimate for ABO.

CHAPTER SUMMARY

There are two estimates derived from pension accounting of interest to analysts other than the economic effects impacting future earnings. One is estimating projected minimum cash flows for credit analysis and the second is estimating the funded status of pension benefit and postretirement benefit plans in an acquisition.

The methods currently available result in estimates that, while possibly the best available, have a high degree of uncertainty. A current project by FASB addresses the subject of disclosures for benefit plans and hopefully will lead to improved reporting that eliminates the need to make highly variable estimates.

CHAPTER 9

Employee Stock Options

INTRODUCTION

Accounting for stock options that are granted as employee compensation may be treated in two different ways under U.S. Generally Accepted Accounting Principles (GAAP). The approaches taken for the two treatments, the intrinsic method and the fair value method, are conceptually and mechanically similar, varying primarily in the way that the options are valued. The difference in valuation is most prominently evidenced in the effect on the firm's operating results.

Currently firms can choose either of the two reporting methods, and until recently, most chose the intrinsic method because it effectively bypassed the income statement and had no immediate effect on earnings per share. It is very likely that the Financial Accounting Standards Board (FASB) and the International Accounting Standards Board (IASB) will converge their standards in the not-too-distant future, requiring that employee stock option grants be expensed using the fair-value method of valuation. Many firms have already begun to implement this approach, while others, such as Microsoft Corporation, have elected to eliminate stock options as a component of their employee compensation plans. Because of the varied and changing approaches that firms currently use, and will use in the future, understanding accounting for employee stock options and its effect on earnings and cash flow is particularly important when trying to compare companies equitably.

THE INTRINSIC VALUATION METHOD

The first treatment, described in *APB Opinion No. 25, Accounting for Stock Issued to Employees* (APB25), is usually referred to as the intrinsic method because of the approach used to value the stock option grant. Under the intrinsic method, the value of an employee stock option is measured as the difference between the exercise price, the amount that the employee is required to pay when exercising the option, and the fair market price on the measurement date, which is usually the date that the option is granted to the employee. Most stock option grants also incorporate a vesting period over which the employee is required to perform services for the employer before being allowed to exercise the option. Conceptually, the intrinsic value of the option is compensation for the services performed during the vesting period. The intrinsic value is recognized as compensation expense over the vesting period.

EXAMPLE 9-1. Compensation Expense under the Intrinsic Method

Compensator Company uses a compensatory stock option plan to compensate certain employees. Under the plan, employees are granted 100,000 options, each having an exercise price of $40.00 on 31-Dec-20X0, when the closing price of Compensator Company's stock is $52.00. The options may be exercised to purchase Compensator Company's $5.00 par value stock, after a three-year vesting period, on or after 1-Jan-20X4. Compensator Company accounts for the employee stock options as follows:

At 31-Dec-20X0, the intrinsic value of the stock option grant is measured as:

The intrinsic value of each option times the number of options granted
($52.00 − $40.00) × 100,000 = 1,200,000

Because the employees have not performed any of the service necessary to vest the options, no financial accounting entry is required on the grant date.

At the end of 20X1, one-third of the vesting period has passed and consequently, Compensator Company recognizes one-third of the intrinsic value of the grant as compensation expense for that period.

dr:	Compensation expense (1,200,000 / 3)	400,000
	cr: Paid-in capital (stock options)	400,000

Similar entries are made to recognize the compensation expense in 20X2 and 20X3 until the entire 1,200,000 has been expensed and recorded as paid-in capital from stock options. The options are exercisable after 31-Dec-20X3. When that occurs, the employees holding the stock options will exchange them, along with cash equal to the $40.00 per share exercise price, for shares of Compensator Company's stock. Assuming for simplicity that all 100,000 outstanding were exercised in 20X4, when Compensator Company common stock is trading at $75.00 per share, Compensator Company records their exercise as a capital transaction, which has no impact on its income statement.

dr:	Paid-in capital (stock options)	1,200,000	
dr:	Cash ($40.00 × 100,000)	4,000,000	
	cr: Common stock ($5.00 × 100,000)		500,000
	cr: Paid-in capital (common stock)		4,700,000

Controversy Associated with the Intrinsic Method

At first glance, the intrinsic method appears as a relatively straightforward means of accounting for the compensation expense of employee stock options. The treatment suffers from the fact that stock options that have no intrinsic value (i.e., out-of-the-money or at-the-money options) on the grant date still have economic value. If, instead of a strike price of $40.00 (in-the-money), the options were granted with a strike price equal to the market price of $52.00 (at-the-money), their intrinsic value at the grant date would have been zero. No compensation cost is ever recognized, and the exercise in 20X4 is still treated as a capital transaction. A controversy arises because the employees have received value in the form of stock worth $75.00 a share by paying in only $52.00 a share, and the difference of $23.00 ($75.00 – $52.00) is never recognized as compensation cost. In effect, income statement recognition is bypassed when "at-the-money" options are granted for employee compensation.

THE FAIR VALUE METHOD

The second treatment, described in *FAS123, Accounting for Stock-Based Compensation* (FAS123), is referred to as the fair value method because of the approach used to value the stock option grant. Although use of the fair value approach is encouraged under FAS123, use of the intrinsic approach of APB25 is still allowed as an alternative. Under the fair value method, the value of an employee stock option is measured by using an option pricing model approach on the measurement date, which is the date that the option is granted to the employee. Similar to the intrinsic method, the fair value is recognized as compensation expense over the vesting period.

USE OF THE INTRINSIC METHOD MAY BE ELIMINATED

The Financial Accounting Standards Board (FASB) is currently evaluating the continued use of the intrinsic method, largely because the granting of at-the-money options allows nonrecognition of compensation expense. The International Accounting Standards Board (IASB) is considering a similar project and it is likely that both bodies will eventually converge to require exclusive use of the fair value method.

Controversy Associated with the Fair Value Method

The controversy associated with the fair value method focuses on the issue of determining the fair value of the stock options granted. FAS123 requires that the fair value of employee stock options be estimated using an option-pricing model such as the Black-Scholes or binomial models. A difficulty arises because employee stock options are subject to significant restrictions that are not considered by any of the existing option-pricing models. Among the most commonly encountered restrictions outside the assumption base of the option-pricing models are employees being barred from exercising the options before the end of the vesting period; requirements that the stock trade above a "trigger" price, higher than the exercise price, before the options may be exercised; and prohibitions against the employees selling, monetizing, or hedging the options. The valuation approach prescribed in FAS123 attempts to accommodate some of the inconsistencies between the types of options addressed by the option-pricing models and the more restrictive employee stock options.

Option-Pricing Model Inputs

Although FAS123 mentions and appears to suggest using either the Black-Scholes or the binomial model, in practice, any option-pricing model may be employed as long as it uses at least the following inputs in the development of the options' fair value:

- Exercise price for the options
- Stock price when the options are granted
- Life of the option
- The volatility of the underlying stock
- Dividends expected to be paid between the grant and exercise dates
- The risk-free rate

Firms are also required to disclose these factors and assumptions on a weighted-average basis in their financial reports.

EVALUATING THE FIRM'S INPUTS TO THE OPTION-PRICING MODEL

The firm's assumptions, used in its option-pricing model, directly impact the estimate of fair value and the amount of compensation expense that the firm recognizes during each year of the vesting period. Items such as the exercise price and the closing stock price on the grant date are essentially "hard numbers," not subject to interpretation or potential estimate error. The other factors, including the life of the options, stock price volatility, expected dividends, and, to a lesser extent, the risk-free rate, are estimates that directly affect the estimated value of the stock options being valued. Although the firm and their auditors ultimately agree on the correct estimates of these inputs, it is sometimes beneficial to review the company's assumptions if employee stock option expense has a significant impact on the firm's operating results. Firms issuing large number of employee stock options often calculate a lower compensation expense by using the more sophisticated binomial option pricing model instead of the simpler Black-Scholes model.

Expected Life of the Options

Options typically have a finite life during which they may be exercised. At the end of their life, they expire and no longer have value. All other factors being equal, longer-lived options are more valuable than shorter-lived options. This also means that longer-lived employee stock options result in the recognition of greater compensation expense than shorter-lived options. When valuing employee stock options, the normal input to the option-pricing model, option life, is replaced with the effective option life. The expected life is the amount of time from the grant until the expected exercise by the employees, based on a number of factors, including the way employees have exercised similar grants in the past, the vesting period, the class of employee, and the stock price volatility. The effective life must be longer than the vesting period and shorter than the option life. Generally, senior employees tend to hold options longer than junior employees. Employees also tend to exercise options earlier when the underlying stock price is more volatile than for stocks having lower price volatility. If the firm estimates too short an effective life, the fair value of the options and the associated compensation expense will be understated. The estimated life should be examined to ensure that the firm's estimates are consistent with the other input factors. Figure 9-1 shows the expected life of an employee stock option relative to the option life and key transaction dates.

Stock Price Volatility

The accounting standard allows some flexibility in the estimate of stock price volatility. Historical data may be used, preferably over the most recent period matching the expected life of the option. For example, the volatility used in the pricing model for an option with an expected life of three years would be derived from the last three years of historic data. Additional flexibility is also allowed in how the data are taken, and any consistent and rational method is justifiable. A firm could use any consistent data set of weekly closes, weekly averages, daily closes, daily averages, etc., and the method selected for some publicly traded firms can have a measurable impact on the valuation of the options. Again, because firms would rather report a lower than a higher compensation expense, they may tend to choose the method resulting in the lowest volatility to produce the lowest possible option value. Firms are not strictly required to use historical data when other circumstances indicate that future price behavior will differ from historical

FIGURE 9·1

Option Timeline

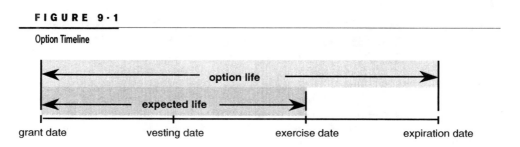

behavior. This leaves the firms a degree of freedom when estimating future volatility. In these cases, in may be prudent to use your own estimate of future stock price volatility and compare the difference in the option values developed using the two different assumptions and the subsequent impact on projected compensation expense.

Expected Dividends

The expected dividend payout between the grant date and the exercise date at end of the expected life reduces the value of the employee stock options. Since the dividends paid come from the anticipated future cash flows existing on the option grant date, if they are paid out prior to exercise, they "escape" from the option holders. The company's estimates for dividend payout should be either consistent with the firm's historical dividend policy or with signaled changes in future dividend policy.

The Risk-Free Rate

FAS123 prescribes the risk-free rate used by U.S. entities as "...the rate currently available on zero-coupon U.S. government issues with a remaining term equal to the expected life of the options."[1] Firms do not have significant latitude when selecting the risk-free rate but can affect the rate used through their estimate of the expected life of the options. A shorter expected option life results in a direct reduction of the option's value, and because shorter-lived zero-coupon issues usually have lower rates, there may be an added effect from a shorter expected life, reducing the estimate of the option's value.

TAX EFFECTS OF EMPLOYEE STOCK OPTIONS

Incentive employee stock options are generally given preferential tax treatment resulting in no consequence to the grantor. Any amount of compensation expense recognized by the company for nondeductible stock options creates a permanent difference so no deferred tax item is recognized. When projecting compensation expense from incentive stock options, adjust earnings before taxes to include the compensation expense before calculating income tax expense as shown in Figure 9-2.

CALCULATION OF DILUTED EARNINGS
PER SHARE FOR COMPANIES EXPENSING
STOCK OPTIONS

When companies elect to expense stock options under FAS123 the fair value of the options is recognized as compensation expense as the options vest. The increased expense reduces both basic and diluted earnings per share. Diluted earnings per share may be further reduced by the incremental shares from the options that are

FIGURE 9·2

Incentive Option Tax Calculation

Investee's Financial Statements

Income Statement	20X0	20X1	20X2	20X3
Revenues	1,000.0	1,100.0	1,210.0	1,350.0
Less: stock option expense	275.0	320.0	340.0	405.0
Less: other expense	420.0	440.0	490.0	510.0
Earnings before taxes	305.0	340.0	380.0	435.0
Addback: stock option expense	275.0	320.0	340.0	405.0
Taxable income	580.0	660.0	720.0	840.0
Income tax expense @ 40%	232.0	264.0	288.0	336.0

granted. To mitigate the "double" effect of expensing stock options, *FAS 128, Earnings per Share*, modifies the treasury stock method used for options granted under stock-based compensation arrangements.

Applicability

The modified treasury stock method applies to fixed awards and to nonvested stock. A fixed award is defined as "an award of stock-based compensation for which vesting is based solely on an employee's continuing to render service to the employer for a specified period of time...that does not specify a performance condition for vesting.[2] The dilutive effect of stock-based awards is considered even if the employee cannot receive or sell the stock until some future date.

Methodology

If awards are granted during the period, any shares issuable are weighted to reflect the portion of the period that they are outstanding. To determine the shares that are issuable, the assumed proceeds used for the treasury stock method are determined as the sum of three items:

1. Any amount that the employee must pay upon exercise. This is usually the option's strike price.
2. The average amount of compensation cost attributed to future service and not yet recognized. This is the fair value of the option that is recorded on the grant date less the portion that has been recognized to date as compensation expense.
3. Any additional tax benefit (burden) that would be credited (debited) to additional paid-in capital if the option were to be exercised. This benefit

(burden) is the amount resulting from any tax deduction in excess of (less than) that recognized for financial reporting purposes.

EXAMPLE 9-2. EPS Calculation with Dilutive Outcome

On 31-Dec-20X1, Compensator Company grants 4,000,000 options having an exercise price of $40.00 per share. The award vests over five years, and each option is determined to have a calculated fair value of $5.75 making a total value of ($5.75 × 4,000,000) = 23,000,000 at the grant date. At the grant date, the company makes no entry.

One year later, on 31-Dec-20X2, the company recognizes one-fifth the value of the total award (23,000,000 / 5) = 4,600,000 as compensation expense. The average market price of the company's stock was $46.00 per share during 20X2. The company has a 40-percent tax rate.

Computation of proceeds for diluted earnings per share:

Amount employees would pay in if all the options were exercised	160,000,000
(4,000,000 × $40.00)	
add: Average unrecognized compensation balance during the year	20,700,000
(23,000,000 + 23,000,000 − 4,600,000) / 2	
add: Additional tax benefit (burden)	400,000
($46.00 − 40.00 − 5.75) × 4,000,000 × 40.0%	
Assumed proceeds	181,100,000

Calculation of incremental shares for diluted EPS

Total shares outstanding under the award	4,000,000
less: Shares assumed repurchased at the market price	3,936,956
(181,100,000 / $46.00 = 3,936,956)	
Incremental shares to be added	63,044

EXAMPLE 9-3. EPS Calculation with Antidilutive Outcome

Same facts as Example 9-2 except that the average market price of the company's stock was $44.00 per share during 20X2. The company has a 40-percent tax rate.

Computation of proceeds for diluted earnings per share:

Amount employees would pay in if all the options were exercised	160,000,000
(4,000,000 × $40.00)	
add: Average unrecognized compensation balance during the year	20,700,000
(23,000,000 + 23,000,000 − 4,600,000) / 2	
add: Additional tax benefit (burden)	(2,800,000)
($44.00 − 40.00 − 5.75) × 4,000,000 × 40.0%	
Assumed proceeds	177,900,000

Calculation of incremental shares for diluted EPS

Total shares outstanding under the award	4,000,000
Shares assumed repurchased at the market price	4,043,182
(177,900,000 / $44.00 = 4,043,182)	
Incremental shares to be added (antidilutive–not considered for diluted EPS)	-0-

ACCOUNTING FOR TARGET STOCK OPTIONS ROLLED OVER IN A PURCHASE ACQUISITION

An infrequently encountered situation occurs when Target Company is acquired in a purchase merger and some, or all, of the existing Target Company employee stock options are converted or exchanged for options in Acquiror Company. When this does occur, the options are often a mixture of both in- and out-of-the-money options and may be either vested or nonvested. Usually, option vesting is accelerated at the acquisition due to change-of-control provisions, allowing the options to settle rather than being rolled over. Not uncommonly, out-of-the money options are simply canceled. The accounting treatment for the less frequent cases, where the options are rolled over, discussed below, varies depending on whether the stock options are vested or nonvested.

Vested Stock Options

In a purchase business combination, Acquiror Company may issue vested stock options in exchange for Target Company's employee stock options. The fair value of the options issued becomes part of the purchase price. Fair value of options for accounting purposes is determined using either a Black-Scholes or binomial option-pricing model for both in-the-money and out-of-the-money options. As previously discussed, the approach is modified to consider the expected life instead of the full life of the options, where expected life is a reasonable estimate of the expected average life before the employees exercise their options.

The increased purchase price, resulting from the inclusion of the fair value of the vested options, increases both goodwill and paid-in capital. For financial reporting purposes, no compensation expense is recognized at the transaction date as a result of rolling over the options. The increase in the purchase price resulting from the fair value of the rollover options is paid for in new options "minted" by Acquiror Company, and their value appears as an increase to Acquiror Company's paid-in capital. Because the increase in paid-in capital directly offsets the increase in goodwill, there is no change in the cash or the debt and equity issued to execute the transaction.

Nonvested Stock Options

If Acquiror Company exchanges nonvested options for Target Company's employee nonvested stock options, then an important differentiation is made between options that are either in-the-money or out-of-the-money. If the options are out-of-the-money, their value is added to the purchase price and the result is the same as for vested options. Both goodwill and paid-in capital increase by an equal amount.

If instead, the unvested options are in-the-money, the accounting becomes slightly more complex. The entire value of the options issued is still considered part of the purchase price, but the unearned portion of the intrinsic value (in-the-money value) of the options is treated as unearned compensation expense. The accounting on the transaction date is to credit Paid-in capital for the value of the options, and then to debit Deferred compensation expense (a contra-equity account) for the unearned portion of the intrinsic value and to debit goodwill for the difference between the two.

The deferred compensation is calculated by multiplying the intrinsic value of the options times a factor equal to the remaining time to vest over the total time to vest (fraction of total vesting period remaining). Looking at Example 9-4, drawn from *FASB Interpretation 44*, the accounting for the deferred compensation expense is explained.

EXAMPLE **9-4. Accounting for Unvested, In-The-Money Options**

On 31-Dec-20X2, Acquiror Company exchanges 10,000 nonvested options valued at 100,000 (10,000 × $10.00) for nonvested Target Company options of equal value. The Target Company options were issued on 31-Dec-20X0 and vest after five years, on 31-Dec-20X5. The Acquiror Company options exchanged also vest after the three remaining years, on 31-Dec-20X5. At the exchange date the options issued are $4.00 in-the-money and consequently have an intrinsic value of: 10,000 × $4.00 = 40,000.

The deferred compensation expense resulting from the exchange is equal to the intrinsic value of the options multiplied by a factor equal to the number of years left to vest divided by the total vesting period or: 40,000 × 3 years to vest / 5-year vesting period = 24,000. The difference between the value of the options and the portion that is recorded as deferred compensation expense increases transaction goodwill.

Because the total value of the options exchanged is considered in the purchase price, we see the effect of the option exchange on the Acquiror's consolidated financials as:

dr.	Goodwill	76,000	
dr.	Deferred compensation expense (contra-equity)	24,000	
	cr. Paid-in capital		100,000

An important aspect of the deferred compensation expense is its dilutive effect on both earnings before interest, taxes, depreciation, and amortization (EBITDA) and net income in postmerger periods. Because it is amortized ratably to compensation expense over the remaining vesting periods, it reduces both EBITDA and net income. Also because a contra-equity account is being amortized, there are no cash flow effects. In the instant case, deferred compensation expense completely amortizes to compensation expense at a rate of 8000 per year in each of the three years remaining in the vesting period.

dr.	Compensation expense	8,000	
	cr. Deferred compensation expense		8,000

Acceleration of option vesting to the deal date captures the cost of rollover options in goodwill, which, no longer being amortized, avoids the postmerger dilution otherwise resulting from amortizing deferred compensation expense. Acceleration also pulls the tax shield associated with the compensation expense into the present, making it in most cases, more valuable than it would be if spread into several future periods. A negative aspect of acceleration is that it undoes the business purpose of the vesting period by eliminating that economic incentive for employees to remain with the acquired firm. Similarly, if a large quantity of unvested in-the-money options is valued using a binomial model instead of the Black-Scholes model, the lower valuation usually returned by the binomial model results in less dilution of postacquisition earnings.

PROJECTING EARNINGS PER SHARE (EPS) FOR OPTION-INTENSIVE FIRMS

The two obvious challenges in projecting a firm's future earnings per share (EPS) are projecting the earnings and projecting the number of shares. Firms having large numbers of options outstanding add a degree of complexity stemming from the nature of the options themselves. Stock prices generally change to maintain a certain multiple of EPS; as the future EPS increases, market forces increase the stock price. A higher stock price means more options are likely to be exercised. The exercise of options means cash is paid in, reducing debt and interest expense, which increases earnings. However, the issuance of new stock to settle the options dilutes the earnings per share, reducing EPS and putting downward pressure on the stock price.

One approach is to simply treat all of the outstanding options as being exercised and combining this result with all of the outstanding shares. This method almost always overstates the number of shares, sometimes even exceeding the number of shares authorized, by assuming that even shares that are far out-of-the-money are exercisable.

The second method is that required for U.S. GAAP, where only the effects of dilutive options and convertibles are considered, using the treasury method. This is probably the best method for determining a "snapshot" of the firm's earnings per share today. Because it assumes that any shares necessary to fill the exercise of options, warrants, or other conversions into common stock are purchased in the open market, then the number of shares assumed as outstanding never exceeds the actual number authorized. The potential problem here is not in the current but in the forecast periods, particularly when attempting to estimate future cash flows because the treasury method never assumes that the firm issues new equity. A second formidable problem is that the treasury method relies on stock price to determine if options are exercised, making the accuracy of future option exercise forecasts contingent on the accuracy of future share price forecasts.

One workable approach for estimating the effect of options on future earnings (remembering that one's success in predicting the future is always limited) is to first project forward basic earnings-per-share and next to project forward stock prices as a multiple of earnings-per-share. The uncertainty entered here is the analyst's estimate of the proper price / earnings multiple. The third step calculates diluted earnings-per-share using the treasury stock method (or the modified treasury stock method for firms that expense employee stock options) based upon the projected forward stock prices. This produces a reasonable estimate of forward diluted earnings-per-share but is sensitive to the analyst's estimate of the forward price / earnings multiple. It also assumes that the firm issues no equity when the options are exercised. If the firm has unissued shares, then additional capitalization can be modeled as a separate layer on top of the base projections.

CHAPTER SUMMARY

Presently firms may choose between two methods when accounting for employee stock options. One method "bypasses" the income statement, effectively letting firms understate their true compensation cost, and the second method expenses the fair value of the options over the "earning period." The current tone of U.S. and international standards setters and regulators is that, in the not-too-distant future, all firms will be required to expense stock options.

Because the expense is a noncash expense that affects EBITDA, it can have important implications for both credit and equity analysis. Ultimately, firms may choose the route taken by Microsoft and others and simply eliminate employee stock options in favor of cash or restricted stock.

CHAPTER 10

Restructuring Charges

INTRODUCTION

The Securities and Exchange Commission (SEC) makes an interesting point regarding restructuring charges: "The term 'restructuring charge' is not defined in the existing authoritative literature."[1] Although we discuss them frequently, the accounting profession has never formally defined them. However, within the scope of U.S. GAAP, certain pronouncements of the Financial Accounting Standards Board (FASB) and the FASB Emerging Issues Task Force (EITF) provide general guidance about "certain costs incurred in a restructuring." Considering incurred costs to be "restructuring costs" for our purposes, we find that they are accounted for differently depending on whether they are incurred as part of a firm's ongoing operations or as a result of a business combination.

The topic of restructuring charges is not a particularly complex or meaty one, but I felt it deserved inclusion on its own for four reasons: The first, of course, is that the term "restructuring charge," while commonly used in financial accounting, is somewhat ambiguous in the authoritative literature, and it might be helpful to clarify it; secondly, restructurings are frequently encountered within all three analytical arenas, M&A, credit, and equity; the third reason is that the FASB recently issued a Statement of Financial Accounting Standards changing the manner in which restructuring charges from a firm's ongoing operations are treated; and lastly, because FASB has proposed changes to the accounting for restructuring charges arising from business combinations. FASB will likely implement the changes in the near future so watch for the Binoculars Icon while reading through the text, as it alerts you to the proposed changes to the accounting standards. International Accounting Standards (IAS) also provide no definition of restructuring costs but define restructuring as "... a programme that is planned and controlled by management, and materially changes either: (a) the scope of a business undertaken by an enterprise; or (b) the manner in which that business is conducted."[2] Because FASB has actually *diverged* from IAS accounting for restructuring costs, the two approaches are treated separately.

FASB'S NEW CHANGES TO FINANCIAL ACCOUNTING FOR RESTRUCTURING CHARGES

Until recently, restructuring charges were recognized as a liability when the firm *committed* to a restructuring plan. This created a conceptual conflict because the "commitment" to a plan was an operating decision and did not create an obligation for the firm to transfer assets or services at some future date. In other words, although a firm says that it plans to exit an activity, it has no legal obligation, and consequently no true liability exists. In June of 2002, FASB issued *Statement of Financial Accounting Standards No. 146, Accounting for Costs Associated with Exit or Disposal Activities* (FAS146), which changed the way that firms recognize liabilities for restructuring charges. Simply stated, the impact of FAS146 is that before its issuance firms recognized liabilities when they committed to a restructuring plan, and now they only recognize liabilities when they actually incur bona fide obligations under a restructuring plan. The new accounting standard only applies to restructuring charges from a firm's ongoing operations, and it does not cover restructuring charges a firm incurs as part of business combinations such as mergers, acquisitions, or leveraged buyouts.

RESTRUCTURING CHARGES—U.S. GAAP

Restructuring charges are costs associated with the exit or disposal of activities and fall into three main classes: one-time benefits paid or provided to employees being involuntarily terminated; the costs of terminating contracts; and the costs of moving employees or consolidating operations. Restructuring liabilities are measured at fair value, and liabilities coming due in future periods are discounted to the present using the credit-adjusted risk-free rate.

One-time Termination Benefits

Over the past two or three years in the financial industry, many analysts have either received their own termination letters or been present when colleagues did as part of mass layoffs, cutbacks, downsizings, or reductions-in-force. The text of the termination letters, in addition to apologies and well wishes for the recipient's future, contained the details of "the package" of one-time termination benefits that the recipient would soon receive. The benefits package might typically include 60 days or some other legal notification period of salary, so many weeks of severance pay calculated as a function of the length of prior service, temporary clerical or word processing support, access to office space, career counseling and job-placement assistance, educational or retraining benefits, etc.

Not meaning to dredge up unpleasant memories for any readers, I chose this example because the costs to the firm of "the packages" it pays out for involuntary terminations are one-time termination benefits, one of the three broad categories of restructuring charges. These types of restructuring charges are recognized when the firm obligates itself to paying specific amounts. The four recognition requirements of FAS146 are met only after the firm:

1. Develops and commits to a termination plan
2. Identifies the employees being terminated (not necessarily by name but by number, job, and location)
3. Provides enough information about the benefit package that involuntarily terminated employees are able to determine the type and amount of benefits they will receive
4. Believes it is unlikely for the plan to change significantly or be canceled

Example 10-1 illustrates how firms recognize liabilities for one-time termination benefits.

EXAMPLE 10-1. Recognition of Liabilities for Termination Benefits

On 15-March-20X1, the management of Downsizer Company decides to reduce the workforce at one of its operating plants due to a long-term shift in its business climate. Downsizer Company management doubts that the plant utilization will ever return to its previous levels. One hundred and twenty-five employees being terminated are identified by name, and the one-time termination benefit is set at $15,000 per employee. By developing the plan, Downsizer Company only meets three of the four requirements necessary for recognizing a one-time termination benefit liability. Two months later, on 15-May-20X1 (the *communication date*), Downsizer Company management notifies the affected employees that they will be terminated on 14-July-20X1 (after the 60-day *minimum retention period*, which coincides with the 60-day *legal notification period*) but will receive a one-time termination benefit payment of $15,000 immediately, regardless of whether or not they stay for the full 60 days until the termination date. Because Downsizer Company now meets all four recognition requirements and the employees are not required to render any future service, Downsizer Company recognizes a liability of (125 × $15,000) = $1,875,000 as the liability associated with the one-time termination benefit.

A slight variation on this occurs if Downsizer Company will not pay the benefit until two months later, on the termination date of 14-July-20X1. On the communication date of 15-May-20X1, Downsizer Company recognizes a liability of (125 × $15,000) = $1,875,000 discounted for two months at the company's credit-adjusted risk-free rate (assume for Downsizer Company that rate is 8 percent) to $1,850,248. In each of the following two months between the communication date and the termination date, Downsizer Company recognizes additional accretion expense of one-half the difference between the full amount of the liability and the discounted value recorded on the communication date ($1,875,000 − 1,850,248 = 24,752 / 2) = $12,376 per month. On the termination date, Downsizer Company has recorded the full amount of the liability ($1,850,248 + 12,376 + 12,376) = $1,875,000, which it settles by paying the terminated employees in cash.

DOWNSIZER COMPANY'S JOURNAL ENTRY AT THE COMMUNICATION DATE, 15-MAY-20X1

dr:	Restructuring expense	1,850,248
	cr: Restructuring liability	1,850,248
memo:	To record the present value of one-time termination benefits	
	(125 × 15,000 = 1,875,000 discounted for 2 months at 8%)	

DOWNSIZER COMPANY'S JOURNAL ENTRY AFTER ONE MONTH, 15-JUNE-20X1

dr:	Accretion expense	12,376
	cr: Restructuring liability	12,376
memo:	To record the first month's accretion expense for the one-time termination benefit liability	

DOWNSIZER COMPANY'S JOURNAL ENTRY AT THE TERMINATION DATE, 14-JULY-20X1

dr:	Accretion expense	12,376
	cr: Restructuring liability	12,376
memo:	To record the second month's accretion expense for the one-time termination benefit liability	

Figure 10-1 shows how Downsizer Company presents the initial recognition and periodic accretion of the restructuring liability for the one-time termination benefits in its monthly unaudited financial statements.

When Downsizer settles the liability by paying the employees in cash, it reverses the restructuring liability.

dr:	Restructuring liability	1,875,000
	cr: Cash	1,875,000
memo:	To record payment of the one-time termination benefit liability	

FIGURE 10·1

Financial Statement Presentation of a Restructuring Liability

Downsizer Company's monthly financial statements			
Income Statement	**May**	**June**	**July**
Revenues	2,000,000	2,000,000	2,000,000
Less: restructuring charge	1,850,248	-	-
Less: accretion expense	-	12,376	12,376
Operating income	149,752	1,987,624	1,987,624
Balance Sheet			
Restructuring liability - beginning	1,850,248	1,850,248	1,862,624
Add: accretion expense	-	12,376	12,376
Restructuring liability - ending	1,850,248	1,862,624	1,875,000

The *communication date* is the date when the company both meets all of the recognition requirements and communicates the termination plan to its employees. Downsizer Company recognizes the fair value of the termination benefit liability on the communication date provided that the employees are not required to work beyond the minimum retention period to receive their termination benefits. The minimum retention period cannot be longer than the legal notification period, which is normally 60 days. Figure 10-2 shows the time line for one-time termination benefits.

FIGURE 10-2

Timeline for One-time Termination Benefits

Communication date:

Downsizer Company informs their employees of the particulars of the plan in sufficient detail for employees to estimate their one-time termination benefits.

Downsizer Company recognizes a liability for the fair value of the termination benefits on the communication date.

Termination date - end of the minimum retention period

Employees are terminated and Downsizer Company settles the one-time termination benefit liability for cash.

If any employees are required to provide service after this date, Downsizer Company recognizes an additional liability for each period of required service after the communication date plus accretion on the liability beginning from the termination date.

15-Mar   15-May   14-Jul

nominally 60 days

Commitment date:

Downsizer Company formulates a plan to involuntarily terminate employees and identifies the number, job functions, location, expected completion date, and benefits package.

Downsizer Company does not recognize a liability.

Minimum retention period:

The minimum retention period cannot be longer than the legal notification period or if there is no legal notification period, 60 days.

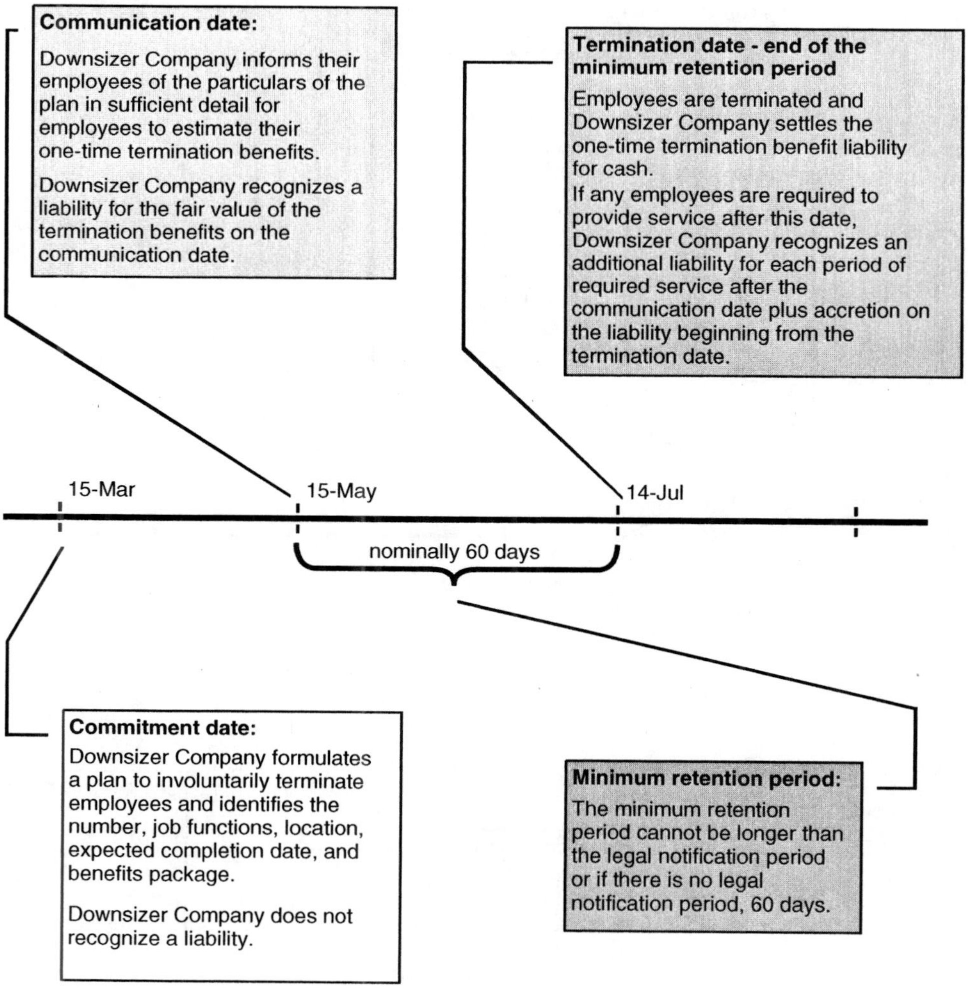

Sometimes firms may require key employees to work beyond the minimum retention period in order to qualify for their termination benefits through a future service period. The future service period begins on the communication date and extends past the minimum retention period to the end-of-service date. Figure 10-3 shows a time line for employees rendering service beyond the minimum retention period.

In these cases, the firm does not recognize a liability on the communication date but instead determines the fair value of the one-time termination benefit by discounting it from the payment date to the communication date (using the credit-adjusted risk-free rate). The fair value of the one-time termination benefit is recognized ratably in each period of future service along with the accretion expense for

FIGURE 10-3

Timeline for One-time Termination Benefits Paid after a Future Service Period

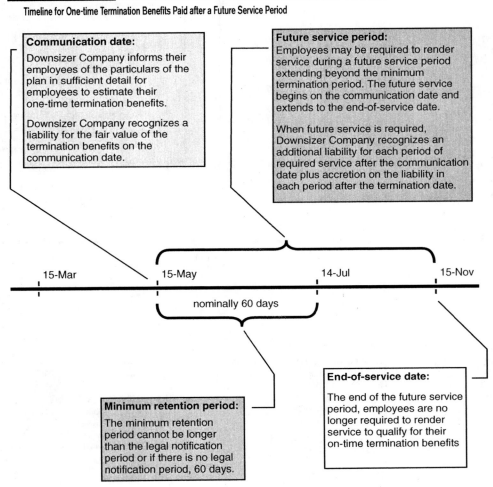

Communication date:

Downsizer Company informs their employees of the particulars of the plan in sufficient detail for employees to estimate their one-time termination benefits.

Downsizer Company recognizes a liability for the fair value of the termination benefits on the communication date.

Future service period:

Employees may be required to render service during a future service period extending beyond the minimum termination period. The future service begins on the communication date and extends to the end-of-service date.

When future service is required, Downsizer Company recognizes an additional liability for each period of required service after the communication date plus accretion on the liability in each period after the termination date.

15-Mar   15-May   14-Jul   15-Nov

nominally 60 days

Minimum retention period:

The minimum retention period cannot be longer than the legal notification period or if there is no legal notification period, 60 days.

End-of-service date:

The end of the future service period, employees are no longer required to render service to qualify for their on-time termination benefits the liability. Example 10-2 shows the recognition of liabilities when employees are expected to provide service after the minimum retention period.

EXAMPLE 10-2. Recognition of Liabilities for Service after the Minimum Retention Period

On 15-March- 20X1, the management of Downsizer Company decides to reduce the workforce at one of its operating plants due to a long-term shift in its business climate. Downsizer Company management doubts plant utilization ever returning to its previous levels and consequently believes that the reduction-in-force is essentially permanent. One hundred and twenty-five employees being terminated are identified by name and their one-time termination benefit is set at $45,000 per employee for each employee that works for the entire six months from the communication date until 15-November-20X1. All employees receive a one-time termination benefit of $15,000 on the termination date of 14-July-20X1 regardless of how long they continue working, but only those employees working through until 15-Novenber-20X1 receive the additional $30,000. Downsizer Company meets all necessary requirements and recognizes a liability of $(125 \times \$15,000) = \$1,875,000$ discounted two months by Downsizer Company's 8-percent credit-adjusted risk-free rate to $1,850,248 because all of the 125 employees are immediately entitled to the $15,000 to be paid in two months on 14-July-20X1.

Even though Downsizer Company will pay additional one-time termination benefits of $30,000 to each employee still working at the end of six months, it does not record any liability for the expected future service on the communication date. Instead, it determines the fair value of the payments *at the termination date* $(125 \times \$30,000) = \$3,750,000$ discounted *four* months at the credit-adjusted risk-free rate of 8% to $3,651,645 and subsequently recognizes that amount ratably over the future service period $(3,651,645 / 6) = \$608,607$ per month for *six* months. Additionally, Downsizer Company recognizes accretion expense of one-fourth the difference between the fair value of the liability on the termination date of 14-July-20X1 and the actual payments made four months later on 15-November-20X1 $(\$3,750,000 - 3,651,645 = 98,355 / 4) = \$24,589$ in each of the four months following the termination date. Another way of stating Downsizer Company's liability is that it immediately owes a $15,000 one-time termination benefit to all 125 employees and an additional $30,000 termination benefit to each employee staying the six months from 15-May-20X1 until 15-November-20X1.

DOWNSIZER COMPANY'S JOURNAL ENTRY AT THE COMMUNICATION DATE, 15-MAY-20X1

dr:	Restructuring expense	1,850,248	
	cr: Restructuring liability		1,850,248
memo:	To record the present value of one-time termination benefits		

$(125 \times 15,000 = 1,875,000$ discounted for 2 months at 8%)

Note that Downsizer does not record any liability for the $30,000 future service payments at the communication date.

DOWNSIZER COMPANY'S JOURNAL ENTRY AFTER ONE MONTH, 15-JUNE-20X1

dr:	Accretion expense	12,376	
	cr: Restructuring liability		12,376

memo: To record the first month's accretion expense for the $15,000 one-time termina-
        tion benefit liability

dr: Restructuring expense   608,607
        cr: Restructuring liability   608,607
memo: To record the future service liability earned from 15-May to
        15-June (3,651,645 / 6) = $608,607

Note: Downsizer does not record any accretion expense for the future service liability
until after the termination date of 14-July-20X1.

DOWNSIZER COMPANY'S JOURNAL ENTRY AT THE TERMINATION DATE, 14-JULY-20X1

dr: Accretion expense   12,376
        cr: Restructuring liability   12,376
memo: To record the second month's accretion expense for the
        $15,000 one-time termination benefit liability

dr: Restructuring liability   1,875,000
        cr: Cash   1,875,000
memo: To record payment of the $15,000 one-time termination benefit liability

dr: Restructuring expense   608,607
        cr: Restructuring liability   608,607
memo: To record the future service liability earned from 15-June
        to 14-July (3,651,645 / 6) = $608,607

DOWNSIZER COMPANY'S JOURNAL ENTRY ONE MONTH AFTER THE TERMINATION DATE, 15-AUGUST-20X1

dr: Restructuring expense   608,607
        cr: Restructuring liability   608,607
memo: To record the future service liability earned from 14-July
        to 15-August (3,651,645 / 6) = $608,607

dr: Accretion expense   24,589
        cr: Restructuring liability   24,589
memo: To record the first month's accretion expense for the
        $30,000 one-time termination benefit future service liability
        ($3,750,000 – 3,651,645 = 98,355/ 4) = $24,589.

Figure 10-4 shows how Downsizer Company presents the initial recognition and periodic accretion of the restructuring liabilities for the one-time termination benefits in its
monthly unaudited financial statements for the employees that it expects to render service
during the future service period.

The restructuring expenses for the $30,000 one-time termination benefit for the rendered
future service total the liability due four months after the termination date of 14-July-20X1.
The structure of the expenses when future service is required is to determine the fair value
of the projected liability discounted back to the termination date (usually 60 days after the
communication date). In this case the projected liability of (125 × $30,000) = $3,750,000 is
discounted back four months from the end of the future service period (15-November-
20X1) to the termination date of 14-July-20X1. The discounted value on the termination
date ($3,651,645) is recognized ratably over the entire six-month future service period from

FIGURE 10-4

Financial Statement Presentation of a Restructuring Liability for Future Service

Downsizer Company's monthly financial statements

Income Statement

	May	Jun	Jul	Aug	Sep	Oct	Nov
Revenues	2,000,000	2,000,000	2,000,000	2,000,000	2,000,000	2,000,000	2,000,000
Less: restructuring charge 1	1,851,100	-	-	-	-	-	-
Less: accretion expense 1	-	11,950	11,950	-	-	-	-
Less: restructuring charge 2	-	609,170	609,170	609,170	609,170	609,170	609,170
Less: accretion expense 2	-	-	-	23,745	23,745	23,745	23,745
Operating income	148,900	1,378,880	1,378,880	1,367,085	1,367,085	1,367,085	1,367,085

Balance Sheet

Cash - beginning	-	148,900	1,527,780	2,906,660	2,398,745	3,765,830	5,132,915
Less: subtractions	-	-	-	1,875,000	-	-	-
Add: additions	148,900	1,378,880	1,378,880	1,367,085	1,367,085	1,367,085	1,367,085
Cash - ending	148,900	1,527,780	2,906,660	2,398,745	3,765,830	5,132,915	6,500,000
Restructuring liability 1 - beginning	1,851,100	1,851,100	1,863,050	1,875,000	-	-	-
Less: subtractions	-	-	-	1,875,000			
Add: accretion	-	11,950	11,950	-	-	-	-
Restructuring liability 1 - ending	1,851,100	1,863,050	1,875.000	-	-	-	-
Restructuring liability 2 - beginning	-	-	609,170	1,218,340	1,851,255	2,484,170	3,117,085
Add: additions	-	609,170	609,170	609,170	609,170	609,170	609,170
Add: accretion	-	-	-	23,745	23,745	23,745	23,745
Restructuring liability 2 - ending	-	609,170	1,218,340	1,851,255	2,484,170	3,117,085	3,750,000

the communication date of 15-May-20X1 to the end of the future service period on 15-November-20X1 at $(3,651,645 / 6) = 608,607$ per month. In each of the four months after the termination date, Downsizer Company recognizes accretion expense equal to one-fourth of the difference between the fair value of the liability at the end of the future service period and its fair value on the termination date: $(3,750,000 - 3,651,645 = 98,355 / 4) = \$24,589$. The restructuring and accretion expenses recognized in each of the six months between the communication date and the end of the future service period total to the full amount of the liability at the end of the future service period.

	Restructuring Expense	Accretion Expense	Total Expense
15-May-20X1	- 0 -	- 0 -	- 0 -
15-June-20X1	608,607	- 0 -	608,607
14-July-20X1	608,607	- 0 -	608,607
15-August-20X1	608,607	24,589	633,196
15-September-20X1	608,607	24,589	633,196
15-October-20X1	608,607	24,589	633,196
15-November-20X1	608,607	24,589	633,196
Total restructuring liability at the end of the future service period			3,750,000

Contract Termination Costs

There are two types of costs associated with contracts that may be recognized as restructuring costs: The first are penalty clause, early termination, or opt-out costs, usually specified in the contract agreement; the second type are contractually obligated amounts that provide no economic benefit to the firm. An example of the second type of costs would be paying rent on a closed factory. If Downsizer Company closes its factory on 15-November-20X1 but the building lease required payment through the end-of-the-year, the rent from 15-November (also called the *cease use date*) to 31-December provides no economic benefit to Downsizer Company and is recognized as a contract termination cost. Similar to one-time termination benefit costs, Downsizer Company recognizes the contract termination cost liability on the communication date, discounted by the credit-adjusted risk-free rate. Downsizer Company would also recognize an accretion expense in each period following the communication date until the liability settlement date. Example 10-3 illustrates Downsizer Company's accounting for contract termination costs as restructuring charges.

EXAMPLE 10-3. Accounting for Contract Termination Costs

On 15-March- 20X1, the management of Downsizer Company decides to close one of its operating plants due to a long-term shift in its business climate. Downsizer Company management doubts plant utilization ever returning to its previous levels and consequently believes that the plant closure is essentially permanent. Downsizer Company rents the building under an annual lease and will continue paying the monthly rent of $200,000 after the *cease use* (plant closure) date of 15-November-20X1 through the end of the year. Downsizer does not expect to be able to sublet the property for the last month and one-half, and consequently none of the rent paid in that period will provide any economic benefit to the firm.

On the communication date of 15-May-20X1, Downsizer Company recognizes a liability for the operating plant's rents for the second half of November and the entire month of December, discounted back at a credit-adjusted risk-free rate of 8 percent. The November rent of ($100,000) discounted back six months from 15-November to 15-May is $96,092 and the December rent of ($200,000) discounted six and one-half months from 1-December to 15-May is $191,546. On the communication date of 15-May-20X1, Downsizer makes the following journal entries.

DOWNSIZER COMPANY'S JOURNAL ENTRY AT THE COMMUNICATION DATE, 15-MAY-20X1

dr:	Restructuring expense	287,638	
	cr: Restructuring liability (November 20X1 rent)		96,092
	cr: Restructuring liability (December 20X1 rent)		191,546
memo:	To record the present value of contract termination costs		

(100,000 discounted for 6 months at 8% + 200,000 discounted for 6.5 months at 8%)

Just as with one-time termination benefits, in each of the periods between recognition and settlement of the liability, Downsizer Company recognizes an accretion expense for each of the two contract termination liabilities equal to the difference between the expected cost and the amount initially recognized on the communication date divided by the number of periods between recognition and settlement. For the portion of the November rent the monthly accretion expense is: $(100,000 - 96,092 = 3908 / 6) = 651$, and for the December rent $(200,000 - 191,546 = 8454 / 6.5) = 1301$.

DOWNSIZER COMPANY'S JOURNAL ENTRY ONE MONTH LATER ON 15-JUNE-20X1

dr:	Accretion expense	1,952	
	cr: Restructuring liability (November 20X1 rent)		651
	cr: Restructuring liability (December 20X1 rent)		1,301
memo:	To record the first month's accretion expense for the contract termination costs associated with building rents after the 15-November-20X1 cease use date.		

Other Associated Costs

The last category of restructuring costs is for those costs associated with consolidating or closing facilities and relocating employees. This is not an exclusive list and many other costs incidental to exiting or disposing of activities probably fall into this category. Some care is needed in segregating costs for disposing of assets because these are generally included as adjustments to the assets' sales price. As with the other restructuring costs, the present value of a restructuring liability is recorded when it is actually incurred, and periodic accretion expense is recognized during the period between recognition and settlement. Example 10-4 illustrates restructuring charges associated with consolidation of facilities as part of an announced restructuring plan.

EXAMPLE 10-4. Other Associated Restructuring Costs

Consolidating Company recently completed construction of its new mid-town Manhattan office building. On 15-Mar-20X1 they commit to a plan to consolidate facilities by disposing of their Wall Street property. All of the staff from Wall Street will be relocated in the new headquarters by 15-November-20X1, and none of the staff will be terminated. On 15-May-20X1 the employees at the Wall Street facility are notified of the impending relocation, and on 15-Jun-20X1, Consolidating Company signs a $180,000 services contract with Moving Company to relocate selected office furniture, files, and equipment to the midtown facility. Terms of the contract are payment of $30,000 at the signing and the balance when the moves are completed on 15-November-20X1. Consolidating Company does not recognize any liability until it enters the contract with Moving Company on 15-Jun-20X1. The expected future cost ($150,000) is discounted back five months from 15-November-20X1 to 15-June-20X1 at 8 percent, so Consolidating Company recognizes a liability of $145,098 on 15-June-20X1. In each of the five subsequent months, Consolidating Company also recognizes accretion expense equal to one-fifth the difference between the initial recognition cost and the expected settlement cost or $(150,000 - 145,098 = 4902 / 5) = 980$.

CONSOLIDATING COMPANY'S JOURNAL ENTRY AT THE CONTRACT DATE, 15-JUN-20X1

dr:	Prepaid moving expense	30,000	
dr:	Restructuring expense	145,098	
	cr: Restructuring liability (Wall Street moving contract)		145,098

cr: Cash	30,000

memo: To record the initial contract payment and present value of
facility consolidation cost (150,000 discounted for 5 months at 8%)

RESTRUCTURING CHARGES—INTERNATIONAL ACCOUNTING STANDARDS

The scope of restructuring charges discussed in FAS146 is contained within two different International Accounting Standards: *IAS37, Provisions, Contingent Liabilities and Contingent Assets*; and *IAS 19, Employee Benefits.* The principal difference between U.S. GAAP and IAS centers around bonuses designed to retain employees to render services during any expected future service periods extending beyond the minimum termination period.

One-time Termination Benefits

The principal differentiation between one-time termination benefits under U.S. GAAP and IAS is that IAS views termination benefits only as those providing no future economic benefit to the firm. Consequently they are immediately recognized to expense. This varies somewhat from U.S. GAAP's treatment of retention payments beyond the minimum retention period. A second important difference is that IAS does not discount current restructuring liabilities, only those that "…fall due more than 12 months after the balance sheet date…"[3]

Contract Termination Costs

IAS accounting for contract service costs is very similar to U.S. GAAP accounting but also allows recognizing a restructuring provision when a *constructive obligation* exists, whereas U.S. GAAP only allows recognition when a present obligation exists. Constructive obligations differ from present obligations in that present obligations require that a past obligating event has occurred that effectively leaves the firm no realistic alternative but to settle the liability. A constructive obligation is one where the firm obligates itself such that its only alternative to settling the liability is reneging on its own pledge.

U.S. GAAP currently allows an acquiring company to recognize restructuring liabilities based on an announced restructuring plan, which creates a constructive obligation. As part of its Business Combinations Project, FASB has already decided that constructive obligations will no longer be recognized as liabilities in business combinations.

Other Associated Costs

IAS focuses on only direct expenditures arising from the restructuring, meaning that the expenditures were brought about solely by the restructuring and that they provide no future economic benefit. One item specifically excluded under IAS but allowed under U.S. GAAP is the costs of relocating continuing staff. Conceptually this is correct within the concept of not allowing expenditures providing future benefits but fails in situations where facilities are being consolidated and the cost of relocating the continuing staff arises to clear a building for disposal.

DISCLOSURE OF RESTRUCTURING CHARGES

The nature of the activity being exited determines the reporting method for restructuring charges. If the exit or disposal activity comes about because of a discontinued operation, then the restructuring charge is taken after the results of income from continuing operations, otherwise the restructuring charge is a component of income from continuing operations. Remember that Results of discontinued operations is one of the three items appearing below earnings from continuing operations. The other two are Extraordinary items and Changes in accounting principle. Although firms generally try to recognize restructuring charges as part of discontinued operations to avoid the negative impact on earnings from continuing operations, the exited activity must meet two tests to be classified as a discontinued operation. The first is that the disposal transaction eliminates both the operations and cash flows of the disposed component from the disposing firm's continuing operations, and the second is that the disposing firm ceases involvement with the disposed component. If the disposal activity fails to meet both tests, then the associated restructuring charges must be included in the determination of income from continuing operations.

RESTRUCTURING LIABILITIES IN BUSINESS COMBINATIONS

Firms often engage in business combinations hoping to recognize future cost savings from closing unnecessary facilities or eliminating redundant positions as part of the economic benefits from the merger or acquisition. When Acquiror Company plans the restructuring activities as part of the acquisition strategy, it recognizes the associated costs of the following on the transaction-adjusted balance sheet on the acquisition date:

- Exiting activities of Target Company
- Involuntarily terminating Target Company employees
- Relocating Target Company employees

However, if the costs provide future benefits to the merged company, they are not recognized as a liability on the acquisition date but rather as expenses in the future periods when they are incurred. The fair value of any restructuring liabilities recognized by Acquiror Company on the acquisition date are included as part of Target Company's total liabilities for the calculation of transaction goodwill.

THE TREATMENT OF RESTRUCTURING LIABILITIES IS CHANGING

The Financial Accounting Standards Board (FASB) is reviewing the treatment of restructuring liabilities as part of the business combinations project. To date, FASB has tentatively decided that acquirers should not recognize restructuring liabilities for planned plant closures or personnel terminations on the acquisition date but to apply the same principles as in FAS146 of recognizing liabilities only when they incur an actual obligation. However, if Target Company had already incurred a liability for restructuring costs, then Acquiror Company assumes that liability along with any others and records them on the transaction date at their fair value. FASB's tentative decisions do not change current accounting until they are incorporated into Financial Accounting Standards through a formal consensus process. When you analyze M&A transactions involving restructuring costs, check the status of FASB's decisions with your accounting advisor.

CHAPTER SUMMARY

Restructuring charges, while not formally defined in authoritative accounting literature, are defined by inference falling into three general categories:

- One-time employee termination benefits
- Contract termination costs
- Other associated costs

The fundamental approach is to recognize the fair value of future payments, discounted to the recognition date using the credit-adjusted risk-free rate and then to recognize accretion expense in each period until the liability is settled.

The recognition rules for employee one-time termination benefits are slightly more intricate when the employees are expected to render service beyond the minimum retention period. In that event, the portion of the one-time termination benefit attributable to the expected future service is discounted to the termination date (the ending date of the minimum retention period), and that value is recognized ratably over the future service period. Accretion expense is only recognized in the periods after the termination date.

IAS accounting is similar to U.S. GAAP with a few notable exceptions. Under IAS employee termination benefits may not benefit future periods and are immediately recognized to expense. U.S. GAAP only allows recognition of restructuring liabilities for present obligations (except in the case of restructurings associated with business combinations), but IAS also allows recognition of restructuring provisions (liabilities) based on constructive obligations. The difference between a present and constructive obligation is that there is usually no reasonable alternative to a present obligation, whereas firms may have reasonable alternatives to constructive obligations. Another difference between the U.S. GAAP and IAS approaches to restructuring obligations is that IAS does not discount current obligations to fair value but recognizes the settlement amount for liabilities expected to settle within 12 months.

The recognition criteria for restructuring charges planned in business combinations are very similar to those used by IAS in that U.S. GAAP currently allows recognition of restructuring liabilities on the acquisition date based on the acquiring company's announced restructuring plan. FASB has already stated their intent to change this as part of the Business Combinations Project to be consistent with the present obligation approach.

CHAPTER 11

Discontinued Operations

INTRODUCTION

When firms report the results of discontinued operations, the impact is often ignored because the results appear "below the line" or after the results of continuing earnings. Consequently there is an incentive for firms to classify the results of loss-generating operations as discontinued operations and conversely, to attempt to retain the results of profitable operations as part of continuing earnings as long as possible. At times, this can be a fairly strong incentive because classification of items as either part of continuing operations or as discontinued operations directly impacts earnings-per-share from continuing operations.

Two other factors support discussing discontinued operations. The first is that classification of a disposed activity as either a discontinued operation or a part of continuing operations involves a degree of accounting judgment. The second factor is that the financial accounting standards governing the reporting of discontinued operations changed within the last two years so, while not brand new, are different than many of us learned in business school.

Whenever there is an incentive to aggressively report an item in financial accounting and that item entails a significant degree of accounting judgment, readers and analysts of the financial reports are well served by an attitude that auditors call "professional skepticism."

HOW RESULTS OF DISCONTINUED OPERATIONS IMPACT EARNINGS FROM CONTINUING OPERATIONS

A good starting point for discussing how classification of items as discontinued operations impact earnings-per-share is reviewing the way the income statement is organized. Figure 11-1 shows how firms are required to report Income from continuing operations, Discontinued operations, Extraordinary items, and Changes in accounting principle on their income statements.

U.S. Generally Accepted Accounting Principles (GAAP) requires firms to present income from continuing operations followed by Results of discontinued operations, Extraordinary items, and Effects of changes in accounting principle. I confess to still using a memory aid from my early accounting classes: **DEC**ember comes at the end of the year—so **D**iscontinued operations, **E**xtraordinary items, and **C**hanges in accounting principle appear in that order at the end of the income statement. The reason that the organization of the income statement is important is that many readers tend to discount or ignore whatever comes after Net income from continuing operations.

Example 11-1 explains how classification of the results from a losing business segment can impact the calculation of earning-per-share depending on whether the segment is classified as a component of continuing operations or as a discontinued operation.

FIGURE 11-1

Organization of the Income Statement–U.S. GAAP

Income Statement

Income from continuing operations

+ Revenues
- Expenses
- Income tax expense

Net income from continuing operations

Discontinued operations

+ Income from discontinued operations
+ Gain on disposal of discontinued operations
- Income tax expense on income and gains from discontinued operations
- Loss from discontinued operations
- Loss on disposal of discontinued operations
+ Income tax benefit on losses from discontinued operations

Net income before extraordinary items and changes in accounting principle

Extraordinary items

+ Extraordinary income (net of taxes)
- Extraordinary expense (net of taxes)

Net income before changes in accounting principle

Changes in accounting principle

+/- Cumulative effect of change in accounting principle (net of taxes)

Net income

EXAMPLE **11-1.** Earnings Impact from Classifying a Business Segment's Activities as Discontinued Operations

Disposer Company operates restaurants in the southeastern and northeastern United States. Half of the restaurants in the Northeast U.S. region have been losing money, and Downsizer Company has decided to sell those restaurants. For the full year 20X0, Downsizer realized income from continuing operations of $1,375,000 composed of the southeastern region's contribution of $1,150,000 and the northeastern region's contribution of $225,000. The northeastern region's results are further broken down as: profitable restaurants—$2,500,000, and unprofitable restaurants—($2,275,000). Downsizer Company has one million shares of common stock issued and outstanding for the entire year and no other equity or derivative issues. Figure 11-2 shows Downsizer Company's earnings-per-share calculation with the results of the unprofitable northeastern region restaurants as part of income from continuing operations and the same calculation except with the results of the unprofitable northeastern region restaurants treated as results of discontinued operations.

Referring to Figure 11-2, in column **A,** Downsizer Company's Earnings per common share is calculated by including the results of all three activities: southeastern region, northeastern region I (profitable restaurants), and northeastern region II (unprofitable restaurants). In column **B** the same operating results are used only this time northeastern region II's results are classified as discontinued operations. That results in Downsizer Company's earnings per common share being more than two-and-one-half times greater than the results including northeastern region II.

SOURCES OF CLASSIFICATION BIAS

Because the managers of firms know how readers of the firm's financial statements weight the information, the managers have an incentive to present "good

FIGURE 11·2

Downsizer Company's Earnings-Per-Share Calculations

Downsizer Company - earnings per share calculation

Income Statement	20X0	20X0
Southeastern region	1,150,000	1,150,000
Northeastern region I	2,500,000	2,500,000
Northeastern region II	(2,275,000)	-
Net income from continuing operations	1,375,000	3,650,000
Results of discontinued operations	-	(2,275,000)
Net income	1,375,000	1,375,000
Basic and diluted EPS	(A)	(B)
Earnings per common share	$1.38	$3.65
Discontinued operations	-	(2.28)
Net income	$1.38	$1.38

news" where it is weighted more heavily and "bad news" where it receives less attention. If a firm's managers had no other basis for choosing where they classified items of income other than to present the best possible picture of the firm's results, they would want all of the "good news" to appear as components of the heavily weighted areas like Net income from continuing operations and all of the "bad news" to be in one of lower-weighted classifications like discontinued operations. More simply stated they would classify all of the items of income and gain as part of continuing operations and all of the loss items as part of discontinued operations.

Of course managers do not have that degree of flexibility and so they need to test circumstances against a set of criteria when classifying items as either part of continuing operations or part of discontinued operations. But classification of items also requires management to apply professional judgment, and when analyzing situations requiring judgment it is always appropriate for us to question whether or not other influences, biases, or incentives exist and whether the judgment applied was subordinated to any of those outside forces. Before making that evaluation, we should start with a good understanding of the classification criteria.

CRITERIA FOR CLASSIFYING ITEMS AS DISCONTINUED OPERATIONS

There are two important aspects to reporting discontinued operations. The first aspect relates to the attributes of the operation being discontinued and how the operation fits into the entity both from an operational and also from a financial reporting perspective. This leads to the concept of a component of the entity (what is really being discontinued?). The second is the reporting entity's actual intent concerning the discontinued operation. This aspect looks at how the firm has or will dispose of the operation (form of disposal) and whether it is a true disposal of both the operations and the associated cash flows (functional disposal).

THE OPERATIONS BEING DISCONTINUED— COMPONENT OF A BUSINESS

Treatment of an item as a discontinued operation requires that it be a *component of the entity* which the *Statement of Financial Accounting Standards No. 144, Accounting for the Impairment or Disposal of Long-Lived Assets*, (FAS144) defines as "...comprising operations and cash flows that can be clearly distinguished, operationally and for financial reporting purposes, from the rest of the entity."[1] This definition of a *component of the entity* is more flexible than the previous criterion that required the firm to exit a line of business. A component can be a great number of different things, depending on how individual companies structure their operations and financial reporting units. This also means that what constitutes a component at one firm may or may not constitute a component at other firms.

DISPOSAL CRITERIA

FAS144 requires that for a component of an entity to be classified as a discontinued operation, it must first be either:

- Already disposed of
- Classified by the entity as "held for sale"

This establishes management's intent concerning the asset or component being disposed. Either it already has disposed of the component or undertaken a series of actions that, even though the firm still holds the component for sale, convincingly conveys to outsiders management's intent to dispose of the asset or component.

Methods of Disposal

Firms generally dispose of components using one of four methods:

- Sales to third parties either wholesale or piecemeal
- Abandonment or cease-use
- Exchanges for other productive assets
- Distribution or spin-off to owners

The most likely of the four methods to be a cause for concern are abandonments. Sales, exchanges, and distributions all require control of the assets or component to pass away from the firm, but abandonments may be accomplished by the firm simply ceasing to use the assets. This can cause misclassification if, in future periods, the firm repossesses the assets and begins using them again. Now, through an easily accomplished act, the firm has changed an abandoned asset into a temporarily idled one, and temporary idling an asset does not qualify for treatment as a disposal.

Assets Held for Sale

The second category is assets that the firm intends to dispose of that are held for sale. Because this is conditioned on management's intentions, FAS144 requires the assets or component to meet six tests to determine if it is truly being held for sale.

1. Management both has the authority to and commits to a plan to dispose of (sell) the component.
2. The component has to be ready to be sold at the time it is recognized as "held-for-sale."
3. The firm has to be actively looking for someone to buy the component and is performing any other actions necessary for the component to be sold.
4. Management has to both believe that someone is willing to buy the component and that the sale can be completed within a year.

5. The firm is asking a price that represents the fair value of the component.

6. It is very unlikely that management is going to change its mind about selling the component.

Disposal In-Fact

To account for a component as a discontinued operation the firm must either have already disposed of the component or meet the criteria for classifying the component as being held for sale. Beyond that are two important additional criteria that the firm must satisfy that determine whether or not the firm has functionally discontinued the operation. The first is that the disposal transaction actually eliminated (or will eliminate after the component is sold) the operations and cash flows of the component. Examples 11-2 and 11-3 are adapted from FAS144 and present some good insights into evaluating this criterion.

EXAMPLE 11-2. Discontinued Operations—Eliminating Operations and Cash Flows[2]

Disposer Company is an operator of restaurants in the northeastern United States and distinguishes the operations and cash flows, operationally and for financial reporting purposes, at the individual restaurant level. Consequently each restaurant is a component of Disposer Company. Based on Disposer Company's strategic plan, the firm's management decides to sell one-half of its restaurants for an unspecified amount of cash and to receive a stream of residual franchise income based on each individual restaurant's revenues. The components are properly classified as held for sale but do not meet the reporting requirements for discontinued operations because the cash flows of the components are not entirely eliminated from Disposer Company's financial accounting results.

EXAMPLE 11-3. Discontinued Operations—Eliminating Operations and Cash Flows

Disposer Company also operates retail stores in the southern United States and distinguishes the operations and cash flows, operationally and for financial reporting purposes, at the individual store level. Consequently each store is a component of Disposer Company. Based on Disposer Company's marketing plan, the firm's management decides to close and sell two of its Atlanta stores and open a new Atlanta superstore. The superstore would continue selling the same products as the current stores but would add home improvement and lawn and garden products.

Even though the stores, as components of Disposer Company, are sold, they do not meet the reporting requirements for discontinued operations because their operations and cash flows are not entirely eliminated from Disposer Company's financial accounting results (simply moved to the superstore).

The second requirement is for the firm to no longer have significant continuing involvement in the component's operation. Continuing involvement in operations can come in the form of contracts, operating agreements, or restrictions on the terms of sale. Example 11-4 postulates one of the many different types of arrangements where firms can dispose of components but still have significant continuing involvement in the component's operations.

EXAMPLE 11-4. Significant Continuing Involvement

Disposer Company is an electric power utility that owns a generating plant and a distribution system. The plant and the distribution system each meet the definition of a component because their operations and cash flows are clearly distinguished for both operational and financial reporting purposes. Disposer sells the generating plant to Investor Company and coincidentally enters into an agreement to operate the plant. Although it will purchase electricity from Investor Company's generating plant at market rates, Disposer Company's sales agreement allows it to sell electricity to meet its own needs before selling to other buyers.

Even though Disposer Company sold the generating plant and eliminated its cash flows and operations, it still maintains a significant involvement in the operations of the generating plant and does not meet the requirements to recognize its disposal as a discontinued operation.

INTERNATIONAL ACCOUNTING TREATMENT OF DISCONTINUED OPERATIONS

International Accounting Standards (IAS) are similar to U.S. GAAP regarding accounting for discontinued operations, but there are a few important differences. One difference that is apparent but not significant is that *International Accounting Standard IAS 35, Discontinuing Operations* (IAS35), refers to discontinued operations as discontinuing operations to emphasize that the classification is made at the beginning of the disposal process and not near the end, as one may infer from discontinued.

Comparing Discontinued Operations

The primary difference between IAS and U.S. GAAP regarding the operation being discontinued is that IAS requires the discontinued operation to constitute a major line of business or geographical operation. U.S. GAAP allows classification of a more liberal range of operations or components being governed only by the ability of Disposer Company to clearly distinguish the operations and cash flows of the component for operational and financial accounting purposes. Example 11-5 illustrates differences between the U.S. GAAP and IAS approaches to classifying discontinued operations.

EXAMPLE 11-5. Discontinued Operations—Comparing Classification under U.S. GAAP and IAS

Disposer Company is an operator of restaurants in the continental United States and distinguishes the operations and cash flows, operationally and for financial reporting purposes, at the individual restaurant level. U.S. GAAP allows Disposer Company to treat each individual restaurant as a component eligible for classification as discontinued operations. IAS prohibits allowing a single restaurant to be classified as a discontinuing operation and instead looks for a more significant part of Disposer Company like a separate line of business or geographical segment, or in this example, the entire Northeast United States restaurant segment. The difference here is all of the restaurants in the northeastern United States versus one of the restaurants in the northeastern United States.

Comparing Recognition Criteria

The second principal difference between U.S. GAAP and IAS relates to the criteria for recognizing a discontinued (discontinuing) operation. Both accounting standards organizations permit recognition when Disposer Company enters into a binding sale agreement. The area differing between U.S. GAAP and IAS is when Disposer Company is allowed to recognize an activity it is planning to dispose of as a discontinued or discontinuing operation. U.S. GAAP requires Disposer Company to first classify the component as a held for sale activity by meeting each of the six criteria of FAS144. IAS35 requires instead of the six specific criteria of FAS144 only that "...the enterprise's (Disposer Company's) board of directors or similar governing body has both (i) approved a detailed, formal plan for the discontinuance and (ii) made an announcement of the plan."[3]

CHAPTER SUMMARY

Managers of firms often have incentives to show the best possible results from continuing operations. Results of continuing operations are often considered by equity investors as a better metric for assessing a firm's economic condition because it is viewed as being a "cleaner" indicator of the firm's expected future performance than net income. That is because net income may contain items that are not expected to occur in future periods, such as the results of discontinued operations, extraordinary gains and losses, and the impact of changes in accounting principles.

When events occur where it is not entirely clear whether a specific transaction should be accounted for as a discontinued operation, it is decided by the professional judgment of the firm's management. If the classification of the operation being disposed of is debatable and it is operating at a loss, then management may be biased to classify it as a discontinued operation and eliminate the negative impact on income from continuing operations. Similarly, if the operation is profitable, then management may be biased to retain it as part of the firm's continuing operations to benefit the results of continuing operations. As analysts it is necessary to view disposal transactions skeptically regarding the impact of classification either as discontinued operations or as part of continuing operations on both income from continuing operations and cash flows from continuing operations.

Companies are able to dispose of operations in one of four ways, through:

- Sales to third parties either wholesale or piecemeal.
- Abandonment or cease-use.
- Exchanges for other productive assets.
- Distribution or spin-off to owners.

This is true both under U.S. GAAP and IAS.

U.S. GAAP also allows companies to classify its operations as held for sale if the circumstances meet all six of the following criteria:

1. Management both has the authority to and commits to a plan to dispose of (sell) the assets.
2. The component has to be ready to be sold at the time it is recognized as "held-for-sale."
3. The firm has to be actively looking for someone to buy the component and is performing any other actions necessary for the component to be sold.
4. Management has to both believe that someone is willing to buy the component and that the sale can be completed within a year.
5. The firm is asking a price that represents the fair value of the component.
6. It is very unlikely that management is going to change its mind about selling the component.

IAS requirements are not as detailed as U.S. GAAP and allow enterprises to classify operations as discontinuing operations after their board of directors (or governing body) has:

- Approved a detailed, formal discontinuance plan
- Announced the plan

CHAPTER 12

Net Operating Loss Deductions

INTRODUCTION

Firms that generate operating losses can often use those losses to offset future (or sometimes past) taxable income. Offsets of taxable income equate to cash in the periods that the tax refunds are realized. The chapter begins by describing the two methods available for firms to utilize their net operating losses (NOLs) and then continues to look at how NOL use is limited by time or in certain M&A scenarios. Finally we look at the relationship between NOLs, deferred taxes, and financial reporting and how to capture the intricacies of those relationships in projection and valuation models.

NET OPERATING LOSS DEDUCTIONS

For financial accounting purposes, companies having a net operating loss (NOL) in any reporting period may recognize a book income tax benefit in that reporting period. However, under current U.S. tax law, companies having a net operating loss (NOL) in any tax year do not receive an immediate tax benefit but, instead, may use the loss as a deduction that reduces their taxable income in other tax years. The Internal Revenue Code (IRC) allows two different schemes for applying the deduction. The first is called "carryback," where losses in the current accounting period are carried back to offset earnings from prior periods. The second is "carryforward," where losses from the current period carry forward to reduce taxable income in future periods.

Net Operating Loss Carryback

The default scheme is the NOL carryback, illustrated in Figure 12-1. This approach uses the net operating losses (NOLs) realized in the current period to offset any

FIGURE 12·1

Default Net Operating Loss Carryback Scheme

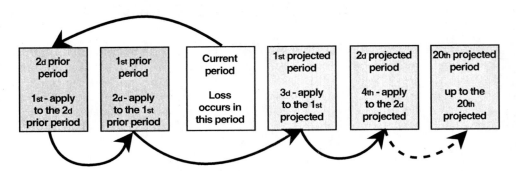

taxable income in the second prior period, resulting in an income tax refund in the current period. If, after reducing the second prior period's taxable income to zero, an NOL still remains, then it is applied to the first prior year. If there was also taxable income in that period, the NOL then reduces that income, also resulting in a refund in the current period. If, after reducing taxable income to zero in the two years preceding the current year, any portion of the NOL still remains unused, that portion is carried forward to offset future taxable income for up to 20 years.

EXAMPLE 12-1. Taxpayer Company Has the Following Historical and Projected Operating Results

	2d prior 20X0	1st prior 20X1	current 20X2	1st proj. 20X3
Taxable income (loss)	1,000.0	500.0	(1,800.0)	5,000.0
Tax rate	30.0%	30.0%	0.0%	40.0%
Cash taxes before NOL carryback	300.0	150.0	0.0	2,000.0
Cash effects of NOL carryback	-	-	(450.0)	(120.0)
Cash taxes after NOL carryback	300.0	150.0	(450.0)	1,880.0
Present value (PV) of tax savings (10% discount rate)			559.1	

Example 12-1 illustrates the use of NOL carrybacks to offset prior period taxable income to generate tax refunds in the current period, 20X2. Taxpayer Company's 1800 net operating loss occurring in 20X2 carries back to 20X0, reduces 20X0 taxable income from 1000 to 0, and results in a tax refund of (1000 × 30%) = 300 in 20X2. After reducing 20X0 earnings to 0, the remaining (1800 − 1000) = 800 of the NOL carries forward to the 1st prior year, 20X1. The NOL applied against 20X1 taxable income reduces it from 500 to 0 and results in the realization of a tax refund of (500 × 30%) = 150 in 20X2. Because there is (800 −500) = 300 of NOL remaining after reducing prior periods income to 0, that unused amount becomes an NOL carryforward that can be used to reduce taxable income in one or more of the next 20 future periods. If the projected earnings are correct, the remaining 300 of NOLs reduce Taxpayer Company's 20X3 taxable earnings to (5000 – 300) = 4700, resulting in a (300 × 40%) = 120 tax savings in 20X3. To reflect the expected future tax benefit, Taxpayer Company records a deferred tax asset of 120 in 20X2. In 20X3, when the tax savings is actually realized by reducing the cash income tax expense, the 120 deferred tax asset is credited and cash is debited for the same amount.

Effects of Post-September 11th Legislation on the Use of NOLs

The Job Creation and Worker Assistance Act of 2000 (JCWWA-2002) modified the rules concerning the use of NOLs to provide additional economic stimulus aimed at off-setting the effects of September 11th. Briefly, under the act, NOLs arising in either 2001 or 2002 may be carried back to the *five* previous tax years instead of the normal two previous tax years. The use of the longer carryback period is made optional, and companies are free to simply choose to continue using the existing rules. (See Figure 12-2.)

Net Operating Loss Carryback Waiver

The second, or alternate scheme, can be viewed as being the same as previously described, but without carryback. Under the alternate scheme, companies must specifically elect to forgo carryback of NOLs to offset prior period earnings. Instead, the NOLs are only used to offset earnings in future periods. The method elected by the company will generally be based on the marginal tax rates in the carryback and carryforward periods and the time-value of money. The decision to carryback or to only carryforward is made for the NOL arising from any single tax year, and is decided independently of the decisions for NOLs arising from other tax years.

FIGURE 12-2

Net Operating Loss Carryforward Scheme

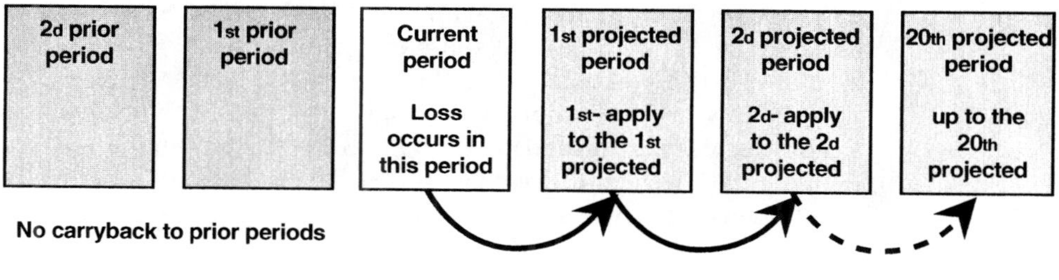

EXAMPLE 12-2. Taxpayer Company has the Following Historical and Projected Operating Results

	2ᵈ prior 20X0	1ˢᵗ prior 20X1	current 20X2	1ˢᵗ proj. 20X3
Taxable income (loss)	1,000.0	500.0	(1,800.0)	5,000.0
Tax rate	30.0%	30.0%	0.0%	40.0%
Cash taxes before NOL carryforward	300.0	150.0	0.0	2,000.0
Cash effects of NOL carryforward	-	-	-	(720.0)
Cash taxes after NOL carryforward	300.0	150.0	0.0	1,280.0
Present value (PV) of tax savings (10% discount rate)			654.5	

In the previous example, Example 12-1, Taxpayer Company used the carryback approach resulting in a 20X2 tax refund of 450 and future tax savings having a present value of 109.1 (120 / (1 + assumed discount rate of 10%) meaning the 20X2 NOL has a present value of (450.0 + 109.1) = 559.1. If Taxpayer Company instead chooses to use the carryforward only method, as shown in Example 12-2, the present value of the tax savings would be 1800 × 40% = 720/(1 + 10% assumed discount rate) = 654.5. In this specific case, the difference between the past and future tax rates created a savings larger than the time value of money lost by waiting until 20X3 to receive the refund.

OTHER TAX CONSIDERATIONS RELATING TO NOLS

Beyond this general explanation of the treatment of net operating losses are a number of other related aspects of taxation that must be considered on a "facts and circumstances" basis. These include but are not limited to:

- Treatment of dividends received by corporate taxpayers
- Effect of capital loss carryovers and tax credits
- Effect of AMT NOLs and credit carryforwards
- Specified liability losses

M&A CONSIDERATIONS RELATING TO NOLS

Section 382 of the Internal Revenue Code limits the use of NOL carryforwards following an ownership change. We normally associate an ownership change with a change-of-control transaction and the IRC defines a corporate ownership change as occurring if any 5-percent shareholder increases his/her ownership by 50 percent over his/her minimum position.

Following an ownership change, the use of NOL carryforwards in each future tax year is limited to the value of the company's stock, just before the ownership change, multiplied by the long-term tax-exempt rate (currently just less than 5 percent). There must also be a continuity of the business enterprise for at least two years.

EXAMPLE 12-3. Limits on the Use of the Target Company's NOLs Following an Acquisition

Acquiror Company buys all the stock of Target Company for 1000. Target Company has NOLs in the amount of 300, and the long-term tax-exempt rate is 5 percent. The NOL deduction that is allowed postacquisition Acquiror Company from Target Company's NOL carryforwards in each year following the acquisition is limited to (1000 × 5%) = 50 until they are either completely utilized or until they expire.

The long-term tax-exempt rate is the highest of the adjusted Federal long-term tax-exempt rates in effect for any month in the three-calendar-month period ending with the calendar month in which the ownership change date occurs[1]. They are published in the Internal Revenue Service (IRS) monthly Revenue Rulings, which are available on the IRS Web site, *www.irs.gov.*

NOL EFFECTS ON FINANCIAL (GAAP) REPORTING

A company having net operating losses in the current period expects to realize a reduction in income taxes payable approximately equal to the amount of the loss deduction times the marginal tax rate. For financial reporting purposes, the effect on taxes payable should be recognized in the current year. This creates temporary differences because the cash flow arising from the same event occurs in different financial reporting and tax periods. Because the company expects to recover the tax benefit of the net operating tax loss in the future, it records a deferred tax asset in the current period. Note in the following examples the difference between the accounting for financial reporting purposes (book accounting) and tax purposes (tax accounting).

EXAMPLE 12-4. Comparison of Book and Tax Accounting for NOLs

Taxpayer Company has 20X0 revenues in the current period of 5000, expenses of 6000, and a marginal tax rate of 40 percent. Taxpayer Company waives carryback, electing to carry-forward all of its NOLs. In 20X1, Taxpayer Company has taxable income of 2000.

20X0	Book Accounting		Tax Accounting
Revenues	5,000.0	Revenues	5,000.0
Expenses	(6,000.0)	Expenses	(6,000.0)
Earnings before taxes	(1,000.0)	Net operating loss	(1,000.0)
Income tax benefit @ 40%	400.0	Taxes payable	0.0
Net income	(600.0)	NOL carryforward	1,000.0

Taxpayer Company funds a deferred tax asset for the temporary timing difference (the 400 refund is expected in the future). This is a noncash transaction because no refund was actually received and no cash was used for funding the deferred tax asset account.

dr: Deferred tax asset   400.0
    cr: Income tax benefit   400.0
memo: To record the deferred tax effect of the current period net operating loss

In 20X1, the next reporting period, Taxpayer Company receives the tax refund. The calculation of book income tax expense is not affected, but income taxes payable (cash taxes) and the deferred tax asset are reduced by the amount of the NOL carryforward used times the marginal tax rate.

20X1	Book accounting		Tax accounting
Revenues	6,000.0	Gross income	2,000.0
Expenses	(4,000.0)	NOL carry forward	(1,000.0)
Earnings before taxes	2,000.0	Taxable income	1000.0
Income tax expense	800.0	Taxes payable	400.0
Net income	1,200.0		

The entry for the 800 book income tax expense reflects paying 400 in cash taxes and reducing the deferred tax asset by the 400 tax reduction relating to the NOL carryforward in 20X1. Note that the reduction on 20X1 cash taxes has no effect on Taxpayer Company's book net income or earnings per share (EPS).

dr:	Income tax expense	800.0	
	cr: Cash		400.0
	cr: Deferred tax asset		400.0
memo:	To record the deferred tax effect of the net operating loss carryforward		

Deferred Tax Assets Associated with NOL Carryforwards

Companies fund a deferred tax asset in cases where the company expects to realize a future tax benefit from the loss carryforward. If the company believes that, more likely than not,[2] future income will be insufficient to allow realizing the full tax benefit, it may decide to fund the deferred tax asset and then simultaneously recognize a valuation allowance account (contra-asset) for the tax benefit it will not realize. This has the effect of eliminating the deferred tax asset because the deferred asset *net* of the valuation account is generally presented on the balance sheet. The notes to the financial statement contain the details of the accounts.

EXAMPLE 12-5. Deferred Tax Asset Valuation Accounts

In 20X0, Taxpayer Company reported an accumulated 1.18-billion-dollar net operating loss but considered that the realization of any future tax benefit was so uncertain that it provided a valuation allowance offsetting the full amount of the associated 451-million-dollar deferred tax asset. Consequently, Taxpayer Company presented a net deferred tax asset of zero on its 20X0 consolidated balance sheet.

Considerations for NOLs in M&A Transactions

If the target in an acquisition has NOL carryforwards and an associated deferred tax asset, the asset may need to be revalued (either by writing it down or by recognizing a valuation allowance account) at the time of the transaction. This arises from the IRC Section 382 limitations on the uses of target NOL carryforwards following an ownership change. The deferred tax asset is written down to reflect the expected future tax benefit after considering the consequences of the IRC Section 382 limitations.

EXAMPLE 12-6. Treatment of deferred tax assets related to target NOLs in an acquisition

On 31-Dec-20X1, Acquiror Company acquires 100 percent of the stock of Target Company for 100 in cash. Prior to the transaction, Target Co. has 50 of NOLs expiring in five years and an associated deferred tax asset of 20. Assume that both Acquiror Company and Target Company use a 40-percent tax rate. The long-term tax-exempt rate is 5 percent, and IRC Section 382 limits the total expected future tax benefit of Target Company's NOL carryforwards to:

$$100 \times 5\% = 5 \text{ deduction} \times 40\% = 2 \text{ tax benefit per year} \times 5 \text{ years}$$
$$= 10 \text{ total expected tax benefit}$$

The deferred tax asset balance sheet account should be reduced by the difference between the preacquisition expected tax benefit and the postacquisition expected tax benefit $(20 - 10) = 10$ when recording the fair value of Target Company on the transaction date.

VALUATION CONSIDERATIONS

When valuing companies having NOL carryforwards, it is often easier to find the present value of the tax shield of the NOL carryforwards separately. This is then added to the present value of the firm calculated without the effects of NOL carryforwards. There are three principal advantages to this approach. The first is alleviating the need to find the earnings before interest and taxes (EBIT) tax rate that correctly reflects the effects of the NOL carryforwards. Secondly, is providing a clearer valuation of the NOL carryforward benefits if they extend beyond the explicit forecast period (i.e., a five-year forecast but NOLs that will require 10 years to recover). Thirdly, is allowing the tax benefits to be valued using a discount rate different than the cost of capital. Acquirors often consider these flows to be less volatile (in some cases almost debtlike) than other free cash flows. Quite commonly, a lower discount rate is used, sometimes as low as the after-tax cost of debt, depending on the probability of realizing the future benefits of the NOLS.

EXAMPLE 12-7. Discount Rate for Valuing NOL Carryforwards

Assume the same facts and results as in Example 12-6 and that Acquiror Company's deduction for Target Company's existing NOLs is expected to be limited to five in each future period.

CASE 1: HIGHLY CERTAIN RECOVERY OF TARGET COMPANY'S NOLS

Following the acquisition of Target Company by Acquiror Company, combined Acquiror-Target Company has projected taxable income of 500 in each of the projected periods following the acquisition, 20X1 through 20X5. Taxable income would have to vary by 495 to make the benefit of the allowed NOL deduction of five to be unrealizable. Realization of the tax benefit of the NOL is highly certain, and it should be valued at a lower discount rate than the firm's other cash flows.

CASE 2: LESS CERTAIN RECOVERY OF TARGET COMPANY'S NOLS

Following the acquisition of Target Company by Acquiror Company, combined Acquiror-Target Company has projected taxable income of five in each of the projected periods following the acquisition, 20X1 through 20X5. Any negative variation in projected taxable income would make some of the benefit of the allowed NOL deduction of five to be unrealizable. Realization of the tax benefit of the NOL is only as certain as projected earnings, and it should be valued at the same discount rate as the firm's other cash flows.

MODELING NOL CARRYBACKS AND CARRYFORWARDS

Incorporating NOLs into a projection/valuation model can be relatively intricate due to two principal factors. The first is that the firm can elect to either carry the NOL back to prior periods and then apply any unused amount as a carryforward in future periods or only carry the NOL forward and apply it to offset income in future periods. The second factor potentially increasing the complexity of the financial modeling is that the firm may make a different election for the NOL occurring in any tax year. For example, the firm may apply the 20X0 NOL against prior period earnings before applying any unused portion against future earnings (the default carryback scheme) and then elect to apply the 20X1 NOL only to offset future earnings without first using it for carryback. The further complicating effects of the longer carryback periods allowed under the *Worker Assistance and Job Creation Act of 2002* (the Act), mentioned earlier, may generally be ignored since the Act only applies to net operating losses incurred in tax years 2001 and 2002. Because the majority of firms incurring NOLs in 2002 have already reported, there is no need to attempt to forecast their treatment of their 2002 NOLs. However, the approach used would be similar to that described except that the losses apply back for five instead of the normal two prior periods.

Approach to Modeling Net Operating Losses

A financial model reflecting the effects of net operating loss carrybacks and carryforwards can be cumbersome to construct but not particularly difficult if several important points are considered to incorporate the methodology dictated by the tax regulations. As shown in Figure 12-3, a step-by-step approach requires first identifying, for the period of interest, whether taxable income or a tax loss exists.

Income—Carryforwards Applied in a Taxable Income Period

Reduce the current period's taxable income by the amount of any NOL carryforwards from prior periods beginning with the oldest first. When modeling this, it is important to apply the "oldest" carryforwards, meaning those from the earliest periods first because carryforwards expire after 20 years if they are unused. Carry forward any unused portions of unexpired NOLs to be applied in the next projected period.

FIGURE12-3

Net Operating Loss Flowchart

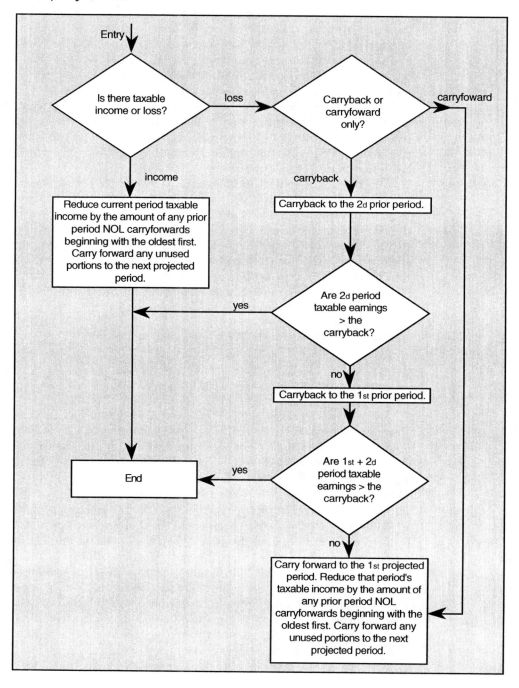

Loss—Carryback Method in a Net Operating Loss Period

The second condition the firm may face is that of a projected or anticipated loss. If a firm has a taxable loss, then it must decide whether it should first carry the loss back and apply it against prior period taxable income or simply carry the entire loss forward. By default NOLs carry back and apply against prior period taxable earnings (if any) in the second prior period. The amount of earnings offset in that period by the NOL is multiplied by the appropriate tax rate and that product is recognized as a tax benefit, a cash tax refund in the loss period.

If the second prior period's earnings are greater than the NOL, then the NOL is fully offset and the process ends. If, instead, the NOL is greater than the second prior period earnings, the remainder is applied against the first prior period's earnings. Again, a cash tax benefit is recognized for the product of the earnings offset in that period times the tax rate.

If the sum of second and first prior period earnings is greater than the NOL, then the NOL is fully applied and the process now ends. If, on the other hand, the NOL is greater than the sum of both the second and first prior period's earnings, the amount remaining is carried forward and applied against earnings in the projected periods. Because no cash is recognized in the current period for the carryforward amount, a deferred tax asset equal to the carryforward amount times the enacted tax rate is recognized instead. Example 12-8 illustrates the use of an NOL to offset prior period taxable income with the remainder being carried forward to projected periods.

EXAMPLE 12-8. Modeling NOL Carryback to Prior Periods

Taxpayer Company realizes a 1250 net operating loss in tax year 20X3. Previous period taxable incomes were 430 in 20X1 and 520 in 20X2. Taxpayer Company's projected earnings are 110 in 20X4, 270 in 20X5 and a 500 loss in 20X6. A 40-percent tax rate applies.

Figure 12-4 shows the modeling for the net operating loss section of Taxpayer Company's income statement. It is possible, in practice, to collapse some of the elements shown to make the model more concise. For purposes of conceptual clarity, this example shows more row-by-row detail than is actually necessary. To model the effects of the 20X3 NOL, the loss is first applied against the earliest period's (20X1) taxable earnings of 430 and the remainder of $(1250 - 430) = 820$ are next applied against the first prior period's (20X2) taxable earnings of 520. This remainder of $(820 - 520) = 300$ is carried forward to the first projected period, 20X4.

In projected periods, the taxable earnings are first reduced by prior period carryforwards, beginning with the oldest and working, in order, to the most recent. In Figure 12-4, the 20X4 taxable earnings of 110 are less than the 300 NOL carryforward, so taxable earnings are reduced to zero, the carryforward is reduced to $(300 - 110) = 190$, and that amount carries forward into 20X5 as the NOL carryforward from *two* periods earlier. In 20X5, taxable earnings of 270 are greater than the NOL carryforward of 190 and taxable income for 20X5 is reduced to $(270 - 190) = 80$ and the NOL carryforward is exhausted.

FIGURE 12-4

Mechanics of Modeling NOL Carryback and Carryforward

Taxpayer's Financial Statements

Income Statement	20X1	20X2	20X3	20X4	20X5	20X6
Earnings before taxes	430.0	520.0	(1,250.0)	110.0	270.0	(500.0)
Net operating loss calculations - Carryforward						
NOL carryforward from 20 periods earlier	-	-	-	-	-	-
Carryforward used in current period	-	-	-	-	-	-
NOL carryforward remaining	-	-	-	-	-	-
(Carryforwards from periods 3 through 19 are treated similarly)						
NOL carryforward from 2 periods earlier	-	-	-	-	190.0	0.0
Carryforward used in current period	-	-	-	-	190.0	-
NOL carryforward remaining	-	-	-	-	0.0	0.0
NOL carryforward from last period	-	-	-	300.0	0.0	0.0
Carryforward used in current period	-	-	-	110.0	-	-
NOL carryforward remaining	-	-	-	190.0	0.0	0.0
NOLs used in the current period	-	-	-	110.0	190.0	-
Earnings before taxes after prior period carryforward	430.0	520.0	(1,250.0)	0.0	80.0	(500.0)
Net operating loss calculations - Carryback						
NOLs created this period	-	-	1,250.0	0.0	0.0	500.0
Carryback to 2d prior year	-	-	430.0	0.0	0.0	0.0
Current period NOLs remaining	-	-	820.0	0.0	0.0	500.0
Carryback to 1st prior year	-	-	520.0	0.0	0.0	80.0
Current period NOLs remaining	-	-	300.0	0.0	0.0	420.0

In 20X6 Taxpayer Company realizes a net operating loss of 500. Because taxable earnings in the second prior period (20X4) have already been reduced to zero by the NOL carryforward from 20X3, the NOL can only be carried back to the first prior period, 20X5, where it can be applied against the 80 of taxable income remaining after reduction by the carryforward from 20X3. The unapplied portion of the 20X6 NOL, (500 − 80) = 420 is carried forward to periods 20X7 and beyond.

Figure 12-5 shows the calculation of the cash and deferred tax items and the deferred tax asset account. Cash taxes are the product of earnings before taxes after prior period carryforwards and the tax rate. In the first period, 20X1, cash taxes are calculated as $(430 \times 40\%) = 172$.

A deferred tax expense or benefit is recorded to reflect changes in the future tax benefit associated with the NOL carryforwards. As new carryforwards are realized, any portion remaining after carrying them back against prior period earnings appear on the current period NOL's remaining line, which is multiplied by the enacted tax rate to determine the amount of the deferred tax benefit. In the last

FIGURE 12·5

Calculating Taxes When Modeling NOL Carryback and Carryforward

Taxpayer's Financial Statements

Income Statement	20X1	20X2	20X3	20X4	20X5	20X6
Earnings before taxes	430.0	520.0	(1,250.0)	110.0	270.0	(500.0)

Net operating loss calculations - Carryforward

	20X1	20X2	20X3	20X4	20X5	20X6
NOL carryforward from 20 periods earlier-			-	-	-	-
Carryforward used in current period	-	-	-	-	-	-
NOL carryforward remaining-			-	-	-	-

(Carryforwards from periods 3 through 19 are treated similarly)

	20X1	20X2	20X3	20X4	20X5	20X6
NOL carryforward from 2 periods earlier-			-	-	190.0	0.0
Carryforward used in current period	-	-	-	-	190.0	-
NOL carryforward remaining-			-	-	0.0	0.0
NOL carryforward from last period	-	-	-	300.0	0.0	0.0
Carryforward used in current period	-	-	-	110.0	-	-
NOL carryforward remaining-			-	190.0	0.0	0.0
NOLs used in the current period	-	-	-	110.0	190.0	-
Earnings before taxes after prior period carryforwards	430.0	520.0	(1,250.0)	0.0	80.0	(500.0)

Net operating loss calculations - Carryback

	20X1	20X2	20X3	20X4	20X5	20X6
NOLs created this period	-	-	1,250.0	0.0	0.0	500.0
Carryback to 2d prior year	-	-	430.0	0.0	0.0	0.0
Current period NOLs remaining	-	-	820.0	0.0	0.0	500.0
Carryback to 1st prior year	-	-	520.0	0.0	0.0	80.0
Current period NOLs remaining	-	-	300.0	0.0	0.0	420.0

Calculation of taxes

	20X1	20X2	20X3	20X4	20X5	20X6
Tax rate	40.0%	40.0%	40.0%	40.0%	40.0%	40.0%
Current income tax expense (benefit) - cash taxes	172.0	208.0	(380.0)	0.0	32.0	(32.0)
Deferred tax expense (benefit)	-	-	(120.0)	44.0	76.0	(168.0)
Income tax expense (benefit) - GAAP taxes	172.0	208.0	(500.0)	44.0	108.0	(200.0)

Balance Sheet	20X1	20X2	20X3	20X4	20X5	20X6
Deferred tax asset - beginning	0.0	0.0	0.0	120.0	76.0	0.0
Deferred tax benefit (expense)	-	-	120.0	(44.0)	(76.0)	168.0
Deferred tax asset - ending	0.0	0.0	120.0	76.0	0.0	168.0

period, 20X6, the current period NOLs remaining of 420 are multiplied by the enacted tax rate of 40 percent to calculate the deferred tax benefit of $(420 \times 40\%) = 168$. In the same period, on the balance sheet, the Deferred tax asset—beginning account balance of zero is increased by the deferred tax benefit of 168 to determine the Deferred tax asset—ending account balance of $(0 + 168) = 168$.

The portion of a period's NOL that is applied as carryback creates a current income tax benefit in the NOL period in the form of a cash tax refund. In 20X3, Taxpayer Company realizes a 1250 loss that is carried back against 20X1 and then 20X2 earnings. The resulting current income tax benefit is the sum of the NOL applied in each of the prior periods multiplied by the tax rate resulting in a cash tax benefit in 20X3 of $(430 + 520 = 950 \times 40\%) = 380$.

In periods such as 20X4, when NOL carryforwards are used to reduce taxable income, the amount of the NOL carryforward applied to reduce cash taxes is recognized as a deferred tax expense. Since 110 of NOLs are used in 20X4, that amount is multiplied by the appropriate tax rate of 40 percent to calculate Taxpayer Company's deferred tax expense of $(110 \times 40\%) = 44$.

Income tax expense for financial reporting purposes, GAAP taxes, is the sum of the current income and deferred tax expenses. In 20X3, GAAP taxes are the sum of the 380 current tax benefit and the 120 deferred tax benefit yielding an income tax benefit of $(380 + 120) = 500$, which appears in the model as negative taxes, indicating that the operating results for the period generate a tax advantage.

CHAPTER SUMMARY

Firms that experience net operating losses generally realize a tax benefit. The benefit is realized in the period that the losses occur if the firm elects to apply the loss against previous earnings or it is realized in future periods if the firm carries the loss forward. Any net operating losses that are not used to offset taxable earnings continue to carry forward to future periods until they are completely offset against taxable earnings or they expire.

In periods when a net operating loss occurs, the provision for taxes (book taxes) appears as negative taxes. Conceptually, negative taxes indicate that a refund is due. Whenever the firm expects to realize the refund in a different period than the NOL, cash and book taxes are reconciled by recognizing a deferred tax asset. When the tax benefit (refund) is realized, the deferred tax asset reverses. If the firm anticipates that the tax benefit will never be realized, due to expiration of the NOL, then the deferred tax asset is eliminated through a valuation account.

When valuing firms with NOLs, the probability of realizing the tax benefit of the NOL drives the value of the NOL. Because of that, it is often beneficial to value the expected cash flows (tax benefits) from the NOLs separately (but not isolated from) the remainder of the firm. This allows selection of a discount rate that reflects the uncertainty of those cash flows.

When a company carrying forward NOLs experiences a change of control, the recoverability of its NOLs is limited to approximately five percent (specifically the long-term tax exempt rate) of the value of the company's stock. This often results in the value of an acquired firm's NOLs being significantly diminished or even eliminated in an acquisition. If the firm is acquired in a deemed asset sale or other taxable transaction, it is possible that the selling company can use some or all of the NOLs to offset the tax burden of the transaction. As we see in the Chapter 14 discussion of IRC Section 338(h)(10) transactions, these cases can create value by shifting the realization of the tax benefit of the NOLs from the future to the present.

CHAPTER 13

Purchase Accounting for Business Combinations

INTRODUCTION

Accounting for business combinations or leveraged buyouts using the purchase method of accounting is mistakenly believed by some to fall only within the responsibilities of M&A analysts. The reality is that the frequency of mergers, acquisitions, and leveraged buyouts makes a solid understanding of this body of knowledge important to credit and equity analysts as well. Fortunately, recent changes to U.S. and Canadian financial accounting rules prescribe that all accounting for business combinations be done using the purchase method of accounting; this eliminates pooling accounting and effectively halves the number of rules that analysts need to remember and apply. The International Accounting Standards Board (IASB) also has a working Business Combinations Project that will very likely converge with U.S. and Canadian standards, making purchase accounting the global norm.

Because the work of the Financial Accounting Standards Board (FASB) and the International Accounting Standards Board (IASB) to revise the accounting standards for business combinations is ongoing, you should pay particular attention to the Binoculars Icon while reading through the text. It alerts you to pending changes to the accounting standards.

The chapter begins by reviewing the conceptual basis underlying purchase accounting. The second section calculates the target company's net identifiable assets using practical examples of purchase price allocation, goodwill calculation, and estimation of deferred tax assets and liabilities. The third part explains the determination of the purchase price, including common questions such as the proper accounting treatment of M&A, debt origination and equity issuance fees, and finally the calculation of transaction goodwill. Lastly we discuss the accretive and dilutive transaction effects on the acquiring company's forward earnings per share (EPS), transaction cash flow effects, and other, less frequently encountered issues, including: "negative goodwill," creation of minority interests, and limitations on purchased net operating losses (NOLs).

PURCHASE ACCOUNTING BASICS

Generally, in a purchase accounting transaction, the purchase price is allocated to each of the assets (and liabilities) being purchased (or assumed) according to their fair value, such that the buyer records each of them at the price paid in the transaction. If the buyer pays more than the fair value of all of the net assets combined, the excess is recorded in an asset account titled Goodwill. Understanding two basic concepts is essential to analyzing transactions using purchase accounting. They are fair value and goodwill.

A third topic reviewed is that of debits and credits. The idea of debits and credits underlies all of financial accounting and is prerequisite to these discussions. However, for those analysts that learned debits and credits mechanistically, I provide a slightly different perspective: debits and credits viewed as a way of understanding cash flows.

The Fair Value Concept

When firms purchase assets they record them on their books at their cost, usually the price that they paid in cash. Over time, most fixed assets are used by the firm to produce revenues, so the firm depreciates, or adjusts downward the book value of the assets to estimate their decrease in value as they are "used up." Some assets that are not consumed in the production of revenues, such as the land a factory is built upon, are not depreciated but remain on the company's books at their purchased or historical cost.

Financial accounting seeks to fairly, yet conservatively, present a firm's position; the firm either keeps recorded values of its fixed assets constant (as in the case of land) or systematically reduces them over the assets' useful lives (as in the case of depreciable or amortizable assets). Sometimes, particularly when a firm has owned a large number of real properties for long periods of time, the firm's assets end up being grossly understated due to appreciation and the effects of inflation. Imagine a company that in the year 1800 purchased a city block in Manhattan or San Francisco for 10,000 dollars and still carries it on its books at its historical cost. Its balance sheet would be understated by tens or maybe hundreds of millions of dollars.

Now imagine that in the present day you are planning to buy that company. Even though its balance sheet reports the value of the property at 10,000 dollars, both you and the seller know the true value is 10 million dollars. Because that really is the true value, you, or anyone else interested in buying the property, would reasonably expect to pay 10 million dollars to acquire it. Ten million dollars represents the market or the fair value of the property. It is the price that two unrelated parties, having different interests, could settle on in what is sometimes called an "arm's length transaction." Here's another way of thinking about this. If the property were sold at an auction attended by everyone interested in buying the property, the auction sale price would represent the true measure of the property's fair value.

The Goodwill Concept

Of course it rarely, if ever, works out that someone pays an amount exactly equaling the sum of the fair values of all of the assets being purchased: The purchase price is almost always higher (the whole is greater than the sum of the parts). The reason for the higher price is that a company is more than just a collection of assets; it is a collection of assets organized to produce a particular product or deliver a specific service. The market values companies as the present value of their expected future cash flows, which is almost always more than the current liquidation value (fair value) of the assets. (Otherwise the owners would realize a greater economic benefit by liquidating the assets and doing nothing, rather than laboring to operate the company.)

Accounting for business combinations does not allow the allocated purchase price for any asset to exceed its fair value: Any excess paid over the fair value of the assets must be accounted for separately. The excess is recorded as goodwill, which is defined as "the excess of the cost of an acquired entity over the net of the amounts assigned to assets acquired and liabilities assumed."[1] Alternatively, goodwill can also be expressed as the excess of the purchase price over the fair value of the net identifiable assets acquired.

Debit and Credit Review

In double-entry accounting, the balance sheet is always kept in balance by making debits equal credits. But debits and credits do not seem to be intuitive concepts for many analysts, so let us think of them in the context of something everyone understands: cash. Rephrasing the original statement, in double-entry accounting, the balance sheet is always kept in balance by making the uses of cash equal the sources of cash. Think of debits as the uses of cash and credits as the sources of cash. Increasing assets uses cash, and so a debit increases assets (debit = use of cash) because we use cash to "buy" the asset. We get cash from borrowing or increasing liabilities, so a credit increases liabilities (credit = source of cash).

At this point someone inevitably asks, "If cash is an asset, how is increasing (debiting) cash on the balance sheet a use of cash?" Think of the assets classified as cash on the balance sheet as being deposits in a checking or savings account, and then think of cash as money in your hand (remember, this whole exercise is conceptual). If you want to increase (debit) your checking account (cash on the balance sheet), you have to *use* the cash that is in your hand (debit = use of cash). Similarly, if you want to have more cash in your hand, you can take an advance on your credit card, increasing (crediting) your personal liability and getting more cash to hold in your hand (credit = source of cash). Whenever we say that uses equal sources, or that debits equal credits, we are saying essentially the same thing.

CALCULATING TARGET COMPANY'S NET IDENTIFIABLE ASSETS

Identifiable assets are the assets separable from the firm either physically or by contractual arrangement. Essentially all of the assets of a firm are identifiable except for goodwill. A company's net identifiable assets are its total assets less goodwill and less the firm's liabilities. Accountants and analysts often approach the calculation of net identifiable assets differently, usually because accountants have direct access to the company's books, whereas analysts often are forced to estimate the balance of some accounts.

The starting point for calculating a target company's net identifiable assets is its balance sheet. One general approach to follow for calculating net identifiable assets is to:

- Eliminate any existing goodwill recorded on the target company's balance sheet.
- Adjust Target Company's assets and liabilities to fair value (by writing them up or down).
- Estimate and record the unrecognized intangible assets that are being purchased.
- Record any unrecognized restructuring charges.
- Recalculate the deferred tax assets and deferred tax liabilities.
- Calculate the identifiable net assets being purchased.

Adjusting Target Company's Balance Sheet

One means of simplifying this task is to reduce the owner's equity accounts into three classes: common equity, preferred equity, and minority interest. Write-ups, write-downs, or eliminations are offset against common equity, and the characteristics of the preferred equity and minority interest are preserved to reflect the facts of the transaction. A second method is ignoring owner's equity altogether when calculating Target Company's net identifiable assets. There is really nothing wrong in using this approach as long as any items of owner's equity that are not being purchased, such as Target Company minority interests or preferred equities, are considered in the final transaction accounting. Figure 13-1 shows the opening balance sheet of Target Company on the transaction date both before making any adjustments and after combining owner's equity accounts and eliminating goodwill. Note that for convenience, the Common equity, Additional paid-in capital and Retained earnings accounts were combined into a single Common equity account and that Target Company's pre-existing Goodwill account was eliminated against the Common equity account.

Adjusting Assets and Liabilities to Fair Value

The next step adjusts Target Company's assets and liabilities to fair value. Technically, this activity is an allocation of the purchase price, so we first check that the

FIGURE 13·1

Target Company's Opening Balance Sheet

Target Company's balance sheet		Adjustments		
Balance Sheet	**Opening**	**Debits**	**Credits**	**Adjusted**
Cash	200.0			200.0
Inventories	300.0			300.0
Accounts receivable	1,000.0			1,000.0
Current deferred tax assets	100.0			100.0
Current assets	1,600.0	0.0	0.0	1,600.0
Property, plant and equipment	3,000.0			3,000.0
Goodwill	700.0		(700.0) b	-
Other intangible assets	2,000.0			2,000.0
Deferred tax assets	400.0			400.0
Total assets	7,700.0	0.0	700.0	7,000.0
Accounts payable	1,100.0			1,100.0
Current portion of long-term debt	1,500.0			1,500.0
Current liabilities	2,600.0	0.0	0.0	2,600.0
Deferred tax liabilities	800.0			800.0
Long-term debt	1,400.0			1,400.0
Total liabilities	4,800.0	0.0	0.0	4,800.0
Minority Interests	100.0			100.0
Preferred equity	200.0			200.0
Common equity	500.0 **b**	700.0	2,100.0 a	1,900.0
Additional paid-in capital	900.0 **a**	900.0		-
Retained earnings	1,200.0 **a**	1,200.0		-
Owner's equity	2,900.0	2,800.0	2,100.0	2,200.0
Owner's equity & liabilities	7,700.0			7,000.0
Total adjustments		2,800.0	2,800.0	

purchase price is greater than the net identifiable assets of the target. The purchase price usually represents a substantial premium over the net identifiable assets, but in the rare cases that it does not, we would need to apply the approach for "negative goodwill" later in this chapter. Staying with the more frequently encountered case of a transaction creating goodwill (because the purchase price is greater than the fair value of the identifiable assets being acquired), our initial task becomes one of estimating the fair values of Target Company's assets and liabilities.

Adjusting the Current Accounts to Fair Value

Recall that current accounts are those assets and liabilities expected to be disposed of or settled within one business cycle. For most industries, within one business cycle means within the next year. Consequently, some balance sheets items, such as deferred taxes and long-term debt, are split between the current or short-term section of the balance sheet and the long-term section. This is done for deferred tax items to show the amount being realized or settled in the next year. Those portions are presented as part of current assets or current liabilities while the remainder stays in long-term assets or long-term liabilities. Similarly, the amount of Target Company's issued debt that is due to be repaid (the principal, not the interest payments) in the next year is moved from the long-term debt section of the balance sheet and presented in the current liability section under the Current portion of long-term debt account. Example 13-1 explains the current portion of long-term debt within the framework of personal finance.

EXAMPLE 13-1. The Current Portion of Long-Term Debt

Assume that you borrow $100,000 from the bank at 5-percent interest to purchase a home using a 30-year mortgage. The bank calculates your monthly loan payment to be $536.82, and in the first year your expected total mortgage payments are ($536.82 × 12 = $6,441.84). The bank also provides you with an amortization schedule indicating that $1,475.37 of your first-year payments is applied to reduce your principal, and the remaining $4,966.47 of your payments is charged as interest expense. At the time the loan is issued to you, you would record it on your "personal balance sheet" as:

dr:	Cash		100,000.00
	cr:	Current portion of long-term debt	1,475.37
		(principal to be repaid in the first year)	
	cr:	Long-term debt (5% 30-year mortgage)	98,524.63
		(100,000.00 – 1,475.37 current portion)	

This requirement for presenting current portions separately is informative for assessing the firm's liquidity and short-term cash flows, but it introduces a level of informational noise when we are using the financial statements for M&A transactions. Adjusting the current accounts and returning the current portions of long-term assets to their parent accounts eliminates the extra noise and simplifies our analysis. Figure 13-2 shows the adjustments to the current accounts returning the current portions of the long-term accounts back to their parent accounts by crediting (debiting) the current portions of assets (liabilities) and debiting (crediting) the underlying long-term accounts by an equal amounts.

Accounts Receivable

Most other current assets are not adjusted and simply brought over at their recorded amounts. There may be exceptions to this general rule, usually associated with accounts receivable and inventories. Companies estimate the amount of their accounts receivable they believe are uncollectible and record that amount as an Allowance for doubtful accounts. Accounts receivable on the balance sheet are shown net of the allowance. If, because of news items, an accountant's reports, or company disclosures, you believe that the firm has not recognized a large enough allowance for

FIGURE 13·2

Target Company's Balance Sheet: Adjusting the Current Accounts

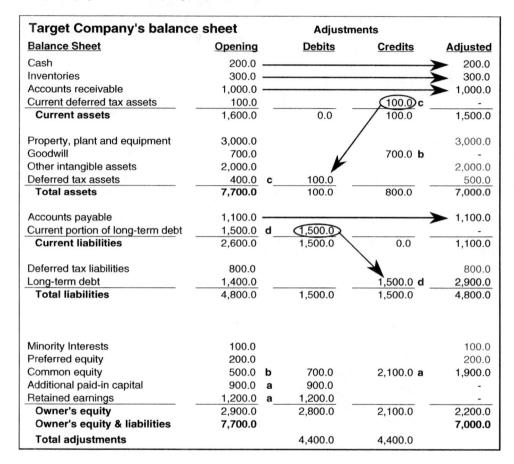

Target Company's balance sheet		Adjustments		
Balance Sheet	Opening	Debits	Credits	Adjusted
Cash	200.0			200.0
Inventories	300.0			300.0
Accounts receivable	1,000.0			1,000.0
Current deferred tax assets	100.0		100.0 c	-
Current assets	1,600.0	0.0	100.0	1,500.0
Property, plant and equipment	3,000.0			3,000.0
Goodwill	700.0		700.0 b	-
Other intangible assets	2,000.0			2,000.0
Deferred tax assets	400.0 c	100.0		500.0
Total assets	7,700.0	100.0	800.0	7,000.0
Accounts payable	1,100.0			1,100.0
Current portion of long-term debt	1,500.0 d	1,500.0		-
Current liabilities	2,600.0	1,500.0	0.0	1,100.0
Deferred tax liabilities	800.0			800.0
Long-term debt	1,400.0		1,500.0 d	2,900.0
Total liabilities	4,800.0	1,500.0	1,500.0	4,800.0
Minority Interests	100.0			100.0
Preferred equity	200.0			200.0
Common equity	500.0 b	700.0	2,100.0 a	1,900.0
Additional paid-in capital	900.0 a	900.0		-
Retained earnings	1,200.0 a	1,200.0		-
Owner's equity	2,900.0	2,800.0	2,100.0	2,200.0
Owner's equity & liabilities	7,700.0			7,000.0
Total adjustments		4,400.0	4,400.0	

doubtful accounts and that even a larger portion of accounts receivable are uncollectible, adjust the Accounts receivable account downward (credit) by the additional amount with an offsetting entry reducing (debiting) the Common equity account.

Inventories

Similar to other current assets, inventories are usually carried over at their recorded value unless one of two situations exists. The first situation arises for companies valuing their inventories using the last-in, first-out (LIFO) instead of the first-in, first-out (FIFO) method. Under the LIFO valuation method, firms assume that the item they bought for inventory today (the last-in) is the next item of inventory they will use or sell (first-out). The FIFO inventory valuation method assumes that the oldest item the firm carries in their inventory (first-in) is the next item they will use or sell (first-out). Under the LIFO valuation method, the inventory balance is usually understated (at least in times of rising prices) because the method assumes that newer, more expensive items are sold first, leaving the older, less expensive items in inventory. Estimating the fair value of the inventory on a FIFO basis requires adjusting the balance sheet Inventory account by the amount of the LIFO reserve. The LIFO reserve, sometimes titled as "adjustment of inventories to a LIFO basis" is disclosed in the inventory footnote to the target's financial statements whenever the target uses the LIFO inventory valuation method. Example 13-2 details the adjustments needed to estimate inventories reported using LIFO valuation to a FIFO basis.

EXAMPLE **13-2. Estimating LIFO Inventories on a FIFO Basis**

Target Company reports its inventories using the LIFO method of inventory valuation. They disclose in the footnotes to their financial statements that the reserve for the LIFO valuation method is 100. Target Company's marginal tax rate is 40 percent. The entries adjusting the reported LIFO inventory to a FIFO valuation basis for analytic purposes are:

dr: Inventory (debited for the LIFO reserve)	100.0	
cr: Deferred tax liability $(100.0 \times 40\%)$		40.0
cr: Common equity $(100.0 \times (1 - 40\%))$		60.0

In periods of falling prices, this adjustment produces opposite results because in those periods, the LIFO valuation method overstates the value of the inventory by assuming the firm uses or sells new, less expensive, first and retains older, more expensive, stock in inventory. Adjusting LIFO-valued inventory to a FIFO valuation basis when prices are falling reduces the carrying amount of the Inventory, the Deferred tax liability and Common equity accounts. In the case of either rising or falling prices, this approach provides the best achievable estimate for the value of the inventory until the firm's accountants provide a more precise estimate based on the results of their detailed audit and valuation of the firm's physical inventory.

A second situation requiring adjustments to the reported inventories is similar to that for accounts receivable; the analyst has knowledge or reason to suspect that the inventories are not fairly stated. This is most likely to occur either in high-tech firms whose inventories tend to become obsolete very quickly or in some older firms that may have accumulated obsolete inventories over a long period of time. In either case, the inventories should be adjusted downward to reflect fair value at the transaction date.

Long-Term Assets

If you are working with the seller, their accountants can provide you with detailed estimates of the fair values of the assets and liabilities. More often than not, you will need to develop your own estimates. Good sources of reference values are recent purchases of similar companies; after you identify comparable transactions, locate the target company's last preacquisition financial statements and the parent's first postacquisition statements for a few transactions. Comparing the two sets of financial statements provides insights into how the reported values of the fixed assets from the pretransaction target statements varied from their fair values reported in the combined company's posttransaction statements.

Estimating the Intangible Asset Write-Up

A second issue addressed by analyzing prior transactions is the recognition of purchased intangible assets. Firms acquire intangible assets in one of two ways; they either purchase them or they create them. Purchased intangible assets are recognized on the company's balance sheet, but self-created intangibles such as client lists, databases, advertising jingles, etc. typically are not recognized. When a company having self-created intangible assets is acquired, the purchaser subsequently recognizes the intangibles that it purchases on its consolidated balance sheet.

Estimating the appropriate amount of the write-ups for these assets is problematic because it varies by industry group and how much time has passed since the target was last acquired or was founded. One common approach is to calculate goodwill as if the transaction included no new intangibles and then to "carve out" a percentage of the goodwill as newly recognized intangible assets. Most M&A practitioners have a sense of an appropriate "carve-out" percentage within their field of specialization, but for transactions where there is little or no experiential basis, research of recent, similar transactions is the best alternative. Again, good data sources include the target company's last preacquisition financial statements and the parent's first postacquisition financial statements for several recent transactions within the same sector. Use the purchase price and target company's balance sheet, fully adjusted except for the intangible asset write-up, to calculate goodwill as if there were no write-up to intangibles. Finally, determine what percentage of that goodwill was recognized as a write-up to intangible assets. Attempt to locate transactions where the target companies were in the same sector and had similar histories and acquisition premia.

Deferred Taxes

Remembering the basic rule for deferred taxes, an excess of the book basis of an asset over its tax basis creates a deferred tax liability. Most acquisitions are stock acquisitions, meaning that the purchaser acquires the stock of the target company. Consequently, the tax bases of the underlying assets are unchanged. This poses our next challenge, estimating the Deferred tax asset and Deferred tax liability accounts. Finding the exact tax bases of the target company's assets is practically never an option. As an alternative, we can make the presumption that the target company's deferred tax assets and liabilities are correctly recorded in its financial statements and adjust these values for the known effects from the transaction.

In the case of asset write-ups, the book basis is increased over the tax basis, creating an additional deferred tax liability. The existing deferred tax liability is adjusted upward to record the effect of the asset write-up. One important exception to this rule occurs when one class of fixed assets being adjusted to fair value is land. Figure 13-3 assumes that the fair value of the fixed assets is 500 higher than the value recorded in Target Company's pretransaction financial statements. On the transaction date, the fixed asset account is adjusted upward by this amount and an additional deferred tax asset of $(500 \times 40\% = 200)$ is recorded. The remaining $(500 - 200 = 300)$ is credited to the combined Common equity account to complete the entry.

Another potentially important effect of the transaction on Target Company's recorded deferred taxes arises from any deferred tax asset recorded by Target Company relating to net operating loss (NOL) carryforwards. The company records a deferred tax asset for the future tax benefit that it expects to realize from offsetting taxable income by the NOL carryforwards. As the future tax benefits occur, the

FIGURE 13-3

Target Company's Balance Sheet: Adjusting the Fixed Asset Account and Deferred Taxes

Target Company's balance sheet		Adjustments		
Balance Sheet	Opening	Debits	Credits	Adjusted
Cash	200.0			200.0
Inventories	300.0			300.0
Accounts receivable	1,000.0			1,000.0
Current deferred tax assets	100.0		100.0 c	-
Current assets	1,600.0	0.0	100.0	1,500.0
Property, plant and equipment	3,000.0 **e**	500.0		3,500.0
Goodwill	700.0		700.0 **b**	-
Other intangible assets	2,000.0			2,000.0
Deferred tax assets	400.0 **c**	100.0		500.0
Total assets	7,700.0	600.0	800.0	7,500.0
Accounts payable	1,100.0			1,100.0
Current portion of long-term debt	1,500.0 **d**	1,500.0		-
Current liabilities	2,600.0	1,500.0	0.0	1,100.0
Deferred tax liabilities	800.0		200.0 **e**	1,000.0
Long-term debt	1,400.0		1,500.0 **d**	2,900.0
Total liabilities	4,800.0	1,500.0	1,700.0	5,000.0
Minority Interests	100.0			100.0
Preferred equity	200.0			200.0
Common equity	500.0 **b**	700.0	2,100 + 300 **a,e**	2,200.0
Additional paid-in capital	900.0 **a**	900.0		-
Retained earnings	1,200.0 **a**	1,200.0		-
Owner's equity	2,900.0	2,800.0	0.0	2,500.0
Owner's equity & liabilities	7,700.0			7,500.0
Total adjustments		4,900.0	4,900.0	

Deferred tax asset account is decreased as a noncash offset to the provision for taxes. When a firm having NOL carryforwards undergoes a change of ownership, such as in an acquisition, the Internal Revenue Code (IRC) limits the rate at which those carryforwards can be utilized in future periods. IRC Section 382 sets the maximum amount of the existing Target Company NOL carryforwards that can be applied in any future period as the long-term tax exempt rate times the stock value on the acquisition date. Example 13-3 calculates the adjustment to Target Company's recorded deferred tax asset resulting from the NOL carryforward limitation following a change of ownership.

EXAMPLE 13-3. Deferred Tax Asset Adjustment from IRC Section 382 Limitations

Target Company currently has 500 in NOL carryforwards expiring in three years. The company expects to offset enough of its taxable income before the end of the three-year period so that it can realize the full tax benefit from the carryforwards. Anticipating the future tax benefit from the NOL carryforwards, Target Company recorded a deferred tax asset of (500 × 40% = 200) as the losses were incurred. Acquiror Company purchases 100 percent of the outstanding Target Company stock for 3000. The long-term tax-exempt rate at the acquisition date was 4.25 percent.

IRC Section 382 limits the utilization of the NOL carryforwards to no more than (3000 × 4.25% = 127.5) in each of the three periods remaining before the NOL carryforwards expire. Acquiror Company can only utilize a total of (127.5 × 3) = 382.5 of Target Company's NOL carryforwards and consequently can only realize a (382.5 × 40%) = 153 tax benefit. At the acquisition date, Acquiror Company would write-down Target Company's existing deferred tax asset of 200 to 153, reflecting the effect of the IRC Section 382 limitation.

dr:	Retained earnings	47.0	
	cr: Deferred tax asset		47.0

IN-PROCESS RESEARCH AND DEVELOPMENT COSTS

U.S. GAAP requires charging the value of in-process research and development assets acquired in a business combination to expense on the transaction date unless they have an alternative future use.[2] As part of the Business Combination Project, FASB tentatively decided to eliminate this requirement and to instead, have firms capitalize acquired in-process research and development assets as assets on the acquisition date. Like other assets, the capitalized research and development assets are tested for impairment in future periods. FASB's decision does not change current accounting for acquired research and development assets until the decision is codified into the financial accounting standards. If you are analyzing a transaction with acquired research and development assets, check the status of this issue with your accounting advisor.

Pension Liabilities

If Target Company sponsors a single-employer defined-benefit pension plan and/or other postretirement benefit plan, then Acquiror Company must recognize a liability (or asset) for the unfunded (or overfunded) portion of the projected benefit obligation (PBO) for defined-benefit pension plans and/or the accumulated postretirement benefit obligation (APBO) for defined-benefit postretirement benefit plans existing on the acquisition date. Note two items here. The first is that if the plans are actually overfunded, then Acquiror Company recognizes a long-term asset (reducing transaction goodwill) instead of a long-term liability (increasing transaction goodwill). The second is that this adjustment should be the net unfunded (or overfunded) amount of the PBO and should eliminate any other pension assets or liabilities on Target Company's balance sheet.

Other Long-Term Liabilities

The fair value of long-term liabilities can be easily determined for issues that trade in the secondary debt market. If Target Company has no publicly traded issues of its own, then the market price of instruments with similar features can be used to determine the fair values of the outstanding debt.

An item that is often overlooked when valuing liabilities being acquired, when the liabilities will remain outstanding after the acquisition, is the effect of the business combination on the credit rating of the instrument. This question was clarified by the Financial Accounting Standards Board (FASB) in July of 2002. At that meeting FASB decided that regarding the purchase method procedures for business combinations that "The fair value of a liability assumed should reflect the credit rating attaching to the liability as a result of the combination."[3] This means that for most business combinations where any target company debt issues are left outstanding, they should be valued at the transaction date using the credit rating they are expected to carry following the acquisition. Example 13-4 describes how the expected change in credit rating affects the fair value of Target Company's liabilities.

> **EXAMPLE 13-4. Effect of Acquiror Company's Credit Rating on Target Company's Outstanding Debt**
>
> Target Company has an outstanding senior debt issue of 100 million that is rated BBB and actively trades in the market at 97. The debt was originally issued at par and consequently is recorded on Target Company's books at 100. Target Company is being acquired by Acquiror Company, who intends to leave Target Company's senior debt issue outstanding. Acquiror Company currently has two other senior debt issues outstanding that are both rated AA. The credit rating agency has indicated that postacquisition, Target Company's outstanding debt issue will be upgraded to AA, reflecting the anticipated financial strength of the combined firm. AA rated debt having similar terms as the outstanding Target Company issue trades in the market at 101. At the transaction date, Target Company's senior debt is written up from its 100 book value to 101, reflecting its fair value with the AA credit rating it receives as a result of the acquisition.

Restructuring Liabilities

Often business combinations result in some acquired facilities, operations, or positions becoming redundant or unnecessary. To some extent, the future cost savings from closing unnecessary facilities or eliminating redundant positions are part of the economic benefits expected from the merger or acquisition. When these activities are planned as part of the acquisition strategy, the acquirer recognizes the associated costs of the following on Target Company's adjusted balance sheet at the transaction date:

- Exiting any of Target Company's activities
- Involuntarily terminating Target Company employees
- Relocating Target Company employees

However, if the costs provide future revenues to the combined company, they are not recognized as a liability on the transaction date but rather as expenses in the future periods in which they are incurred. When calculating Target Company's net identifiable assets, the fair value of any restructuring liabilities recognized at the transaction date are included as part of the target's total liabilities.

 THE TREATMENT OF RESTRUCTURING LIABILITIES IS CHANGING

FASB is reviewing the treatment of restructuring liabilities as part of the business combinations project. In June of 2002, FASB issued *FAS146, Accounting for Costs Associated with Exit or Disposal Activities* (FAS146), dealing with restructuring liabilities incurred other than through business combinations.[4] The effect of that standard was to narrow the scope from recognizing liabilities for planned future activities to recognizing liabilities only after they represent a binding obligation on the firm. FASB tentatively decided that acquirers should not recognize restructuring liabilities for planned plant closures or personnel terminations on the acquisition date but to apply the same principles as in FAS146. If the acquisition target had incurred a liability for restructuring costs, then the acquiror assumes that liability and records it on the transaction date.

THE NET IDENTIFIABLE ASSETS CALCULATION

After eliminating Target Company's goodwill and adjusting its accounts to fair value, all that remains is determining the difference between the identifiable assets and liabilities. The difference represents Target Company's net identifiable assets, which is, conceptually, the fair value of the company being purchased. Any excess of the purchase price paid above that fair value is recorded as transaction goodwill.

CALCULATING THE PURCHASE PRICE

The second part of the goodwill calculation requires determining the price paid to purchase the target company. The cost of the transaction can generally be broken down into three different parts: the fair value of the consideration given, the fair value of contingent payments, and the direct costs of acquiring the target entity. The costs of acquiring the target are commonly characterized as fees.

TRANSACTION FEES

There are three types of fees commonly encountered in business combinations: equity issuance fees; financing fees; and legal, accounting, and M&A advisory fees (which are often collectively referred to as advisory fees). Some analysts engage in a practice of simply aggregating all of the fees into a single item. Because each of the three classes of fees is accounted for differently, the aggregated treatment leads to an incorrect calculation of goodwill but more importantly results in understating the dilutive effect of the transaction in the forward periods.

Equity Issuance and Registration Fees

FAS141, Business Combinations, just like its predecessor standard, *APB16, Business Combinations*, specifically excludes equity issuance and registration fees from the calculation of the purchase price in a business combination. Rather, the issuance and registration fees are treated as a direct reduction to the fair value of the equities being issued. These costs are not as operating expenses and consequently do not flow through the income statement. When showing the issuance of equity in an M&A analysis, it is a good practice to footnote or otherwise annotate proceeds reduced due to registration and issuance fees. For example, the entry:

| dr: | Cash | 998.0 | |
| | cr: Common equity 1,000,000 @ $1.00 per share | | 998.0 |

is confusing to the reader because one million times one dollar is obviously not $998,000. A more informative presentation is:

dr:	Cash	998.0	
	cr: Common equity 1,000,000 @ $1.00 per share		998.0
	(recorded net of registration and issuance fees of 2.0)		

because it explicitly discloses the equity issuance fee and answers a question that you can reasonably anticipate the reader will ask, "Why is a million not a million?" International accounting standards differ from U.S. GAAP on this point and include the equity issuance and registration costs as part of a business combination's purchase price.[5]

INTERNATIONAL AND U.S. ACCOUNTING STANDARD CONVERGENCE

The current International Accounting Standards Board (IASB) exposure draft for revisions to *International Accounting Standard No. 22, Business Combinations* (IAS 22) proposes changing the current IAS approach to accounting for equity issuance and registration fees to align with the U.S. GAAP approach. Although the IASB exposure draft does not change current accounting practices, the focus of FASB and IASB to align U.S. and International Accounting Standards makes it very likely that IAS 22 will change the accounting for equity issuance fees to treat them as a reduction to the proceeds realized. If you are analyzing a business combination transaction being conducted under IAS, check the status of the IASB exposure draft with your accounting advisors.

Financing Fees

Investment banks charge a financing fee, sometimes also called an underwriting fee, when they issue debt for firms. The fees are typically 2 to 4 percent of the face value of the debt issue and are not considered part of the direct costs of a business combination. Instead the fees are recorded in a Deferred financing fees asset account and are amortized as an operating expense over the life of the underlying debt. Example 13-5 illustrates how deferred financing fees are recorded on the transaction date and later expensed against operating income.

EXAMPLE **13-5. Recording and Periodic Expensing of Deferred Financing Fees**

Acquiror Company issues 1000 of senior debt to finance the acquisition of Target Company. The syndicating bank charges a 2.5-percent financing fee for the debt issue, separate from any advisory fees. The debt has a five-year term and is issued at par on the transaction date, 31-December-20X0 with a face rate of 5 percent. At the transaction date, Acquiror Company records the debt issuance, proceeds, and deferred financing fee asset on its consolidated balance sheet.

dr:	Cash		975.0	
dr:	Deferred financing fees		25.0	
	cr:	Senior debt 5% 20X5		1,000.0

Figure 13-4 details how the deferred financing fee asset is amortized over the life of the underlying debt. Note that the periodic amortization expense is treated separately from interest expense.

At first glance, treating the amortization of the deferred financing fees separately from interest expense may seem inconsistent with the treatment afforded the amortization of a discount or premium realized at issuance. The distinguishing difference is that a discount or a premium is an adjustment to the price of the bond based on its rate of interest and risk relative to the current market pricing. Unlike the points that you might pay for a home mortgage, the financing fee is not a form of interest prepayment but is really more like the equity issuance fee, a service charge for the administrative mechanics of registering, syndicating, and issuing the debt. Because debt has a finite life, the financing fee is amortized over its life. Because they are amortized as a component of operating expense, financing fees are dilutive to future earnings, however; the impact is usually relatively small.

FIGURE 13·4

Acquiror Company's Financial Statements: Expensing the Amortization of the Deferred Financing Fee Asset

Acquiror's Financial Statements - Accounting for the deferred financing asset

Income Statement	20X1	20X2	20X3	20X4	20X5
EBITDA	1,900.0	2,100.0	2,300.0	2,500.0	2,700.0
Less: Amortization of deferred financing fees	5.0	5.0	5.0	5.0	5.0
EBIT	1,895.0	2,095.0	2,295.0	2,495.0	2,695.0
Less: Interest expense (1,000 @ 5%)	50.0	50.0	50.0	50.0	50.0
EBT	1,845.0	2,045.0	2,245.0	2,445.0	2,645.0
Less: Taxes @ 40%	738.0	818.0	898.0	978.0	1,058.0
Net income	1,107.0	1,227.0	1,347.0	1,467.0	1,587.0

Balance Sheet - Assets					
Deferred financing fees asset - beginning balance	25.0	20.0	15.0	10.0	5.0
Less: Amortization from Income statement	5.0	5.0	5.0	5.0	5.0
Deferred financing fees asset - ending balance	20.0	15.0	10.0	5.0	-

Cash Flows					
Net income	1,107.0	1,227.0	1,347.0	1,467.0	1,587.0
Add: Amortization of deferred financing fees	5.0	5.0	5.0	5.0	5.0
Cash from operations	1,112.0	1,232.0	1,352.0	1,472.0	1,592.0

Legal, Accounting, and M&A Advisory Fees

Legal, accounting, and M&A advisory fees usually add up to a few percent of the total transaction price. Of the three classes of fees, they are the only one that is correctly included as a component of the equity purchase price. Because they are included entirely within the purchase price, for transactions creating goodwill, the advisory fees increase goodwill on a dollar-for-dollar basis. Example 13-6 illustrates the inclusion of advisory fees on the calculation of goodwill.

EXAMPLE **13-6.** Effect of Advisory Fees on the Calculation of Goodwill

Acquiror Company purchases all of the outstanding stock of Target Company for 3000 and pays advisory fees of 40. Target Company has total net identifiable assets of 2500 at the acquisition date. Goodwill for the transaction is calculated as the difference between the cost of Target Company and its net identifiable assets.

	With Fees	Without Fees
Equity purchase price	3,000	3,000
Legal, accounting and M&A advisory fees	40	0
Total cost of Target Company	3,040	3,000
Less: Target Company's net identifiable assets	2,500	2,500
Transaction goodwill created	540	500

Note that each dollar of advisory fees equates directly to an additional dollar of recorded transaction goodwill.

U.S. GAAP IS LIKELY TO CHANGE

As one of the milestones in the ongoing *Business Combinations: Purchase Method Procedures* project, FASB has decided that "Acquisition-related costs paid to third parties (for example: finder's, advisory, legal, accounting, and other professional fees that are attributable to negotiating or completing the business combination) are not part of the exchange transaction and should be expensed as incurred."[6] This is a change from current GAAP, but FASB's tentative decisions do not change current accounting until they are subjected to further deliberation and incorporated in the *Statements of Financial Accounting Standards.* Contact your accounting advisor to check the status of this issue. Table 13-1 summarizes the current and proposed treatments for the three classes of fees under both U.S. GAAP and IAS.

FAIR VALUE OF THE CONSIDERATION GIVEN

The purchase price paid for a transaction is the fair value of the consideration given where fair value is "The amount for which an asset (or liability) could be bought (or incurred) or sold (or settled) in a current transaction between two willing parties, that is, other than in a forced liquidation sale."[7] The purchase price or portion of the purchase for acquisitions made for cash is easily determined because it is the amount of cash given. However, debt instruments, equity securities, or other assets are more commonly used as currency in business combination transactions.

In cases where publicly traded securities are used, the market price is considered to be the best indication of fair value. Unfortunately, the market's short-term reaction to news and events can introduce "noise" that makes determining the true market price difficult to discern. Consequently, the market prices in a range of dates around the transaction date are examined to determine the best estimate of the fair value of securities being exchanged. Example 13-7 illustrates how to calculate the purchase price.

EXAMPLE 13-7. Calculating the Purchase Price

Target Company has 100 shares of common stock outstanding trading at $18.00 per share. Acquiror purchases all of Target's outstanding stock for $2.50 cash and 2 shares of Acquiror Company common stock. At the transaction date, Acquiror Company stock trades in the market at $13.75 per share. The purchase price is calculated as:

$2.50 cash per share × 100 shares	250
2 shares of Acquiror stock @ $13.75 per share × 100	2,750
Total consideration for 100 Target shares	3,000

TABLE 13·1

Current and Proposed Fee Treatment under U.S. GAAP and IAS

Class of fee	U.S. GAAP	IAS
Equity issuance and registration fees for equity issued in a business combination No change is proposed to U.S. GAAP and if the proposed change to IAS is enacted, U.S.GAAP and IAS would align.	**Current** Treats equity issuance and registration fees incurred for stock issued during a business combination as reductions to the proceeds of the issuance and not as a component of the purchase price. **Proposed** No change	**Current** Treats equity issuance and registration fees incurred for stock issued during a business combination as direct acquisition costs and includes them as a component of the purchase price. **Proposed** Treats equity issuance and registration fees incurred for stock issued during a business combination as reductions to the proceeds of the issuance and not as a component of the purchase price.
Financing fees for debt issued in a business combination No change is proposed to U.S. GAAP and if the proposed change to IAS is enacted, U.S.GAAP and IAS would not completely align.	**Current** Treats financing fees as providing future benefits extending over the lifetime of the debt. The fees are capitalized as a deferred financing fee asset and amortized as a component of operating expenses over the lifetime of the debt. **Proposed** No change	**Current** Treats financing fees incurred for debt issued during a business combination as direct acquisition costs and includes them as a component of the purchase price. **Proposed** Treats financing fees incurred for debt issued during a business combination as transaction costs reducing the proceeds of the issuance and not as a component of the purchase price.
Advisory fees incurred in a business combination No change is proposed to IAS and if the proposed change to U.S.GAAP is enacted, U.S.GAAP and IAS would not completely align.	**Current** Treats advisory fees incurred during a business combination as direct acquisition costs and includes them as a component of the purchase price. **Proposed** Treats advisory fees incurred for debt issued during a business combination as costs expensed in the period incurred and not as a component of the purchase price.	**Current** Treats advisory fees incurred during a business combination as direct acquisition costs and includes them as a component of the purchase price. **Proposed** No change

FAIR VALUE OF EQUITY SECURITIES ISSUED WILL BE MEASURED AT THE TRANSACTION DATE

The Financial Accounting Standards Board (FASB) decided as part of the Business Combinations Project that the definition of the acquisition date should be clarified to indicate that it is the date that the acquirer gains control over the target and that the fair value for equity securities issued as consideration to effect a business combination is measured on the acquisition date.

CALCULATING GOODWILL

Once the purchase price and net identifiable assets have been calculated, calculating goodwill is simply a matter of differencing the two, provided that the purchase price is greater than the fair value of the net identifiable assets. The case where the value of the net identifiable assets exceeds the purchase price is addressed in the following discussion on negative goodwill.

Example 13-8 shows the calculation of goodwill and the entry for recording the transaction on the acquisition date.

EXAMPLE **13-8. Calculating Goodwill and Recording the Transaction**

Target Company has 100 shares of outstanding common stock trading at $24.00 per share. Acquiror purchases all of Target's outstanding stock for $2.50 cash and two shares of Acquiror Company common stock. At the transaction date, Acquiror Company stock trades in the market at $13.75 per share, and Target Company has 2500 of net identifiable assets. Acquiror Company also pays 40 in advisory fees for the transaction. The purchase price is calculated as:

$$100 \times (\$13.75 \times 2 = \$27.50 + \$2.50 = \$30.00) = 3,000.0 + 40.0 = 3,040.0$$

Because the purchase price is greater than the net identifiable assets of the target, goodwill is created in the transaction and is the difference between the purchase price and the target's net identifiable assets:

Purchase price	3,040.0
Less: target's net identifiable assets	2,500.0
Transaction goodwill created	540.0

The journal entry recording the transaction is:

dr:	Net identifiable assets		2,500.0	
dr:	Goodwill		540.0	
	cr:	Cash		290.0
		(advisory fees + purchase money: 40 + 250 = 290)		
	cr:	Common stock		2,750.0

NEGATIVE GOODWILL

To this point we have limited our discussion to the most common acquisition scenario where the purchase price exceeds the value of the net identifiable assets. In fact, the standard accounting definition of goodwill is the *excess* of the consideration given (purchase price) *over* the value of the net identifiable assets received. In liquidation, distress, or other "bargain" situations, it sometimes occurs that the excess of the purchase price over the net identifiable assets is negative, commonly referred to as "negative goodwill," also referred to as the excess of fair value over cost.

Conceptually negative goodwill does not make sense. In efficient markets there are few bargains, so we approach these situations from the perspective that the valuations of the assets are probably overstated. The negative goodwill is allocated to the assets, reducing their recorded values until the negative goodwill is reduced to zero.

Allocating Negative Goodwill by Reducing the Acquired Asset Values

Some of the assets, such as cash and marketable securities, are clearly recorded at their fair value and it makes no sense reducing them. This is true of other assets where we have a high certainty that they are recorded at fair value. *FAS141, Business Combinations*, lists five classes of assets that are not written down when allocating negative goodwill. They are:

- Current assets
- Securities recorded using the cost method (trading, available for sale, and held-to-maturity)
- Deferred tax assets
- Prepaid pension assets
- Assets being held for sale

All of the other assets are written down by a pro rata amount of the negative goodwill. Example 13-9 explains how the acquired assets of Target Company are written down on a pro rata basis to allocate the excess of the fair value of the assets received over the cost (negative goodwill).

EXAMPLE 13-9. Allocating Negative Goodwill under U.S. GAAP

Again, Target Company has 100 shares of common stock outstanding trading at $24.00 per share. Acquiror Company purchases all of Target's outstanding stock for $2.50 cash and two shares of Acquiror Company common stock. Except this time, Acquiror Company stock trades in the market at $10.00 instead of $13.75 per share on the transaction date. Target Company still has 2500 of net identifiable assets. Acquiror Company also pays 40 in advisory fees for the transaction. The purchase price is calculated as:

$$100 \times (\$10.00 \times 2 = \$20.00 + \$2.50 = \$22.50) = 2,250.0 + 40.0 = 2,290.0$$

Because the value of Target Company's net identifiable assets (2500.0) is greater than the purchase price (2290.0), the difference between the purchase price and the target's net identifiable assets results in negative goodwill:

Target Company's net identifiable assets	2,500.0
Less: Purchase price	2,290.0
Negative goodwill	210.0

Allocating the negative goodwill by writing down Target Company's assets on a pro rata basis is a three-step process:

1. Determining which classes of assets may be written down (remember, U.S. GAAP does not allow negative goodwill allocation to current and four other classes of assets).
2. Determining the fraction (percentage) that each class of allocable assets makes of the total allocable assets.
3. Allocating the negative goodwill by writing down each class of allocable assets according to its percentage of the total.

Target Company's assets are shown in the first column of Figure 13-5, adjusted to fair value on the transaction date. The first step is to determine which classes of Target Company's assets may be written down. U.S. GAAP does not allow allocating negative goodwill to current assets or deferred tax assets, hence Target Company's only eligible asset classes are: Property, plant and equipment and Other intangible assets.

The second step is determining the percentage that each eligible asset class is of the total assets eligible for allocation of negative goodwill. Target Company has two eligible classes totaling (3500 + 2000) = 5500. Property, plant and equipment comprises (3500 / 5500) = 63.6% of the eligible assets and Other intangible assets is the remaining (2000 / 5500) = 36.4% of the eligible assets.

The last step is the pro rata allocation of the negative goodwill to write down Target Company's assets. Because we need to allocate 210.0 for negative goodwill, we write down

FIGURE 13-5

Allocating Negative Goodwill to Target Company's Assets

Target Company's assets		Allocation of negative goodwill		
Assets	Adjusted	Percentage	Credits	Final
Cash	200.0			200.0
Inventories	300.0			300.0
Accounts receivable	1,000.0			1,000.0
Current deferred tax assets	-			-
Current assets	1,500.0	0.0	0.0	1,500.0
Property, plant and equipment	3,500.0	63.6%	133.6	3,366.4
Goodwill	-			-
Other intangible assets	2,000.0	36.4%	76.4	1,923.6
Deferred tax assets	500.0			500.0
Total assets	**7,500.0**		210.0	**7,290.0**

Target Company's Property, plant, and equipment account by its pro rata share of (63.6% × 210.0) = 133.6 from 3500.0 to 3366.4 and the Other intangible assets account by its pro rata share of (36.4% × 210.0) = 76.4 from 2000.0 to 1923.6.

These allocations reduce Target Company's net identifiable assets from 2500 to 2290, making them equal with the purchase price of 2290. Because the difference between the fair value of the acquired net assets and the purchase price is now zero, there is no longer any negative goodwill.

Treating Negative Goodwill under International Accounting Standards (IAS)

International Accounting Standards do not require a pro rata write down of eligible asset classes but instead suggest that asset valuations be re-examined to ensure that they are not overstated and liabilities be examined to ensure that none are omitted. Any negative goodwill is recognized at the acquisition date and treated in one of two ways. The first is amortizing it as a component of income over the weighted-average life of the acquired depreciable or amortizable identifiable assets. The second method is similar to U.S. GAAP in that the negative goodwill at the acquisition date is recognized as income at the acquisition. Example 13-10 illustrates the amortization of negative goodwill over the weighted-average life of the acquired depreciable and amortizable identifiable assets.

EXAMPLE 13-10. Amortizing Negative Goodwill under International Accounting Standards

Following the facts of Example 13-9, Target Company has 100 shares of common stock outstanding trading at $24.00 per share. Acquiror Company purchases all of Target's outstanding stock for $2.50 cash and two shares of Acquiror Company common stock. Except this time, Acquiror Company stock trades in the market at $10.00 instead of $13.75 per share on the transaction date. Target Company still has 2500 of net identifiable assets. Acquiror Company also pays 40 in advisory fees for the transaction. The purchase price is calculated as:

$$100 \times (\$10.00 \times 2 = \$20.00 + \$2.50 = \$22.50) = 2{,}250.0 + 40.0 = 2{,}290.0$$

Because the value of Target Company's net identifiable assets (2500.0) is greater than the purchase price (2290.0), the difference between the purchase price and the target's net identifiable assets results in negative goodwill:

Target Company's net identifiable assets	2,500.0
Less: Purchase price	2,290.0
Negative goodwill	210.0

Target Company has depreciable Property, plant and equipment assets of 3500 with 4-year useful lives and amortizable Other intangible assets of 2000 with 9.5-year useful lives. The weighted-average useful life of the depreciable and amortizable identifiable assets is (3500 × 4 + 2000 × 9.5) / (3500 + 2000) = 33,000 / 5500 = 6 years. Acquiror Company records the transaction negative goodwill as a contra-asset account at the acquisition date and subsequently recognizes it ratably as a component of income as (210 / 6) = 35 per year.

Negative Goodwill Exceeding the Acquired Asset Values

Conceivably, the excess of the fair value of the net assets received over the purchase price (negative goodwill) could exceed the total assets eligible for allocation of negative goodwill. In these cases, U.S. GAAP requires that the eligible assets be written down to zero, and the acquiring entity recognize any remaining unallocated negative goodwill as an extraordinary gain on its income statement for the acquisition period. Allowable treatments under IAS are the same as previously described, recognition as income either at the acquisition date or ratably over the weighted-average useful life of the depreciable or amortizable identifiable assets.

AMORTIZATION OF GOODWILL

U.S. GAAP no longer allows goodwill to be amortized as an operating expense. Instead it is carried at its historical value and periodically tested for impairment. Currently, IAS requires that goodwill be amortized over its useful life, which is generally expected, for financial accounting purposes, to be 20 years. Consequently, two identical transactions, one accounted for using U.S. GAAP and the other accounted for using IAS, could result in different forward earnings results due to the amortization of goodwill. The acquirer using U.S. GAAP would carry the transaction goodwill at its acquisition date value, whereas the acquiror using IAS would reduce its earnings in each postacquisition period by the amount of the goodwill amortization. The amortization of goodwill dilutes the acquiror's forward earnings. Conversely, firms electing the option under IAS to recognize negative goodwill ratably to income experience an accretive effect from the increase in income.

The International Accounting Standards Board released an exposure draft (ED3) as part of its Business combinations project. The draft proposes aligning the treatment of goodwill under IAS with current U.S. GAAP. In other words, once the proposed exposure draft is accepted, IAS would require goodwill to be carried at its historical cost and periodically tested for impairment. Because this is still in the proposal stage, check with an accounting adviser for business combinations recorded under IAS.

Tax Amortization of Goodwill

Note that the rules for amortization of goodwill are different for financial reporting and taxation purposes. For federal tax purposes there are two classes of goodwill, deductible and nondeductible. Generally all goodwill is nondeductible unless it arises from an asset sale or a deemed asset sale under Internal Revenue Code (IRC) Section 338(h)(10). Tax-deductible goodwill is amortized, for tax purposes, over a statutory 15-year amortization period. The financial reporting treatment of goodwill is not affected by whether or not it is tax deductible.

Whenever nondeductible goodwill is recorded, it has a tax basis of zero, so its book basis is always greater. Normally when an asset's book basis exceeds its tax basis, it requires recognition of a deferred tax liability. *FAS109, Accounting for Income Taxes*, specifically excepts "…the portion of goodwill for which amortization is not deductible for tax purposes, …".[8]

Tax-deductible goodwill is another matter. As the goodwill is amortized for tax purposes, its tax basis is reduced using a straight-line amortization method to zero over a 15-year period. The book carrying amount is not amortized, and the book value remains constant throughout the full 15-year period (assuming that no impairment of the goodwill occurs in that period). Consequently, the excess of the book basis over the tax basis increases each year, requiring recognition of a larger-and-larger deferred tax liability, until the goodwill is fully amortized at the end of 15 years. The associated deferred tax liability remains on Acquiror Company's books until its book basis is reduced either by Acquiror Company writing down the book value of the goodwill because it becomes impaired or by Acquiror Company itself being acquired by another entity. Figure 13-6 shows the relationship between the book basis and the tax basis of tax-deductible goodwill over its 15-year

FIGURE 13·6

Book Basis versus the Tax Basis of Tax-deductible Goodwill

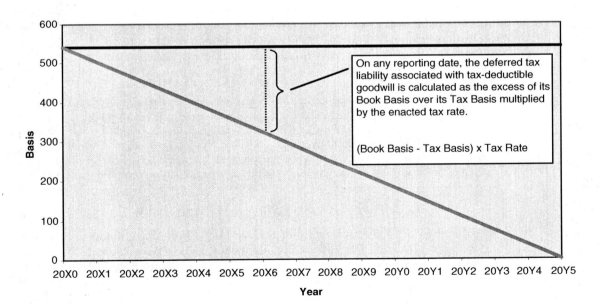

Tax Basis versus Book Basis - Tax-Deductible Goodwill

On any reporting date, the deferred tax liability associated with tax-deductible goodwill is calculated as the excess of its Book Basis over its Tax Basis multiplied by the enacted tax rate.

(Book Basis - Tax Basis) x Tax Rate

statutory amortization period. Example 13-11 illustrates Acquiror Company's deferred tax accounting for the amortization of tax-deductible transaction goodwill.

EXAMPLE 13-11. Deferred Tax Effects from Temporary Differences in Book and Tax Bases of Tax-deductible Goodwill

Target Company has 100 shares of common stock outstanding trading at $24.00 per share. Acquiror purchases all of Target's outstanding stock for $30.00 cash in a 338(h)(10) deemed asset sale on 31-December-20X0. Acquiror Company also pays 40 in advisory fees for the transaction. The purchase price is calculated as:

$$100 \times (\$30.00) = 3,000.0 + 40.0 = 3,040.0$$

Because the purchase price is greater than the net identifiable assets of the target, goodwill created in the transaction is the difference between the purchase price and the target's net identifiable assets. As a deemed asset sale, the goodwill created in the transaction is tax deductible and amortizable over a 15-year statutory life.

Purchase price	3,040.0
Less: Target Company's net identifiable assets	2,500.0
Tax-deductible transaction goodwill created	540.0

The goodwill is amortized for tax purposes over 15 years using a straight-line method so that the tax amortization expense recognized in each of the 15 years is $(540 / 15) = 36$. The goodwill is not amortized for financial reporting purposes.

ACQUIROR COMPANY'S 20X1 FINANCIAL STATEMENTS

Tax Year 20X1	Book reporting		Tax reporting
Revenues	100.0	Revenues	100.0
Goodwill amortization	0.0	Goodwill amortization	36.0
Pretax financial income	100.0	Taxable income	64.0
Income tax expense @ 40%	40.0	Cash taxes @ 40%	25.6
Net income	60.0		

Goodwill basis	Book reporting		Tax reporting
Beginning 31-Dec-20X0	540.0		540.0
Less: 20X1 amortization	0.0		36.0
Ending 31-Dec-20X1	540.0		504.0

The financial reporting entry recording 20X1 taxes is:

dr:	Income tax expense		40.0	
	cr:	Deferred tax liability (36.0 × 40%)		14.4
	cr:	Cash		25.6

Acquiror Company determines the 14.4 increase to the Deferred tax liability account by calculating the expected account balance as the excess of the book basis over the tax basis times the tax rate $(540 - 504) \times 40\% = 14.4$ and then subtracting any existing deferred tax liability already recorded for this asset. Continuing in 20X2 through 20Y5 (15 years),

Acquiror Company recognizes straight-line amortization (36.0 = 540 divided by 15) for tax purposes and no amortization for book purposes. At the end of the fifteenth year, 20Y5, the goodwill has a book basis of 540 and a tax basis of zero. Acquiror Company has recognized the full deferred tax asset of $(540 \times 40\%) = 216$.

ACCRETION AND DILUTION OF EARNINGS

After the acquisition date, the projected earnings of both Acquiror Company and Target Company are reported on a combined basis. If they increase on a per-share basis, the transaction is accretive to (increases) earnings, and if they decrease on a per-share basis the results are dilutive to (decreases) earnings. Determining the accretion or dilution of earnings from a business combination is a four-step process:

1. Analyze the expected operating structure of the combined company and determine the best approach for projecting Target Company's operating results.

2. Based on the outcome of the first step, either combine Target Company's results with Acquiror Company's for the transaction period and then project the combined operating results forward or project Target Company's and Acquiror Company's operating results separately and then combine the projections in each forecast period.

3. The third step is accounting for the effects of the transaction on the earnings of the combined firm. This includes items such as synergies, costs of synergies, changes in interest and dividends, amortization of transaction items, etc. An item that is often overlooked in the initial analysis is that the transaction usually eliminates Target Company's unrecognized pension items: unrecognized prior service cost, unrecognized gain or loss, and unrecognized net obligation. Consequently, if Target Company's net periodic pension expense contains material amortization of the unrecognized items, then recognition of those items on the acquisition date reduces Target Company's pension expense going forward and is accretive to the transaction.

4. Lastly is to analyze the difference between Acquiror Company's stand-alone per-share earnings results and those of the combined entity's. The amount by which they are positive (or negative) is generally presented as a percentage of accretion (or dilution).

Approaches to Projecting the Combined Firm's Operating Results

The first step in projecting the forward earnings of the combined entity is to decide which approach more fairly represents the operating structure of the combined company: whether the value-drivers such as revenues, cost of goods sold, etc., should be combined at the transaction date and then projected forward as a single projection; or whether the value-drivers for each of the entities should continue being projected separately and the separate projections combined in each period to forecast the combined entities operating results. I prefer the latter method for three reasons. The first reason being that it is the more flexible because growing both Acquiror Company's and Target Company's value-drivers at the same rate yields the same outcome as first combining them and then growing them forward at that same rate, and you still retain the option of changing the rates. The second reason is that most acquisitions are just that, acquisitions and not true mergers. Even in the case of true mergers, the melding of the firms occurs over some time, and it is very likely that the two entities will retain some of their individual attributes for one to three years after the acquisition. Finally, projecting the operating results of the two firms individually and then adjusting them for synergies and transaction effect provides a much clearer view of where the value is being created (or destroyed) in the business combination.

Target's Forward Earnings Projections

If the circumstances of the acquisition suggest that the Acquiror and Target are more fairly projected as separate entities, then the next step in determining the impact of the transaction on Acquiror Company's earnings-per-share is combining the projected income statements of Acquiror Company and Target Company. If Acquiror Company and Target Company both use the same fiscal year, then combining their income statements is relatively straightforward. If they are on different fiscal years, then Target Company's projected income statements must first be *calendarized* or adjusted to coincide with Acquiror Company's fiscal year. Example 13-12 illustrates the approach used to estimate Target Company's earnings results to Acquiror Company's fiscal year. Note that in a business combination the combined firm remains on the acquirer's fiscal year.

EXAMPLE **13-12.** Calendarizing Target Company's Projected Annual Operating Results to Acquiror Company's Fiscal Year

Acquiror Company is acquiring Target Company in an all-stock transaction. Acquiror Company's fiscal year end is 31-December and Target Company's is 30-April. After the acquisition, Target Company will continue to operate as a wholly owned subsidiary and will change its fiscal year end to coincide with Acquiror Company's. Prior to the transaction, the results of the combined firm are projected by first calendarizing Target Company's projected financial statements to Acquiror Company's fiscal year-end (31-December). This is done by estimating the portion of Target Company's results for the parts of each of its two fiscal years corresponding to Acquiror Company's fiscal year and combining them to synthesize a "new" fiscal year. Figure 13-7 visually illustrates the calendarization process.

Assume that Target Company projects net income of 1200 for fiscal year 20X1, ending 30-April-20X1 and 1800 for fiscal year 20X2, ending 30-April-20X2. Calendarize Target Company's earnings to a 31-December fiscal year-end by constructing an artificial year comprised of the last four months (January through April) of Target Company's fiscal year 20X1 and the first eight months (May through December) of Target Company's fiscal year 20X2.

FIGURE 13·7

Calendarizing Target Company's Projected Operating Results to Acquiror Company's Fscal Year

Acquiror Company Fiscal Year 20X1

| Jan | Feb | Mar | Apr | May | Jun | Jul | Aug | Sep | Oct | Nov | Dec |

Target Company Fiscal Year 20X1
Net income = 1,200.0

Target Company Fiscal Year 20X2
Net income = 1,800.0

| May | Jun | Jul | Aug | Sep | Oct | Nov | Dec | Jan | Feb | Mar | Apr | May | Jun | Jul | Aug | Sep | Oct | Nov | Dec | Jan | Feb | Mar | Apr |

4 / 12 of 20X1 results + 8 / 12 of 20X2 results
Net income = 400.0 + Net income = 1,200.0

Target Company Calendarized Year 20X1
Net income = 1,600.0

| Jan | Feb | Mar | Apr | May | Jun | Jul | Aug | Sep | Oct | Nov | Dec |

NOTE: To simplify this discussion, we only look at calendarizing the Net income account but in practice, all of the income statement accounts would also be calendarized. Balance sheet accounts may also be estimated using linear interpolation between statement dates, but a more common practice is to use the last statement date before the transaction and adjust it according to the external accountant's report.

On an annual basis we estimate Target Company's calendarized fiscal year 20X1 (ending 31-December-20X1) results to be four-twelfths of its fiscal year 20X1 results (4 / 12 × 1200) = 400 plus eight-twelfths of its fiscal year 20X2 results (8 / 12 × 1800) = 1200 totaling (400 + 1200) = 1600 for the calendarized year ending 31-December-20X1.

This process would be repeated for each of Target Company's projected years so that its operating results could be combined with Acquiror Company's to project the operating results of the combined firm. A potential source of error from this approach is that it assumes that Target Company's annual earnings occur ratably throughout the year. This is often not the case, and if projections are available for shorter periods, either monthly or quarterly, they can provide better estimates. Example 13-3 explains the calendarization process when quarterly instead of annual projections are available.

EXAMPLE 13-13. Calendarizing Target Company's Projected Quarterly Operating Results to Acquiror Company's Fiscal Year-end

The nature and timing of the transaction are the same as they were in Example 13-12, as are Target Company's annual projections for net income of 1200 for fiscal year 20X1, ending

30-April-20X1 and 1800 for fiscal year 20X2, ending 30-April-20X2. Additional information is available projecting Target Company's quarterly results for the same periods.

TARGET COMPANY'S PROJECTED QUARTERLY RESULTS:

Fiscal Period	20X1	20X2
Q1 (May – Jul)	220.0	420.0
Q2 (Aug – Oct)	280.0	440.0
Q3 (Nov – Jan)	300.0	450.0
Q4 (Feb – Apr)	400.0	490.0
Annual total	1,200.0	1,800.0

Again we calendarize Target Company's earnings to a 31-December fiscal year-end by constructing an artificial year comprised of the last four months (January through April) of Target Company's fiscal year 20X1 and the first eight months (May through December) of Target Company's fiscal year 20X2. Because quarterly data are available, our estimate is based on one-third of Q3 of 20X1 ($1/3 \times 300 = 100$) plus Q4 of 20X1 (400), Q1 of 20X2 (420), Q2 of 20X2 (440) and two-thirds of Q3 of 20X2 ($2/3 \times 450 = 300$) and totals 1660. Figure 13-8 provides a visualization of how the quarterly data are combined to estimate Target Company's calendarized fiscal year 20X1 (ending 31-December-20X1).

The estimate of Target Company's calendarized 20X1 net income using the quarterly data is presumably a better estimate than that derived from the annual projections. Differences between estimates derived from annual and quarterly

FIGURE 13-8

Calendarizing Target Company's Projected Annual Operating Results to Acquiror Company's Fiscal Year

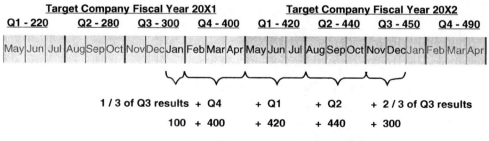

data are larger for high-growth and highly seasonal targets. In transactions where these types of targets are being acquired or the transaction is highly levered, it is common to see the first three to five post-transaction years projected on a quarterly basis changing to annual projections for all later years.

Projecting the Combined Company's Operating Results

If the expected structure of the combined firm fully absorbed Target Company, then Target Company's operating results for the period prior to the transaction can simply be combined with Acquiror Company's and then projected forward. The expected growth rates are usually the same as for Acquiror Company alone. If the combined firm's results are projected forward on a quarterly basis, then the last quarters preceding the acquisition are typically combined for both Target Company and Acquiror Company, even if they do not end on the same date because they will be within two months of each other. If the projections are made on annual data, then calendarize Target Company's historical data to Acquiror Company's last historical year before combining and projecting operating results. If Target Company and Acquiror Company are projected separately, then combine their operating results in each projected period.

GAAP Approach to the Earnings of the Combined Firm

Under U.S. GAAP or IAS, the earnings of Target Company up until the acquisition date are considered to be "purchased" by Acquiror Company. The only portion of Target Company's contributions to earnings for the transaction period is that occurring between the transaction date and the end of the acquisition period, often referred to as the *stub period*. Example 13-14 shows the GAAP calculation of Combined Company's earnings.

NOTE: The term stub period does not have a universal definition. You may find it used to describe the posttransaction portion of a fiscal year (as we use it in this work) and alternatively to describe just the opposite, the pretransaction portion of a fiscal year. The issue becomes not whether one is correct or incorrect but rather is everyone involved in the discussions for the transaction using a common meaning? Whenever potentially ambiguous terms occur, take the time to define them with other parties. If they occur in transaction spreadsheet models, include a transactions sheet or at least define them using the cell comment function.

EXAMPLE 13-14. GAAP Earnings Calculation for a Mid-Year Acquisition

Acquiror Company acquires 100 percent of Target Company as a wholly owned subsidiary on 30-June-20X1. Both Acquiror Company and Target Company have fiscal years ending 31-December. Acquiror earns 2000 in 20X1 and Target earns 800, 350 in the preacquisition period from 1-January to 30-June and 450 in the postacquisition *stub period* from 1-July to 31-December. In its 20X1 consolidated income statement, Acquiror Company recognizes (2000 + 450) = 2450 of earnings.

Projecting Synergies and Transaction Effects

The term *synergies* is often used synonymously with *cost savings*, but for analytical purposes they should always be treated individually. Cost savings typically result from the elimination of redundant positions, equipment, processes, or facilities. It is a relatively straightforward task to identify cost savings opportunities and to estimate their value with a high degree of certainty. Project cost savings separately as a reduction to expenses (usually to selling, general and administrative) in future periods. Net cost savings are also subject to overestimation when the associated costs of implementing them are not properly considered. These include items such as pension settlement costs, severance, and unemployment costs.

Synergies are a different matter and generally are thought of as the additional revenues that the combined firm can realize because of access to new marketing channels, increased cross-selling opportunities, the ability to mine each other's customer lists, etc. Synergies are often projected as a percentage of the acquiror's stand-alone revenues but could also be projected as a percentage of the target's revenues, depending on the expected nature of the synergies.

One common and important source of error is the underestimation (sometimes to the point of omission) of synergy *costs*. Synergies, like any other revenue, have underlying cost components of cost of goods sold and selling, general and administrative expenses that must also be projected. A good rule of thumb is that the margin for synergies should be about the same as the margin on other revenues. Another item often overlooked is the capital investment effect of synergies. If synergies result in increased sales, producing those sales may require additional capital expenditures (for purchasing the production equipment), resulting in additional depreciation expense (for the purchased equipment). The synergy depreciation is an additional operating expense, and both it and the capital expenditures must be included when calculating the combined firm's cash flows. I prefer to project synergies forward as a separate addition to revenues and the synergy costs as a separate component of expenses. These two items are often the source of optimistic projection, and the due diligence process is facilitated if they are clearly and separately disclosed.

Several transaction-related costs or benefits potentially affecting future earnings to be considered are :

- Changes in interest expense from retiring old debt (increases earnings) or from issuing new transaction debt (decreases earnings)
- Changes in deferred financing fee amortization expense from retiring old debt (increases earnings) or from issuing new transaction debt (decreases earnings)
- Changes in preferred equity dividends from buying in old preferred equity (increases earnings) or from issuing new transaction preferred equity (decreases earnings)
- Changes in depreciation of fair value write-ups to tangible assets (decreases earnings) or write-downs to tangible assets (increases earnings)

- Changes in amortization of recognition of new intangible assets (decreases earnings), fair value write-ups to intangible assets (decreases earnings) or write-downs to intangible assets (increases earnings)
- Changes in the minority interests in earnings from buying-in old minority interests (increases earnings) or making a partial acquisition, creating new minority interests (decreases earnings)
- Changes in taxes from combining two entities with different marginal tax rates into a single entity paying at Acquiror Company's tax rate
- Amortization of transaction goodwill for transactions performed under IAS (deceases earnings)
- Amortization of restructuring charges benefiting future periods such as bonus payments to retain key employees through transition periods (decreases earnings)
- Other one-time or nonrecurring transaction-related costs and benefits

Calculating Transaction Accretion or Dilution Effects

Calculating the transaction accretion or dilution to Acquiror Company's earnings per share requires first adjusting the combined firm's operating results (already adjusted for synergy effects) to reflect the additional transaction costs and benefits. Next compare the per-share earnings of the combined firm with Acquiror Company's stand-alone earnings per share to determine the percentage of accretion or dilution to earnings occurring as a result of the transaction.

Remember that any common shares, warrants, options, or convertibles issued by Acquiror Company in the transaction are weighted to reflect the portion of the acquisition year they were outstanding (denominator effect). This is important because it compensates for the fact that Target Company's contribution to earnings in the acquisition year is only for the posttransaction stub period (numerator effect). Example 13-15 calculates the acquisition year accretion/dilution to Acquiror Company's earnings when it purchases Target Company in an all-stock transaction.

EXAMPLE 13-15. Calculating Accretion or Dilution in the Acquisition Period

Acquiror Company acquires 100 percent of Target Company as a wholly owned subsidiary on 30-June-20X1. Both Acquiror Company and Target Company have fiscal years ending 31-December. Acquiror earns 2000 in 20X1 and Target earns 800, 350 in the preacquisition period from 1-January to 30-June and 450 in the postacquisition *stub period* from 1-July to 31-December. In its 20X1 consolidated income statement, Acquiror Company recognizes (2000 + 450) = 2450 of earnings for the combined firm.

For the entire pretransaction period, Acquiror Company has 100 shares outstanding, and it issues 40 new common shares on the acquisition date to acquire Target Company. There are no expected synergies or additional costs or benefits resulting from the transaction. To determine the accretion or dilution to Acquiror Company's earnings per share, first calculate Acquiror Company's stand-alone EPS as its stand-alone earnings (2000) divided by its stand-alone weighted-average shares outstanding (100 × 100% of the acquisition year):

$$\text{EPS} = \frac{\text{Acquisition year stand-alone earnings}}{\text{Weighted-average shares outstanding}} = \frac{2,000}{100} = \$20.00 \text{ per share}$$

Second, calculate the combined company's EPS as Acquiror Company's full-year earnings (2000) plus Target Company's stub-period contribution to earnings (450) divided by the combined company's weighted-average shares outstanding ($100 \times 100\%$ of the acquisition year $+ 40 \times 50\%$ of the acquisition year) = 120:

$$\text{EPS} = \frac{\text{Acquisition year combined earnings}}{\text{Weighted-average shares outstanding}} = \frac{2,450}{120} = \$20.42 \text{ per share}$$

Lastly, Acquiror Company's stand-alone and combined earnings per share are compared to determine whether and to what extent the transaction is accretive or dilutive to earnings.

$$\text{Percentage of Accretion (Dilution)} = \frac{\text{Change in Acquiror's earnings-per-share}}{\text{Acquiror's stand-alone earnings-per-share}} =$$

$$\frac{\text{(Combined EPS} - \text{Stand-alone EPS)}}{\text{Stand-alone EPS}} = \frac{(\$20.42 - \$20.00)}{\$20.00} = 2.1\% \text{ accretive}$$

If Acquiror Company's stand-alone EPS is greater than the combined company's EPS, the result is a negative percentage and the effect of the transaction is dilutive to (reduces) Acquiror Company's EPS. By using the weighted average number of shares, the combined company's earnings per share are kept comparable with subsequent years, even though only Target Company's stub period earnings are used in the acquisition year.

PRO FORMA PRESENTATION (AS IF COMBINED)

There are several different methods for constructing pro forma presentations, but for firms registered with the Securities and Exchange Commission (SEC), Regulation S-X, Section 210.11 requires Acquiror Company to disclose specific pro forma information to investors following a significant business combination accounted for under the purchase method. SEC states its regulatory objective for requiring pro forma financial information disclosure as being able to "…provide investors with information about the continuing impact of a transaction by showing how it might have affected historical financial statements if the transaction had been consummated at an earlier time."[9] Generally, the pro forma financial statements show the firm's historical results restated as if the transaction had occurred three years prior.

The SEC requires the pro forma financial information to show the combined results of Acquiror Company and Target Company as if the transaction had occurred on the first day of the acquisition period. Another way of looking at the pro forma requirement is to combine the results from continuing operations from the two firms, less the contributions of any operations sold or discontinued in the transaction and burdened by the capital cost for the combined entity using the transaction date capital structure. Although it is not required for SEC filings, this same approach is often performed for analytical trending, particularly for credit analysis, by creating pro forma financial statements for the acquisition period and the preceding three historical years.

STATEMENTS OF CASH FLOWS FOLLOWING BUSINESS COMBINATIONS

Show the transaction-related cash flows as a line item (or items) separate from the entity's other cash flows. Transaction-related cash flows are generally classified as either cash flows from investments or from financing activities. A common question arising in transactions is the classification of financing fees because GAAP requires the fees to be recorded as an asset and amortized over the life of the debt. The amortization of the fees is a noncash expense, which is added back to operating income. The initial cash payment of the financing fees on the transaction date is classified as a cash (out) flow from financing activities.[10]

It is also often desirable to modify the GAAP construct for the statement of cash flows in the acquisition period and to begin the statement of cash flows on the acquisition date. This simplifies the due diligence work for lenders trying to ensure that adequate debt service (interest expense and principal repayment) ability exists posttransaction. The "fresh start" approach lends itself to clearer analysis of the combined firm's cash flow picture in the acquisition period by eliminating the "noise" from the preacquisition cash transactions.

LIMITATIONS ON THE USE OF TARGET COMPANY'S NET OPERATING LOSS (NOL) CARRYFORWARDS

As Chapter 12 discusses, Section 382 of the Internal Revenue Code (IRC) limits the use of NOL carryforwards following an acquisition or other ownership change accounted for using the purchase method.

Following an acquisition or other purchase-method business combination, the use of NOL carryforwards in each future tax year is limited to the value of the company's stock, just before the ownership change, multiplied by the long-term tax-exempt rate (currently just less than 5 percent).

NOTE: The long-term tax-exempt rate is the highest of the adjusted Federal long-term rates in effect for any month in the three-calendar-month period ending with the calendar month in which the ownership change date occurs.[11] They are published in the IRS monthly Revenue Rulings, which are available on the IRS Web site, *www.irs.gov.*

The importance for financial accounting on the transaction date is the adjustment of the deferred tax asset recorded by Target Company associated with its NOL carryforwards. Because Acquiror Company executes a corporate ownership change (the IRC defines a corporate ownership change as occurring if any 5-percent shareholder increases its ownership by 50 percent over its minimum position), it limits its ability to use the NOLs in future periods. If the amount of Target Company's NOL carryforward is large and/or its remaining life is short, Acquiror Company may not be able to use the entire NOL carryforward before it expires. (Remember that NOL carryforwards have a 20-year lifetime.) In this case, Acquiror Company adjusts the book value of the deferred tax asset recorded by Target Company for the expected future tax benefit of the NOL carryforward downward on the acquisition date to reflect the reduced tax benefit that the combined company expects to realize. Example 13-16 explains how Acquiror Company reduces the fair value of Target Company's recorded deferred tax asset because of IRC Section 382 limitations on the use of Target Company's NOL carryforwards.

EXAMPLE 13-16. Adjustment of Deferred Tax Assets Because of IRC Section 382 Limitations

Acquiror Company buys all the stock of Target Company for 1000. Target Company has NOLs in the amount of 300 expiring in four years and has recorded a deferred tax asset of $(300 \times 40\%) = 120$ for the NOLs. The long-term tax-exempt rate is 5 percent. The NOL deduction allowed postacquisition Acquiror Company from Target Company's NOL carryforwards in each year following the acquisition is limited to $(1,000 \times 5\%) = 50$ until they are either completely utilized or until they expire. Because the NOLs expire in four years, Acquiror Company expects to use only $(50 \times 4) = 200$ of Target Company's NOLs, and the remainder $(300 - 200) = 100$ will expire. Consequently, at the acquisition date, Acquiror Company recognizes a valuation allowance for the NOLs that it expects to expire unused of $(100 \times 40\%) = 40$ to reduce the fair value of the recorded deferred tax asset from 120 to $(120 - 40) = 80$.

EFFECTS ON MINORITY INTERESTS IN BUSINESS COMBINATION TRANSACTIONS

Business combination transactions change minority interests' positions by either creating new minority interests or eliminating existing minority interests by buying them in. A new minority interest is created when Acquiror Company purchases more than 50 percent but less than 100 percent of Target Company's outstanding common equity. Acquiror Company recognizes the portion that it does not acquire as minority interests on its consolidated balance sheet. If the equity portion that is not bought in is preferred equity, then Acquiror Company records that portion as a minority interest in preferred equity. Minority interests are eliminated whenever existing Target Company minority interests are bought in by Acquiror Company as part of the business combination transaction.

Creating Minority Interests in a Business Combination

When Parent Company acquires less than 100 percent of Target Company in a partial acquisition, the portion of Target Company's common equity remaining in the hands of others is recognized on Parent Company's consolidated balance sheet as a minority interest. Under current U.S. GAAP purchase accounting rules, the purchased portion of Target Company's identifiable net assets are revalued to fair value on the acquisition date while the remaining (unpurchased) portion left outstanding is recorded at book value.

RECOGNITION OF GOODWILL IN MINORITY INTERESTS TRANSACTIONS MAY CHANGE

FASB decided in late 2002 that "The full goodwill method should be used to recognize goodwill in the acquisition of less than 100 percent controlling interest in the acquired entity."[12] Although FASB decisions are not incorporated into GAAP until the underlying Financial Accounting Standards are amended and reissued, it is likely that this decision will be codified. Whenever you analyze partial acquisitions, contact your accounting advisors to determine the status of this item. Examples 13-17 and 13-18 present the differences between recording a partial acquisition using the partial goodwill and full goodwill methods.

EXAMPLE 13-17. Recording a Partial Acquisition Using the Partial Goodwill Method

Target Company is a publicly traded corporation having assets with a book value of 200 and fair value of 300, common equity of 100, and liabilities whose book values equal their fair values of 100. On 31-Dec-20X0, Acquiror Company acquires 75 percent of the common stock of Target Company in the open market for 250 cash. The remaining 25 percent of Target Company remains in the hands of others. Parent Company records the transaction on 31-Dec-20X0 as follows:

dr:	Target Company assets		275.0	(1)
dr:	Transaction goodwill created		150.0	(4)
	cr:	Target Company liabilities	100.0	(2)
	cr:	Cash (paid out in transaction)	300.0	(2)
	cr:	Minority interests (created in transaction)	25.0	(3)
memo:	(1)	75 percent of Target Company assets purchased are written up to fair value.		

$$300 + (300 - 200) \times 75\% = 75 + 200 = 275$$

(2) Target Company liabilities and cash paid in the transaction are recorded at book / fair value.

(3) Minority interests are recorded as 25 percent of Target Company net identifiable assets at existing book value.

$$(200 - 100) \times 25\% = 25$$

(4) Transaction goodwill is recorded as the excess of the purchase price over the fair value of Target Company's net identifiable assets.

$$300 - (275 - 100) - 25 = 150$$

EXAMPLE 13-18. Recording a Partial Acquisition Using the Full Goodwill Method

Assume the same facts as Example 13-17, except Acquiror Company records the transaction using the full goodwill method.

dr:	Target Company assets		300.0		(1)
dr:	Transaction goodwill created		150.0		(4)
cr:	Target Company liabilities			100.0	(2)
	cr:	Cash (paid out in transaction)		300.0	(2)
	cr:	Minority interests (created in transaction)		50.0	(3)
memo:	(1)	100 percent of Target Company assets purchased are written up to fair value of 300.			
	(2)	Target Company liabilities and cash paid in the transaction are recorded at fair value.			
	(3)	Minority interests are recorded as 25 percent of Target Company net identifiable assets at fair value.			

$$(300 - 100) \times 25\% = 50$$

(4) Transaction goodwill is recorded as the excess of the purchase price over the fair value of Target Company's net identifiable assets.

$$300 - (300 - 100) - 50 = 150$$

Creating a Minority Interest in Preferred Equity

A less-common transaction creates a minority interest in preferred equity when Acquiror Company purchases a controlling interest in Target Company but leaves some of Target Company's preferred equity outstanding. Example 13-19 shows how such a situation is recorded.

EXAMPLE 13-19. Recording an Acquisition of a Controlling Interest with Preferred Stock Left Outstanding

Assume that on 31-Dec-20X0 publicly traded Target Company has assets having both a book and fair value of 200, liabilities having both book and fair values of 100, common equity of 75, and preferred equity of 25. On 1-Jan-20X1, Acquiror Company purchases 100 percent of the common equity of Target Company for 75 but leaves the preferred equity outstanding, recording the transaction as:

dr:	Target Company assets		200.0		(1)
	cr:	Target Company liabilities		100.0	(1)
	cr:	Cash (paid out in transaction)		75.0	(1)
	cr:	Minority interests in preferred equity (created in transaction)		25.0	(2)
memo:	(1)	Target Company's assets and liabilities and cash paid in the transaction are all recorded at fair value.			
	(2)	25 of Target Company preferred equity still outstanding is recorded at book value as Minority interests in preferred equity.			

CHAPTER SUMMARY

Accounting for business combinations under U.S. GAAP uses the purchase method. The purchase method records Target Company's identifiable assets and liabilities at fair value, and the excess of the purchase price over the net identifiable assets is recorded as an asset called goodwill. Transaction goodwill is positive whenever the purchase price exceeds the fair value of the net identifiable assets. Under U.S. GAAP transaction, goodwill is carried on Acquiror Company's books at its historical value and periodically tested for impairment. In any period that it is determined to be impaired, it is written down against operating earnings.

In some situations, the fair value of the net identifiable assets may exceed the cost of the acquired assets, resulting in "negative goodwill." Under U.S. GAAP, negative goodwill is allocated ratably to reduce the book value of Target Company's acquired assets other than:

- Current assets
- Securities recorded using the cost method (trading, available for sale and held-to-maturity)
- Deferred tax assets
- Prepaid pension assets
- Assets being held for sale

Acquiror Company recognizes any negative goodwill remaining after reducing the eligible acquired assets to zero as an extraordinary gain in the acquisition period. IAS treats goodwill differently than does U.S. GAAP. Under IAS, both goodwill and negative goodwill are recorded at the acquisition date and amortized as either an expense (goodwill) or a component of income.

Goodwill created in certain transactions, such as asset purchases or deemed asset purchases under IRC Section 338, is tax deductible. Tax-deductible goodwill is amortized for tax purposes but not book purposes, resulting in the recognition of a deferred tax liability equal to the enacted tax rate times the excess of the book basis over the tax basis.

The accretion or dilution of Acquiror Company's earnings-per-share occurring because of the transaction is measured by projecting changes to Acquiror Company's stand-alone forecast earnings per share, such as:

- Changes in interest expense from retiring old debt (increases earnings) or from issuing new transaction debt (decreases earnings)
- Changes in deferred financing fee amortization expense from retiring old debt (increases earnings) or from issuing new transaction debt (decreases earnings)
- Changes in preferred equity dividends from buying in old preferred equity (increases earnings) or from issuing new transaction preferred equity (decreases earnings)
- Changes in depreciation of fair value write-ups to tangible assets (decreases earnings) or write-downs to tangible assets (increases earnings)
- Changes in amortization of recognition of new intangible assets (decreases earnings), fair value write-ups to intangible assets (decreases earnings), or write-downs to intangible assets (increases earnings)

- Changes to the minority interests in earnings from buying in old minority interests (increases earnings) or making a partial acquisition creating new minority interests (decreases earnings)
- Changes in taxes from combing two entities with different marginal tax rates into a single entity paying at Acquiror Company's tax rate
- Amortization of transaction goodwill for transactions performed under IAS (deceases earnings)
- Amortization of restructuring charges benefiting future periods such as bonus payments to retain key employees through transition periods (decreases earnings)
- Other one-time or nonrecurring transaction-related costs and benefits

Accretion or dilution is usually expressed as a percentage of Acquiror Company's stand-alone projected earnings per share.

In the acquisition period, purchase accounting combines the Acquiror Company's full-year earnings results with Target Company's posttransaction or stub period earning results to determine the combined company's results. Because any additional shares of Acquiror Company issued in the transaction are weighted, per-share metrics are comparable from period to period. Other metrics, not on a per-share basis, are not comparable, so pro forma results are often presented allowing comparison of period-to-period results on an "as if combined" basis.

CHAPTER 14

Deemed Asset Sales under IRC Sections 338(h)(10) or 338(g)

INTRODUCTION

When a company is acquired through an acquisition of its stock, gains and losses are then calculated using the basis of the stock. The tax bases of the underlying assets and liabilities that make up the company are unchanged by the transaction. A deemed asset sale is a feature of the U.S. Internal Revenue Code (IRC) allowing a stock sale to be treated as an asset sale. In other words, the stock of the company is sold, but taxes are paid as if the individual assets were sold, and consequently the tax bases of the underlying assets are "stepped-up" to reflect the allocated sale price.

At first the advantage of a transaction where taxes are paid sooner rather than later is not apparent until we consider net operating losses (NOLs). NOLs have a finite life and expire if they cannot be used to offset taxable income. Additionally, the IRC restricts the rate at which they may be applied following a change of control transaction. In fact, one outcome of many stock purchase transactions is that the potential future tax benefit of Target Company's NOLs is permanently lost. A deemed asset sale under Section 338(h)(10) can mitigate or eliminate this undesirable outcome by offsetting the NOLs against any gain on the deemed asset sale. The 338(h)(10) election often provides the double benefit of preserving the tax benefit of NOLs that would have otherwise been lost and accelerating realization of those benefits to the present. A third benefit of a 338(h)(10) election is that any goodwill or intangible assets recognized because of the transaction are tax deductible, unlike goodwill created or purchased self-created intangible assets recognized in no-step-up stock acquisitions.

OVERVIEW OF THE SECTION 338(H)(10) ELECTION

At first glance, a discussion of the treatment a stock purchase as a deemed asset sale for federal tax purposes may seem out of place in an accounting textbook.

FIGURE 14·1

Section 338(h)(10) Transaction

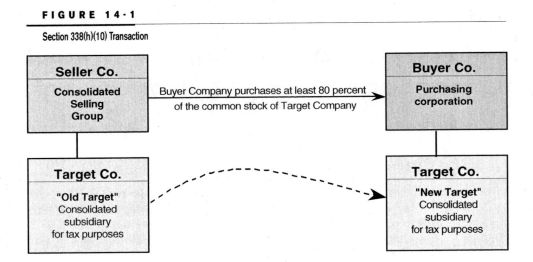

Analysts that have attempted to find explanations of the taxation and financial reporting mechanics of deemed asset sales and how to model them should certainly appreciate their inclusion here.

To clarify the discussion of Section 338 transactions as shown in Figure 14-1 and the following discussions, we look at three corporate entities, the first two being: Target Company, an at-least 80-percent-owned subsidiary of the second entity, Seller Company, who consolidates Target Company's results for federal tax purposes. Buyer Company is the third entity and purchases the stock of Target Company from Seller Company.

Inside and Outside Basis

Usually, when the stock of Target Company is purchased for cash or other consideration such as relief from indebtedness, Seller Company pays taxes on the difference between the realized selling price of the stock and its adjusted basis (outside basis). The tax bases of Target Company's underlying assets (inside bases) pass, unchanged, into the hands of Buyer Company, the purchaser. This is sometimes referred to as a "no-step-up" transaction because the tax bases of Target Company's assets and liabilities are the same after the transaction as they were before the transaction, even though the bases for financial reporting purposes (book bases) may change as a result of the transaction.

If both Seller Company and Buyer Company jointly elect, the stock sale may be deemed (for tax purposes) under IRC Section 338(h)(10), to be an asset sale. As a deemed asset sale, Seller Company (or Buyer Company) pays tax on the difference between the deemed (imputed) sale price of the assets and their tax bases. The deemed sale price is allocated to the assets sold, which steps up their tax bases in the hands of Buyer Company. The federal tax code allows cost recovery of the basis of an asset through either depreciation or amortization deductions. Consequently, the higher deductions realized from stepping up the bases of the assets results in reduced cash taxes in the periods following a step-up transaction.

Tax Burden of Deemed Asset Sale Transactions

In general, Target Company is treated as transferring all of its assets to Buyer Company in exchange for consideration that includes discharge of its liabilities in a single transaction on the acquisition date. Because this is a taxable event, a tax liability is created as a consequence of the sale, and the sale agreement specifies which party (Buyer Company or Seller Company) absorbs the economic cost of the tax.

Regardless of whether Buyer Company or Seller Company bears the burden for the sale taxes, the sale price may be negotiated to make Seller Company indifferent as to whether the transaction is structured as a stock sale or a deemed asset sale under Section 338(h)(10). This usually means that Buyer Company concedes some of the economic benefits of the tax benefits it realizes from the Section 338(h)(10) transaction to Seller Company in the form of a higher purchase price than would normally be negotiated for a taxable stock transaction. Because the deemed asset sale treatment cannot be elected unilaterally but must be made mutually and simultaneously by both parties to the transaction, Seller Company has leverage in the negotiations to force Buyer Company to "share" some of the tax benefits in exchange for Seller's agreement to elect treatment under Section 338(h)(10).

BENEFITS OF SECTION 338(h)(10) SALES

Because the transaction is treated as a deemed asset sale, the bases of the purchased assets are stepped up; however, they may not be stepped up above their individual fair values. In the case where there is a residual of the purchase price over the fair market values of the assets purchased, the residual of the purchase price not used to step up assets is allocated to goodwill. Generally, this allows Buyer Company to take higher tax depreciation than it would under a stock sale where the assets remain at their old tax bases. The advantage to Buyer Company is the present value of the tax shield created by the depreciation of the bases step-ups.

Tax-Deductible Goodwill

A significant tax impact of a Section 338(h)(10) transaction is that any goodwill created in the transaction is tax deductible. Under a straight stock purchase or "no-step-up" transaction, goodwill recognized in the transaction is not tax deductible. An obvious advantage to Buyer Company (the purchaser) over a stock purchase is the present value of the tax savings from the tax-deductible goodwill created, amortized over a statutory 15 years. A sometimes overlooked subtlety is that, because the benefit is from the tax-deductible goodwill *created* in the transaction, if the target had preexisting *tax-deductible* goodwill, then only the incremental increase between the transaction goodwill and the target's preexisting tax-deductible goodwill can be considered as a *transaction* benefit.

Following the implementation of *FAS142, Goodwill and Other intangible Assets,* goodwill is no longer amortized for financial reporting (book) purposes. In the case of tax-deductible goodwill, this results in a difference between the tax and book bases because the tax basis is reduced each period by the amount of the periodic cost recovery, whereas the book basis remains unchanged.

To account for excess of the book basis over the tax basis, a deferred tax liability is recognized equal to the excess, of the book basis over the tax basis, times the enacted tax rate. The tax amortization of the goodwill in each of the 15 periods subsequent to the deemed asset sale increases the difference between the book and tax bases, resulting in the recognition of a deferred tax expense calculated as the amortization times the enacted tax rate. This deferred tax expense increases the deferred tax liability account increases in each period.

Tax-Deductible Intangible Assets

Intangible assets that are self-created by a taxpayer, such as client lists, patents, copyrights, and trademarks, are excluded from IRC Section 197 and are generally nondeductible. In a stock purchase transaction, the characterization of these intangibles is unchanged for tax purposes because it is the stock of the firm that is being purchased and not the individual assets. If a deemed asset sale is elected under Section 338(h)(10), the intangibles previously created by the old Target Company become *purchased* intangible assets, and Buyer Company is permitted a cost recovery deduction for those purchased intangibles under IRC Section 197 following the deemed asset sale. Like goodwill, the economic benefit to Buyer Company from a Section 338(h)(10) transaction, compared to a stock purchase, is the present value of the future tax savings from amortization of the cost of any previously nondeductible intangible assets. Also like goodwill, all other Section 197 intangible assets are amortized over a statutory 15-year period without regard to their actual economic life. Because the amortization of the intangible assets for financial reporting purposes is determined by their expected useful lives, it is entirely likely that the amortization periods for book and tax purposes will differ. The unequal amortization periods and resulting periodic amortization expenses create a difference between the book and tax bases of the intangible assets. Buyer Company accounts for the tax effects of the book-tax difference by recognizing deferred tax items in each of the subsequent accounting periods.

NOL Carryforwards

If an acquisition target has existing net operating loss carryforwards (NOLs), then these may be used to offset all or a portion of Seller Company's gain from the deemed asset sale. A common error that occurs in estimating the economic value of a Section 338(h)(10) transaction is to include the entire tax savings from the NOLs as part of Seller Company's economic benefit from the transaction. The most accurate estimate of Seller Company's benefit is the difference between the benefit realized from using the NOLs to offset transaction gain and the benefit that would have been realized had the transaction not occurred. In cases where Seller Company is projected to completely use Target Company's NOLs in future periods, the advantage for Seller Company's comes from the *earlier* recognition of the tax benefit from the NOLs and is the difference between the tax savings on the sale gain offset by the NOLs and the present value of the tax savings of using the NOLs in the future. The economic benefits of a Section 338(h)(10) election may be significantly greater when it is unlikely that Seller Company can realize the full tax benefits of Target Company's NOLs because projected future earnings are not adequate to allow recovery of the NOLs before they expire.

Accretion/Dilution in Deemed Asset Sale Transactions

Goodwill and some intangibles, such as those having indefinite useful lives, are not subject to amortization for financial reporting (book) purposes. Consequently, there is no reduction to book earnings from their amortization and no reduction to reported total income tax expense because for financial reporting purposes, the cash tax shield realized from those items creates (and is recognized as) a deferred tax liability.

EXAMPLE **14-1. Book and Tax Effects of a Deemed Asset Sale Transaction**

Buyer Company purchases Target Company on 31-Dec-20X0, and both Seller Company and Buyer Company elect treatment as a deemed asset sale under Section 338(h)(10). The single asset recorded in the transaction is goodwill in the amount of 1500. The combined group realizes the financial results shown below. Because the transaction goodwill is tax deductible and book goodwill is not, book earnings are not impacted by its amortization, whereas the tax results are affected.

BUYER-TARGET COMBINED COMPANY OPERATING RESULTS

Tax Year 20X1	Book reporting		Tax reporting
Revenues	1,000.0	Revenues	1,000.0
Amortization	-.-	Amortization	(100.0)
Earnings before taxes	1,000.0	Taxable income	900.0
Income tax expense @ 40.0%	(400.0)	Current tax expense	(360.0)
Net income	600.0		

To reflect the fact that the tax basis of goodwill is reduced below the book basis of goodwill, the financial reporting entry includes a deferred tax item:

dr:	Income tax expense	400.0	
	cr: Cash		360.0
	cr: Deferred income tax liability (100.0 × 40.0%)		40.0
memo:	To record the cash and deferred components of income tax expense.		

DETERMINING THE SALE PRICE FOR A SECTION 338(h)(10) ELECTION

In a purchase of Target Company's stock, the sale price is usually very straightforward. It is the price paid for the stock that, for Seller Company, represents the amount realized for the sale. Under a deemed asset sale, the amount realized is calculated a little differently because we are treating the transaction as if all of the assets were sold (even if we are only buying 80 or 90 percent of the company). The amount realized also considers that Seller Company is discharged from all of Target Company's liabilities, which may even include the tax liability from the sale itself. The result is the aggregate deemed sale price (ADSP).

Aggregate Deemed Sale Price (ADSP)

In a deemed asset sale, Target Company is deemed to have sold all of its assets to Buyer Company. The ADSP is the amount for which Target Company is deemed to have sold its assets to Buyer Company. The IRC prescribes the method for calculating ADSP and is determined by first grossing up the sale price to reflect 100 percent of the assets, subtracting the selling costs incurred by the selling shareholders and then adding the total liabilities assumed by Buyer Company.

EXAMPLE **14-2.** Calculation of the Aggregate Deemed Sale Price

Target Company is a wholly owned and consolidated subsidiary of Seller Company. Buyer Company purchases 90 percent of Target Company's outstanding stock for 9000. The tax bases of the assets being sold are 1000. Selling costs for Target Company's shareholders were 200, and the fair value of the Target Company's liabilities was an accounts payable of 400 and a 5000 note. Under the terms of the sales agreement, Seller Company is responsible for the tax consequences of the sale, and Seller Company's tax rate is 34 percent.

$$\text{ADSP} = \text{G (grossed-up sale price less selling costs)} +$$
$$\text{L (target's liabilities other than any tax liability for the deemed sale)}$$

ADSP is calculated as:

grossed-up sale price (9,000 / 90%)	10,000
less: selling costs	- 200
add: assumed liability	+ 400
add: assumed liability	+ 5,000
Aggregate deemed sale price (ADSP)	15,200

At a 34 percent tax rate, the tax consequence paid by Seller Company is:

$$(15,200 - 1,000) \times 34\% = 4,828$$
$$(\text{ADSP} - \text{total bases of all the assets}) \times \text{tax rate}$$

Alternatively, Buyer Company and Seller Company could, by agreement, specify that Buyer Company, instead of Seller Company, assumes responsibility for the tax consequences of the sale. In that case, ADSP is increased to include the assumed tax liability. Using the other facts from above, rearrange the tax code formula for ADSP[1] to a more usable form:

ADSP = G (grossed-up sale price less selling costs) +
         L (Target Company's liabilities other than any tax liability for the
         deemed sale) +
         $Tr \times (ADSP - B - N)$ where:

Tr is Seller Company's tax rate, B is the bases of the assets deemed sold, and N are the amount of NOL carryforwards used to shield gain on the sale.

It is important to note, especially when modeling this transaction, that in this form the calculation is circular because ADSP appears on both sides of the equation, causing both ADSP and the tax consequence of the sale $Tr \times (ADSP - B - N)$ to increase with each iteration. Solving for ADSP:

$$ADSP = (G + L - Tr \times (B + N) / (1 - Tr)$$

ADSP is calculated as: =

grossed-up sale price (9,000 / 90%)	10,000
less: selling costs −200	
add: assumed liability	+ 400
add: assumed liability	+ 5,000
add: sale tax liability (22,515 − 1,000) × 34%	+ 7,315
Aggregate deemed sale price (ADSP)	22,515

In Example 14-2, deciding to have Buyer Company, instead of Seller Company, assume the tax consequence (liability) from the sale results in a (7315 − 4828) = 2487 higher tax burden for the transaction.

Calculating Seller Company's Gain or Loss on the Sale

Taxable gain from a stock sale is the selling price less the adjusted basis of the stock (which includes its selling cost). The gain on the sale may usually be reduced by any loss carryforwards of Seller Company. Tax is calculated at Seller Company's 34-percent tax rate for the remaining gain.

In an asset sale, the gain or loss for each asset within the seven asset classes is individually calculated and then characterized as capital or ordinary. A reasonable simplification for analyzing transactions is to calculate gains and losses on each class (as opposed to calculating gains and losses for each individual asset) and then to net the seven gains and losses from the classes together. Again, the gain on the sale may usually be reduced by any loss carryforwards of Seller, and the tax is calculated at Seller's tax rate for the remaining gain.

When determining the tax effects of a Section 338(h)(10) election, the taxable gain is based on the calculated ADSP and not the cash sale price. This creates a higher tax burden in the cases where the transaction includes assumption of Target Company's liabilities by Buyer Company because the value of the discharged liabilities is treated as income to the selling group. Depending on the form of the transaction, the assumed liabilities may or may not include the tax liability that results from the sale.

Calculating Buyer Company's Bases for Depreciation and Amortization

Buyer Company recovers the cost of the purchased assets through depreciation or amortization of their adjusted cost bases. In a Section 338(h)(10) transaction, the cost basis of the individual assets is determined by allocating the adjusted grossed-up basis (AGUB) of the transaction to each of the seven individual classes of assets. Available AGUB is allocated first to the most liquid asset class, Class I, Cash and equivalents, up to the amount of their fair value. Any remaining AGUB that has not been allocated to Class I assets is allocated sequentially to each of the remaining asset classes. Any residual AGUB that is allocated to asset classes I through VI is finally allocated to Class VII, Goodwill.

Adjusted Grossed-Up Basis (AGUB)

The AGUB of the assets acquired in the sale is the same as the ADSP except for the effects of acquisition and selling costs. Selling costs are subtracted for the calculation of ADSP and acquisition costs are added for the calculation of AGUB. ADSP and AGUB also vary if the transaction involves nonrecently purchased stock (not a common occurrence).

Buyer Company depreciates each of the assets as if they were just placed into service after being purchased for a cost equal to their allocated portion of AGUB. When comparing the difference between a stock sale and a Section 338(h)(10) election, only the present value of the step-up from the asset sale is considered because the existing bases continue to be depreciable for a stock sale.

This approach incorporates another reasonable simplification. In actuality, the assets pretransaction bases may be depreciable over a shorter number of years under a stock sale than they would be under the "fresh-start" that results from a Section 338(h)(10) election.

Example 14-3. Calculation of theAdjusted Grossed-Up Basis[2]

Buyer Company purchases 100 percent of the stock of Target Company for 2000. Buyer Company and Seller Company both elect to treat the transaction as a deemed asset purchase under Section 338(h)(10). As part of the transaction, Buyer Company also assumes 690 of Target Company's outstanding liabilities and agrees to pay the 300 tax liability arising from the transaction. Additionally, Buyer Company incurs 10 of advisory fees associated with the transaction. The AGUB of Target Company's purchased assets is:

Grossed-up basis (2,000 / 100%)	2,000
Acquisition costs	10
Assumed liability	690
Transaction tax liability	300
Adjusted grossed-up basis (AGUB)	3,000

EXAMPLE 14-4. Allocation of the Adjusted Grossed-Up Basis[3]

Continuing the facts and results of Example 14-3, assume that on the day following the transaction, Target Company has assets with fair market values as shown below. The equipment is modified accelerated cost-recovery (MACRS) property having both a three-year tax and economic life. The equipment originally cost 1800 and was placed in service 18 months prior to the transaction. The AGUB of 3000 is allocated to each asset by class, in order, beginning with Class I.

Class	Asset	Fair value	Allocated basis	Remaining AGUB
I	Cash	200	200	2,800
II	Marketable securities	300	300	2,500
III	Accounts receivable	600	600	1,900
IV	Inventory	300	300	1,600
V	Equipment	900	900	700
V	Land	400	400	300
VI	Customer list	150	150	150
VII	Goodwill	0	150	0

The tax basis that this process allocates to each of the assets in this process represents that asset's new depreciable or amortizable tax basis. The amount by which the new allocated tax basis exceeds the pretransaction tax basis is the amount of the step-up realized from the deemed asset sale transaction.

Asset Amortization Bases

If the Class VI asset, Customer list, was a self-created intangible asset, then its tax basis was zero on the transaction date. On the day after the transaction, the Customer list becomes a purchased Section 197 intangible asset whose allocated basis of 150 is recoverable through tax-deductible straight-line amortization of 10 per year over a statutory 15-year period. Similarly, the goodwill created is also tax deductible and recoverable in the same fashion over the same statutory recovery period. If Buyer Company is a 34-percent taxpayer whose appropriate discount rate is 10 percent, the economic benefit from the tax-deductible intangible asset and goodwill alone is the present value of the tax savings of $(10 + 10 = 20 \times 34\%)$ = 6.8 in each of the 15 posttransaction periods, or approximately 51.7.

If Buyer Company had purchased the stock of Target Company and not elected treatment as a deemed asset sale under Section 338(h)(10), the tax bases of the assets would not have changed, and the transaction goodwill recognized would not have been tax deductible. The tax savings realized from the deemed asset sale makes the economic outcome of the transaction more appealing to Buyer Company

Asset Depreciation Bases

The tax bases of depreciable assets such as the equipment are also stepped up in a deemed asset sale transaction. In Figure 14-2, the depreciation schedule of Target Company's three-year modified accelerated cost-recovery (MACRS) equipment is shown for both its pretransaction original and its posttransaction stepped up bases. Because MACRS uses a midyear convention, only one-half of the first year's depreciation is allowed and full recovery of three-year property occurs over a four-year period.

Figure 14-2 shows how the step up of the tax basis of an asset produces an economic benefit for Buyer Company. If the transaction had been undertaken as a stock purchase without a Section 338(h)(10) election, the tax basis would have remained unchanged and the asset depreciation continued under the original depreciation schedule. Because MACRS accelerates depreciation for tax purposes, the tax basis of 400 remaining on the transaction date is significantly lower than the financial reporting basis and the fair market value. If the transaction is treated as a deemed asset sale, the asset's tax basis steps up from 400 to 900. The economic benefit to Buyer Company is the 134.8 present value of the tax savings from the step-up in basis of (900 − 400) = 500, not the tax savings from the entire basis of 900 because 400 of that amount was depreciable under the original schedule.

FIGURE 14·2

Original and Stepped-Up Depreciation Schedule

Depreciation schedule: 3-year property					
Original depreciation	**20X0**	**20X1**	**20X2**	**20X3**	**20X4**
Equipment - beginning	-	400.0	133.3		
Depreciation	-	266.7	133.3		
Equipment - ending	400.0	133.3	-	-	-
Stepped-up depreciation					
Equipment - beginning	-	900.0	600.0	200.0	66.7
Depreciation	-	300.0	400.0	133.3	66.7
Equipment - ending	900.0	600.0	200.0	66.7	-
Effect of step-up					
Increase in tax-deductible depreciation		33.3	266.7	133.3	66.7
Tax benefit @ 34% tax rate		11.3	90.7	45.3	22.7
Present value @ 10% discount rate	134.8				

MODELING SECTION 338(h)(10) TRANSACTIONS

Modeling the financial accounting of a deemed asset sale is nearly identical to modeling an acquisition. The primary difference lies in the calculation of the deferred tax items because the tax and book bases are stepped up under Section 338(h)(10), making the tax bases of assets equal to their book bases. Because the differences between book and tax bases are eliminated, there is no need to recognize a deferred tax asset or liability for those items. Any deferred tax items existing on Target Company's balance sheet because of book/tax differences are generally eliminated by the transaction.

Target Company Net Operating Losses (NOLs)

In any business combination involving a Target Company having net operating loss (NOL) carryforwards, the deferred tax asset associated with the carryforwards must usually be reduced to reflect the fact that Section 382 limits the future use of the carryforwards. That remains true for deemed asset sale transactions, which must also be modeled to eliminate any deferred tax asset associated with Target Company NOLs that Seller Company uses to reduce gain from the sale. The deferred tax asset is reduced using a valuation allowance for the unrecoverable future tax benefit (unrecoverable amount of the NOL × the enacted tax rate).

Modeling Economic Benefits and Burdens

One key objective when modeling a deemed asset sale transaction is to accurately estimate the benefits and burdens of the transaction and to identify who bears or enjoys them. Often the best starting point is first looking at the economic outcomes of a stock sale transaction. Next, the same analysis is performed for a Section 338(h)(10) transaction, and the two outcomes are compared. This analysis results in a range of prices for the transaction: at one end Seller Company is indifferent between a stock sale and a deemed asset sale because there is a price that provides the same economic outcome. At the other end of the range is a price where Buyer Company is indifferent for the same reason. Ideally, the final negotiated price "sharing" the benefits of the Section 338(h)(10) election falls within the analyzed range.

EXAMPLE 14-5. Basic Section 338(h)(10) Price Analysis

Seller Company holds 100 percent of the stock of Target Company, which it consolidates for financial reporting and federal income tax purposes. Seller Company's basis in the stock is 50,000 when Buyer Company offers to purchase Target Company for 100,000. Target Company consists of a single Class V asset with a five-year MACRS recovery period, an adjusted basis of 25,000, and a fair market value of 50,000. Both Seller Company and Buyer Company are 40-percent taxpayers and Buyer Company's cost of capital is 8 percent.

In Figure 14-3 the economic outcome to both Seller Company and Buyer Company are shown. A basic taxable stock sale leaves Seller Company with 80,000, the selling price less income taxes on the gain, and requires only that Target Company be given up. Seller Company's gain is calculated as the gross income from the sale less the adjusted basis of the stock, (100,000 – 50,000) = 50,000, because it is the stock that is being sold. The same transaction leaves Buyer Company only with Target Company and requires the payout of 100,000. The inference in this basic analysis is that any other offering must provide Seller Company with the same net benefit as this transaction, and likewise, cost Buyer Company no more than the net value being paid.

Seller Company's total benefit from a stock sale includes:

Purchase price
less: selling costs
less: tax on the gain from the sale
less: the present value of the future tax savings that would have produced by any loss carryforwards used to reduce the sale gain.

SELLER COMPANY'S INDIFFERENCE PRICE

If Buyer Company and Seller Company both agree to elect to treat the transaction as a deemed asset sale, then Seller Company's gain must be calculated differently. For a Section 338(h)(10) transaction, the taxable gain is the gross sale proceeds less the adjusted bases of the assets, (100,000 – 25,000) = 75,000 because it is the assets that are deemed to be sold. However, the selling price of 100,000, less taxes of (75,000 ¥ 40%) = 30,000, only leaves Seller Company with 70,000, which is less than the 80,000 realized on the stock sale. Seller Company would clearly favor the outcome of the stock sale unless the selling price was raised to 116,667. Figure 14-4 shows that, at that price, Seller Company realizes a gain of (116,667 – 25,000) = 91,667 yielding a tax burden of (91,667 ¥ 40%) = 36,667 and a net economic benefit of (116,667 – 36,667) = 80,000, the same as the taxable stock sale. Seller Company is indifferent between a taxable stock sale of 80,000 and a deemed asset sale for 116,667 because, after taxes, the result is 80,000 to Seller Company.

Seller Company's total benefit from a deemed asset sale includes:

Purchase price
add: target liabilities assumed
less: selling costs
less: tax on the gain from the sale
less: the present value of the future tax savings that would have produced by any loss carryforwards used to reduce the sale gain.

FIGURE 14-3

Seller Company's and Buyer Company's Economic Outcomes from a Stock Sale

Seller's economic outcome	
Selling price	100,000.0
Adjusted basis of stock	50,000.0
Taxable gain on sale	50,000.0
Tax on sale @ 40%	20,000.0
After-tax proceeds from sale	80,000.0

Target's economic outcome	
Purchase price	100,000.0
Tax burden	0.0
Total price paid	100,000.0
Tax benefits from step up	0.0
Total price paid less benefits	100,000.0

FIGURE 14·4

Seller Company's Indifference Price

Seller's stock sale outcome		Seller's §338(h)(10) outcome	
Selling price	100,000.0	Selling price	116,667.0
Adjusted basis of stock	50,000.0	Adjusted basis of assets	25,000.0
Taxable gain on sale	50,000.0	Taxable gain on sale	91,667.0
Tax on sale @ 40%	20,000.0	Tax on sale @ 40%	36,667.0
After-tax proceeds from sale	80,000.0	After-tax proceeds from sale	80,000.0

BUYER COMPANY'S INDIFFERENCE PRICE

Using the same facts as the preceding analysis for Seller Company's indifference price, a similar approach leads to the Buyer Company's indifference price. That price is determined by increasing the purchase price by the present value of the other economic benefits that Buyer Company realizes. These benefits include the tax savings for the step-up depreciation of (50,000 – 25,000) = 25,000 and for the amortization of transaction goodwill determined as the excess of the price paid over the fair market value of the assets purchased. The purchase price at which Buyer Company is indifferent between a taxable stock purchase or a Section 338(h)(10) election is shown in Figure 14-5 as 126,602.

A purchase at this price creates tax-deductible goodwill of (126,602 – 50,000) = 76,602 that is recovered using straight-line amortization over the 15 years following the transaction at a rate of (76,602 / 15) = 5106.8 producing a tax savings of (5106.8 × 40%) = 2042.7 in each period. The present value of those tax savings is 18,170.6, calculated by using Buyer Company's 8-percent cost of capital as the discount rate. The transaction also steps up the basis of the Class V asset from 25,000 to 50,000, and the additional 25,000 of basis is depreciated over the six years following the transaction. The tax savings from the additional tax-deductible depreciation has a present value of 8431.4. The total economic value of the additional depreciation and amortization tax savings is (18,170.6 + 8,431.4) = 26,602. Buyer Company is indifferent between purchasing Target Company in a stock transaction for 100,000 or paying 126,602 for Target Company in a deemed asset sale transaction and realizing 26,602 of additional economic benefits.

Buyer Company's total burden from a deemed asset sale includes:

Purchase price
less: present value of tax savings from amortizing goodwill created by the transaction
less: present value of tax savings from amortizing intangible asset basis step-up
less: present value of tax savings from depreciating asset basis step-up

SECTION 338(h)(10) TRANSACTION PRICE RANGE

As Figure 14-6 illustrates, the results of analyzing the Seller Company's and Buyer Company's indifference prices identifies a range where both parties may realize better outcomes from electing Section 338(h)(10) treatment of the transaction. In the range between 116,667, Seller Company's indifference price and 126,602, Buyer Company's indifference price, both parties benefit by negotiating a purchase price falling within that range. If the outcome of the analyses indicates that there is no range of mutual benefit, then a deemed

FIGURE 14·5

Buyer Company's Indifference Price

Buyer's stock sale outcome	
Purchase price	100,000.0
Tax burden	0.0
Total price paid	100,000.0
Tax benefits from step up	0.0
Total price paid less benefits	100,000.0

Buyer's §338(h)(10) outcome	
Purchase price	126,602.0
Tax burden	0.0
Total price paid	126,602.0
Tax benefits from step up	26,602.0
Total price paid less benefits	100,000.0

FIGURE 14·6

Transaction Price Range

A §338(h)(10) election gives Buyer Co. a better outcome than a stock purchase if the purchase price is less than 126,602

Only Seller Co. enjoys a better outcome

Both parties realize a better outcome in this range of prices

Only Buyer Co. enjoys a better outcome

A §338(h)(10) election gives Seller Co. a better outcome than a stock purchase if the purchase price is greater than 116,667

116,667   126,602

asset sale transaction would not occur because both Seller Company and Buyer Company must simultaneously agree to the Section 338(h)(10) election.

CHAPTER SUMMARY

When Seller Company sells the assets of its subsidiary, Target Company, it is subjected to tax on any gains at the corporate level. When those gains are either distributed to the shareholders as dividends, or realized by the shareholders as capital gains, they are taxed a second time. Because of the double taxation, selling the assets of a subsidiary usually has less desirable tax consequences for the shareholders of a corporation.

On the other hand, Buyer Company, the purchaser of a subsidiary, would rather purchase the assets and subsequently capture the tax benefits of the stepped-up tax bases through the tax benefit of higher depreciation and amortization deductions. Ideally, Buyer Company would also like to preserve the future tax benefit of any subsidiary NOLs and not have them subject to the Section 382 limitations.

A Section 338(h)(10) election provides benefits for both Seller Company and Buyer Company when the tax benefit from using the NOLs in the present instead of the future (or losing them altogether) plus the present value of the step-up depreciation and amortization is greater than the increased tax burden of the Section 338(h)(10) election over a plain stock sale. Any benefit from a Section 338(h)(10) transaction over a stock sale is usually "split" between Buyer Company and Seller Company because both parties must agree, in advance, to elect the transaction. Whenever a firm is selling a subsidiary with substantial NOLs, a Section 338(h)(10) election should always be analyzed as a potential approach to creating value for the shareholders.

ABO *Accumulated benefit obligation.* The actuarial present value of benefits (whether vested or nonvested) attributed by the pension benefit formula to employee service rendered before a specified date and based on employee service and compensation (if applicable) before that date. The accumulated benefit obligation differs from the projected benefit obligation in that it includes no assumption about future compensation levels.[1]

ADSP *Aggregate deemed sale price.* The aggregate deemed sale price is defined in Income Tax Regulations Section 1.338-4(a) as "…the amount for which old target is deemed to have sold all of its assets in the deemed asset sale."

AGUB *Adjusted grossed-up basis.* The adjusted grossed-up basis is defined in Income Tax Regulations Section 1.338-5(a) as "… the amount for which new target is deemed to have purchased all of its assets in the deemed purchase…"

APB *Accounting Principles Board Opinion.* The Accounting Principles Board preceded the Financial Accounting Standards Board (FASB). The *Accounting Principles Board Opinions* are incorporated in FASB's *Original Pronouncements* and are part of the basis of U.S. Generally Accepted Accounting Principles.

APBO *Accumulated postretirement benefit obligation.* The actuarial present value of benefits attributed to employee service rendered to a particular date. Prior to an employee's *full eligibility date*, the *accumulated postretirement benefit obligation* as of a particular date for an employee is the portion of the *expected postretirement benefit obligation* attributed to that employee's service rendered to that date; on and after the full eligibility date the *accumulated* and *expected postretirement benefit obligations* for an employee are the same.[2]

ARB *Accounting Research Bulletin.* Accounting Research Bulletins were the work of two committees of the American Institute of Certified Public Accountants (AICPA). When the APB superceded those two committees, it carried forward the ARBs as a continuing part of the basis of U.S. GAAP. Subsequently, when FASB superceded the APB, it too carried the Accounting Research Bulletins forward and incorporated them as part of *Original Pronouncements.*

at-the-money In reference to stock options, it is an option whose exercise, or strike, price is equal to the market value of the underlying stock. An equity option having a $40.00 per share exercise price is "at-the-money" when the underlying equity is trading at $40.00 per share.

Carryback "Deductions or credits that cannot be utilized on the tax return during a year that may be carried back to reduce taxable income or taxes payable in a prior year. An operating loss carryback is an excess of tax deductions over gross income in a year; a tax credit carryback is the amount by which tax credits available for utilization exceed statutory limitations."[3]

carryforward "Deductions or credits that cannot be utilized on the tax return during a year that may be carried forward to reduce taxable income or taxes payable in a future year. An operating loss carryforward is an excess of tax deductions over gross income in a year; a tax credit carryforward is the amount by which tax credits available for utilization exceed statutory limitations."[4]

communication date Under a plan to involuntarily terminate employees, the *communication date* is the earliest date that the terminating firm meets all of the requirements to recognize a liability for the one-time benefit costs of the termination plan and has communicated the details of the one-time benefit arrangements to its employees.

contra accounts Contra accounts are offsetting accounts that are normally presented on the face of the financial statements or in footnote disclosures. Accumulated depreciation is an example of a contra asset account because it offsets the Property, plant, and equipment account. Similarly, the Deferred tax valuation account offsets the Deferred income tax asset account.

curtailment "A *curtailment* is an event that significantly reduces the expected years of future service of present employees or eliminates for a significant number of employees the accrual of defined benefits for some or all of their future services."[5]

EBITDA *Earnings before interest, taxes, depreciation, and amortization.* EBITDA is often used as a proxy for cash flows from operations. One of the shortcomings of EBITDA as a metric is that it is strictly an analytic term and consequently has no formal accounting definition. When using EBITDA for comparative purposes, it is important to understand how it is being derived and to adjust it if necessary to be comparable with the other firm's EBITDA.

EBO *Expected benefit obligation.* Actuarial present value as of a particular date of postretirement benefits expected to be paid to or for a current plan participant.[6] The term EBO is generally used in FASB's literature collectively as the expected benefit obligation arising from both pension and other postretirement plans. In that sense it includes the Projected benefit obligation discussed under FAS87 and the Expected postretirement benefit obligation of FAS106. It is unusual to find the term EBO outside of FASB literature.

effective tax rate Companies sometimes disclose an *effective tax rate* as part of the required disclosure reconciling the differences between actual and statutory income taxation. Effective tax rates are generally equal to the firm's statutory federal rate reduced by the effects of tax credits and other tax preference items. Effective tax rate is calculated as the Provision for income taxes divided by Earnings before income taxes (EBT). The effective tax rate is not used for calculating deferred income tax items; they are calculated using the enacted statutory tax rate.

EPBO *Expected postretirement benefit obligation.* The actuarial present value as of a particular date of the benefits expected to be paid to or for an employee, the employee's beneficiaries, and any covered dependents pursuant to the terms of the postretirement benefit plan.[7]

EPS *Earnings per share* is defined in U.S. GAAP as "The amount of earnings attributable to each share of common stock. For convenience, the term is used in [FAS128] to refer to either earnings or loss per share."[8]

ERISA The Employee Retirement Income Security Act of 1974 (as amended). ERISA is the law governing the administration of employee retirement (pension) plans.

FASB *Financial Accounting Standards Board.* FASB is the designated standards board in the United States for establishing financial accounting and reporting standards. More information about FASB's mission is available from their Web site at *www.fasb.org.*

FIFO *First-in, first-out.* An inventory valuation method where the oldest (first-in) inventory is considered to be expended before more recently acquired inventory. FIFO is the most commonly encountered inventory valuation method.

FIN *Financial Accounting Standards Board Interpretations.* Interpretations by the Financial Accounting Standards Board clarifying the application of financial accounting standards and pronouncements.

full eligibility date The date at which an employee has rendered all of the service necessary to have earned the right to receive all of the benefits expected to be received by that employee (including any beneficiaries and dependents expected to receive benefits).[9]

future service period Regarding restructuring charges, when employees are required to render service beyond the minimum retention period (normally 60 days) in order to be eligible for certain involuntary termination benefits, they render the service during the future service period. The future service period begins on the communication date and extends until the employees meet the requirements for the termination benefits.

GAAP *Generally Accepted Accounting Principles* are the rules, standards, laws, and common practices that firms must adhere to when preparing financial statements for presentation to auditors or to outside users.

goodwill The excess of the cost of an acquired entity over the net of the amounts assigned to assets acquired and liabilities assumed. The amount recognized as goodwill includes acquired intangible assets that do not meet the criteria [in FAS141] for recognition as assets apart from goodwill.[10] A slightly more practical definition is: The excess of the total purchase price given over the fair value of the net identifiable assets (net assets less existing goodwill) received.

IAS *International Accounting Standards.* The series of accounting pronouncements, *International Financial Reporting Standards (IFRSs)*, published by the International Accounting Standards Board (IASB).

IASB *International Accounting Standards Board.* The standards setting body for International Accounting Standards whose function parallels that of the Financial Accounting Standards Board. Both boards regularly confer on issues of financial accounting and are committed to converging International Accounting Standards and Financial Accounting Standards. More information about IASB's mission is available from their Web site at *www.iasb.org.uk*.

IFRSs *International Financial Reporting Standards. IFRSs* are the series of the International Accounting Standards Board's (IASB's) published accounting pronouncements constituting *International Accounting Standards.*

IRC *Internal Revenue Code.* The enacted legislation governing income taxation in the United States. The IRC is codified in Title 26 of the United States Code.

IRS *Internal Revenue Service.* The *Internal Revenue Service* is the branch of the U.S. Treasury Department responsible for administering U.S. tax law. More information about IRS's mission is available from their Web site at *www.irs.gov*.

legal notification period Relating to employee terminations, the *Worker Adjustment and Retraining Notification Act (WARN)* requires employers to give employees 60-day notice prior to plant closings or mass layoffs. Laws of the individual states or specific collective bargaining agreements may require different legal notification periods, but they may never be less than the 60 days required under *WARN*. (*Title 20, Code of Federal Regulations, Part 639, Section 5.*)

LIFO *Last-in, first-out.* An inventory valuation method where the most recently acquired (last-in) inventory is considered to be expended before older inventory.

long-term tax-exempt rate As used to compute the Internal Revenue Code Section 382 limitation for the deductibility of net operating loss carryforwards following a change of control, the long-term tax-exempt rate is the highest of the adjusted federal long-term rates in effect during the three-month period comprised of the transaction month and the two preceding months.

MACRS *Modified Accelerated Cost Recovery System.* A system of accelerated tax depreciation using classes of properties instead of individual asset lives as the basis for depreciation. MACRS divides properties into 3, 5, 7, 10, 15, and 20-year classes and depreciates 3- through 10-year properties using the 200-percent declining balance method and 15- and 20-year properties using the 150-percent declining balance method. MACRS assumes no salvage value for assets and defaults to the midyear convention. An exception to the mid-year convention occurs in circumstances where Taxpayer Company places a disproportionate amount of new assets (greater than 40 percent) in service in the last quarter of the year in which case the mid-quarter convention is required.

minimum retention period The period between notification and termination of employment when employees may be expected to continue rendering service. The *minimum retention period* cannot exceed the legal notification period under the *Worker Adjustment and Retraining Notification Act (WARN)* if it applies or 60 days if *WARN* is not applicable.

net identifiable assets A firm's *net identifiable assets* are its net assets (total assets minus total liabilities) minus recorded goodwill. In a business combination under the purchase method of accounting, assets are first restated to fair value before calculating the net identifiable assets acquired in the transaction.

net periodic pension cost The amount recognized in an employer's financial statements as the cost of a pension plan for a period. Components of net periodic pension expense are service cost, interest cost, actual return on plan assets, gain or loss, amortization of unrecognized prior service cost, and amortization of the unrecognized net obligation or asset existing at the date of initial application of [FAS87].[11]

NOL *Net operating loss.* "…the excess of the deductions allowed for by [the Internal Revenue Code] over the gross income."[12]

NOLs *Net operating losses.* The same as net operating loss carryforwards.

Old target Defined in Income Tax Regulations Section 1.338-2(b)(17) as the "…target for periods ending on or before the close of the target's acquisition date." This means the target while it is still in the hands of the seller as part of the seller's consolidated selling group.

P&L *Profit and loss (statement).* An alternate name for the Income statement.

PBGC The Pension Benefit Guarantee Corporation.

PBO *Projected benefit obligation.* The actuarial present value as of a date of all benefits attributed by the pension benefit formula to employee service rendered prior to that date. The projected benefit obligation is measured using assumptions as to future compensation levels if the pension benefit formula is based on those future compensation levels (pay-related, final-pay, final-average-pay, or career-average-pay plans).[13]

phantom goodwill Goodwill that is recognized only on an Investor's working papers for investments consolidated using the equity method of accounting.

phantom write-ups Write-ups of assets to fair value only on an Investor's working papers and not on the balance sheet for investments consolidated using the equity method of accounting. Equity method write-ups are amortized against earnings in investments of affiliates to avoid overstating the equity method investment.

PIK *Payment-in-kind.* Payment of interest due on debt investments by crediting the investor with additional face amounts of the debt instead of paying cash interest. Payment of dividends due on equity investments (usually preferred equity) by crediting the investor with additional shares of the equity instead of paying cash dividends. The interest due on debt is paid with additional debt and the dividends due on equity are paid with additional equity, so these types of instruments are called "payment-in-kind" because the payment received by the investors is the same form as the investments. The payments are commonly referred to as either accreting interest or accreting dividends.

present value The value of a future obligation discounted (reduced) at an appropriate discount rate to reflect the present time value of the money.

PV *Present value.* The value of a future cash flow discounted to the present using a discount rate.

realize In accounting terminology, realize is a concept relating to *when* revenues should be recorded in the income statement. The realization principle also extends to other forms of cash flows.

recognize In accounting parlance, events or items are recognized by recording them in either the financial accounting books, the tax books, or both. For example, if Taxpayer Company recognizes an expense, it "goes on" the income statement. When recognizing an asset, it records the value of the asset on the company's balance sheet.

SAB *Staff Accounting Bulletin.* The SEC staff issues interpretations of rules concerning accounting-related disclosure requirements. Periodically the *SABs* are codified into the regulations and become part of Title 17 of the Code of Federal Regulations. *SABs* are treated as part of Generally Accepted Accounting Principles for companies required to file statements with the SEC.

salvage value The amount for which an asset can be sold or disposed of at the end of its useful depreciable life. When assets are depreciated for financial accounting purposes, they are depreciated from their cost basis to their salvage value. Depreciation for tax purposes under accelerated cost-recovery methodologies such as MACRS generally assumes a zero salvage value to maximize the cost-recovery (depreciation) expense. When a fully depreciated asset is sold, the salvage value is recognized for tax purposes as a taxable gain on the sale of an asset.

SEC *Securities and Exchange Commission.* The *Securities and Exchange Commission* is the U.S. government agency regulating all aspects of the securities and commodities markets. Through the Office of the Chief Accountant, the *SEC* interacts with and authorizes other accounting organizations to develop U.S. Generally Accepted Accounting Principles. More information about SEC's mission is available from their Web site at *www.sec.gov.*

settlement "A transaction that (a) is an irrevocable action, (b) relieves the employer (or the plan) of primary responsibility for a pension benefit obligation, and (c) eliminates significant risks related to the obligation and the assets used to effect the settlement."[14]

straight-line depreciation For financial reporting purposes, a depreciation schedule where the basis of the underlying asset is expensed ratably (equally) in each period of its useful life. For income tax reporting purposes, a cost recovery schedule where the tax basis of the underlying asset is expensed ratably (equally) in each period of its class life.

temporary differences When accounting for income taxes, *temporary differences or taxable temporary differences* are differences "…between the tax basis of an asset or liability and its reported amount in the financial statements that will result in taxable or deductible amounts in future years when the reported amount of the asset or liability is recovered or settled, respectively."[15] Temporary differences commonly arise because of differences between the depreciation rates used for book purposes and those used for tax purposes.

termination date The later of the last day of the minimum retention period or the legal notification period for employees that are not required to render service to earn entitlement to their one-time termination benefits or the day on which (usually the end of the future service period) employees complete any required service to earn full entitlement to a their one-time termination benefits.

valuation allowance "The portion of a deferred tax asset for which it is more likely than not that a tax benefit will not be realized."[16]

vested benefits Benefits for which the employee's right to receive a present or future pension benefit is no longer contingent on remaining in the service of the employer.[17]

working papers The accounting records that firms and auditors use for recording financial information that is required to calculate and support the financial statements. The financial reporting working papers are not published nor made available to outsiders and include depreciation schedules, unrecognized pension items, amortization schedules, etc.

CHAPTER 1

1 Financial Accounting Standards Board, APB Opinion Number 18, The Equity Method of Accounting for Investments in Common Stock, March 1971, para. 6b. *(Bullet points added).*

2 Financial Accounting Standards Board, APB Opinion Number 18, The Equity Method of Accounting for Investments in Common Stock, March 1971, paragraph 16.

3 Financial Accounting Standards Board, APB Opinion Number 18, The Equity Method of Accounting for Investments in Common Stock, March 1971, paragraph 17.

4 Financial Accounting Standards Board, APB Opinion Number 18, The Equity Method of Accounting for Investments in Common Stock, March 1971, paragraph 17.

5 Financial Accounting Standards Board, APB Opinion Number 18, The Equity Method of Accounting for Investments in Common Stock, March 1971, paragraph 17.

6 Financial Accounting Standards Board, FASB Interpretation No. 35, Criteria for Applying the Equity Method of Accounting for Investments in Common Stock, May 1981, paragraph. 3.

7 Financial Accounting Standards Board, FASB Interpretation No. 35, Criteria for Applying the Equity Method of Accounting for Investments in Common Stock, May 1981, paragraph 9.

8 Financial Accounting Standards Board, FASB Interpretation No. 35, Criteria for Applying the Equity Method of Accounting for Investments in Common Stock, May 1981, paragraph 13.

9 U.S. Securities and Exchange Commission, Division of Corporation Finance, *Current Accounting and Disclosure Issues*, August 31, 2001, paragraph II.N.

10 U.S. Securities and Exchange Commission, Division of Corporation Finance, *Current Accounting and Disclosure Issues*, August 31, 2001, paragraph II.N.

11 Financial Accounting Standards Board, FASB Interpretation No. 35, Criteria for Applying the Equity Method of Accounting for Investments in Common Stock, May 1981, paragraphs 7–9.

12 Financial Accounting Standards Board, *Statement of Financial Accounting Standards No. 95, Statement of Cash Flows*, November 1987, paragraph 22.b.

13 Financial Accounting Standards Board, *Statement of Financial Accounting Standards No. 95, Statement of Cash Flows*, November 1987, paragraph 16.b.

CHAPTER 2

1 Financial Accounting Standards Board, *Minutes of the October 30, 2002 Board Meeting*, Financial Accounting Standards Board, Norwalk, CT., November 4, 2002, discussion item 2.

2 Financial Accounting Standards Board, *Minutes of the October 30, 2002 Board Meeting*, Financial Accounting Standards Board, Norwalk, CT., November 4, 2002, discussion item 1.

3 Financial Accounting Standards Board, *Statement of Financial Accounting Standards No. 141, Business Combinations*, Financial Accounting Standards Board, Norwalk, CT., June 2001, paragraph 14.

CHAPTER 3

1 Financial Accounting Standards Board, *Statement of Financial Accounting Standards No. 109, Accounting for Income Taxes*, Financial Accounting Standards Board, Norwalk, CT., February 1992, paragraph 8.

2 Financial Accounting Standards Board, *Statement of Financial Accounting Standards No. 109, Accounting for Income Taxes*, Financial Accounting Standards Board, Norwalk, CT., February 1992, paragraph 10.

CHAPTER 4

1 Financial Accounting Standards Board, *Statement of Financial Accounting Standards No. 109, Accounting for Income Taxes*, Financial Accounting Standards Board, Norwalk, CT., February 1992, paragraph 17.e.

2 Financial Accounting Standards Board, *Statement of Financial Accounting Standards No. 109, Accounting for Income Taxes*, Financial Accounting Standards Board, Norwalk, CT., February 1992, paragraph 17.e.

CHAPTER 6

1 Testimony of Steven A. Kandarian, Executive Director of the Pension Benefit Guarantee Corporation, before the Committee on Education and the Workforce, United States House of Representatives, September 4, 2003.

2 Testimony of Steven A. Kandarian, Executive Director of the Pension Benefit Guarantee Corporation, before the Committee on Education and the Workforce, United States House of Representatives, September 4, 2003.

3 Financial Accounting Standards Board, *Statement of Financial Accounting Standards No. 87, Employers' Accounting for Pensions*, Financial Accounting Standards Board, Norwalk, CT, December 1985, paragraph 264.

4 Financial Accounting Standards Board, *Statement of Financial Accounting Standards No. 87, Employers' Accounting for Pensions*, Financial Accounting Standards Board, Norwalk, CT, December 1985, paragraph 264.

5 Financial Accounting Standards Board, *Statement of Financial Accounting Standards No. 87, Employers' Accounting for Pensions*, Financial Accounting Standards Board, Norwalk, CT, December 1985, paragraph 264.

6 Financial Accounting Standards Board, *Statement of Financial Accounting Standards No. 106, Employers' Accounting for Postretirement Benefits Other Than Pensions*, Financial Accounting Standards Board, Norwalk, CT, December 1990, paragraph 518.

CHAPTER 9

1 Financial Accounting Standards Board, *Statement of Financial Accounting Standards No. 123, Accounting for Stock-Based Compensation*, Financial Accounting Standards Board, Norwalk, CT., October 1995, paragraph 19.

2 Financial Accounting Standards Board, *Statement of Financial Accounting Standards No. 123, Accounting for Stock-Based Compensation*, Financial Accounting Standards Board, Norwalk, CT., October 1995, paragraph 395.

CHAPTER 10

1 U.S. Securities and Exchange Commission, *SEC Staff Accounting Bulletin: No. 100—Restructuring and Impairment Charges*, U.S. Securities and Exchange Commission, Washington, DC, November 24, 1999, Topic 5, paragraph P.

2 International Accounting Standards Board, *International Accounting Standard IAS 37, Provisions, Contingent Liabilities and Contingent Assets*, International Accounting Standards Committee Foundation, London, U.K., July 1998, paragraph 10.

3 International Accounting Standards Board, *International Accounting Standard IAS 19, Employee Benefits*, International Accounting Standards Committee Foundation, London, U.K., 2002, paragraph 139.

CHAPTER 11

1 Financial Accounting Standards Board, Statement of Financial Accounting Standards No. 144, Accounting for the Impairment or Disposal of Long-Lived Assets, August 2001, paragraph 41.

2 Adapted from: Financial Accounting Standards Board, Statement of Financial Accounting Standards No. 144, Accounting for the Impairment or Disposal of Long-Lived Assets, August 2001, paragraphs A27-A30.

3 International Accounting Standards Board, *International Accounting Standard IAS 35, Discontinuing Operations*, International Accounting Standards Committee Foundation, London, U.K., April 1998, paragraph 16(b).

CHAPTER 12

1 Internal Revenue Code of 1986 (as amended) §382(f)(1).

2 Financial Accounting Standards Board, *Statement of Financial Accounting Standards 109 - Accounting for Income Taxes*, paragraph. 97 defines "...*more likely than not* to mean a level of likelihood greater than 50 percent."

CHAPTER 13

1 Financial Accounting Standards Board, Statement of Financial Accounting Standards No. 142, Goodwill and Other Intangible Assets, Norwalk, CT., June 2001, paragraph F1.

2 Financial Accounting Standards Board, FASB Interpretation No. 4, Applicability of FASB Statement No. 2 to Business Combinations Accounted for by the Purchase Method, Financial Accounting Standards Board, Norwalk, CT., February 1975, paragraph 5.

3 Financial Accounting Standards Board, *FASB Action Alert No. 02-29*, Financial Accounting Standards Board, Norwalk, CT., July 31, 2002, pg.3.

4 Emerging Issues Task Force Issue No. 95-3, *Recognition of Liabilities in Connection with a Purchase Business Combination*, Financial Accounting Standards Board, Norwalk, CT., July 21, 1995.

5 International Accounting Standards Board, *International Accounting Standard 22, Business Combinations*, Financial Accounting Standards Board, London, U.K., 1998, paragraph 25.

6 Financial Accounting Standards Board, Business Combinations: Purchase Method Procedures Summary of Tentative Decisions (August 2001 through July 17, 2003), Norwalk CT., Milestone 3.

7 Financial Accounting Standards Board, *Statement of Financial Accounting Standards No. 141, Business Combinations*, Norwalk, CT., June 2001, paragraph F1.

8 Financial Accounting Standards Board, *Statement of Financial Accounting Standards No. 109, Accounting for Income Taxes*, Norwalk, CT., February 1992, paragraph 30.

9 Title 17 Code of Federal Regulations, *Commodity and Securities Exchanges*, Part 210, Section 210.11-02, U.S. Government Printing Office, Washington, DC, April, 2002.

10 Emerging Issues Task Force Issue No. 95-13, *Classification of Debt Issues Costs in the Statement of Cash Flows*, Financial Accounting Standards Board, Norwalk, CT., September 20–21, 1995.

11 IRC §382(f)(1).

12 Financial Accounting Standards Board, *Minutes of the October 30, 2002 Board Meeting*, Financial Accounting Standards Board, Norwalk, CT., November 4, 2002, discussion item 1.

CHAPTER 14

1 Income Tax Regulations, Corporate Liquidations, Section 1.338-4(f)(ii)

2 Income Tax Regulations – Corporate Liquidations, Reg. §1.338-6(d), Example 1(i).

3 Income Tax Regulations – Corporate Liquidations, Reg. §1.338-6(d), Example 1(v).

GLOSSARY

1 Financial Accounting Standards Board, *Statement of Financial Accounting Standards No. 87, Employers' Accounting for Pensions*, Financial Accounting Standards Board, Norwalk, CT, December 1985, paragraph 264.

2 Financial Accounting Standards Board, *Statement of Financial Accounting Standards No.106, Employers' Accounting for Postretirement Benefits Other Than Pensions*, Financial Accounting Standards Board, Norwalk, CT, December 1990, paragraph 518.

3 Financial Accounting Standards Board, *Statement of Financial Accounting Standards No. 109, Accounting for Income Taxes*, Financial Accounting Standards Board, Norwalk, CT, February 1992, paragraph 289.

4 Financial Accounting Standards Board, *Statement of Financial Accounting Standards No. 109, Accounting for Income Taxes*, Financial Accounting Standards Board, Norwalk, CT, February 1992, paragraph 289.

5 Financial Accounting Standards Board, Statement of Financial Accounting Standards No. 88, Employers' Accounting for Settlements and Curtailments of Defined Benefit Pension Plans and for Termination Benefits, Financial Accounting Standards Board, Norwalk, CT, December 1985, paragraph 6.

6 Financial Accounting Standards Board, *Statement of Financial Accounting Standards No.106, Employers' Accounting for Postretirement Benefits Other Than Pensions*, Financial Accounting Standards Board, Norwalk, CT, December 1990, paragraph 518.

7 Financial Accounting Standards Board, *Statement of Financial Accounting Standards No.106, Employers' Accounting for Postretirement Benefits Other Than Pensions*, Financial Accounting Standards Board, Norwalk, CT, December 1990, paragraph 518.

8 Financial Accounting Standards Board, *Statement of Financial Accounting Standards No. 128, Earnings per Share*, Financial Accounting Standards Board, Norwalk, CT, February 1997, paragraph 171.

9 Financial Accounting Standards Board, *Statement of Financial Accounting Standards No. 106, Employers' Accounting for Postretirement Benefits Other Than Pensions*, Financial Accounting Standards Board, Norwalk, CT, December 1990, paragraph 518.

10 Financial Accounting Standards Board, *Statement of Financial Accounting Standards No. 141, Business Combinations*, Financial Accounting Standards Board, Norwalk, CT, June 2001, Appendix F1.

11 Financial Accounting Standards Board, *Statement of Financial Accounting Standards No. 87, Employer's Accounting for Pensions*, Financial Accounting Standards Board, Norwalk, CT, December 1985, paragraph 264.

12 Internal Revenue Code of 1986 (as amended) §172(c).

13 Financial Accounting Standards Board, *Statement of Financial Accounting Standards No. 87, Employers' Accounting for Pensions*, Financial Accounting Standards Board, Norwalk, CT, December 1985, paragraph 264.

14 Financial Accounting Standards Board, Statement of Financial Accounting Standards No. 88, Employers' Accounting for Settlements and Curtailments of Defined Benefit Pension Plans and for Termination Benefits, Financial Accounting Standards Board, Norwalk, CT, December 1985, paragraph 3.

15 Financial Accounting Standards Board, *Statement of Financial Accounting Standards No. 109, Accounting for Income Taxes*, Financial Accounting Standards Board, Norwalk, CT., February 1992, paragraph 289.

16 Financial Accounting Standards Board, *Statement of Financial Accounting Standards No. 109, Accounting for Income Taxes*, Financial Accounting Standards Board, Norwalk, CT., February 1992, paragraph 289.

17 Financial Accounting Standards Board, *Statement of Financial Accounting Standards No. 87, Employers' Accounting for Pensions*, Financial Accounting Standards Board, Norwalk, CT, December 1985, paragraph 264.

INDEX